SKETCHES OF
ENGLISH LIFE
AND
CHARACTER

BY

MARY R. MITFORD
AUTHOR OF "OUR VILLAGE"

WITH
SIXTEEN REPRODUCTIONS
FROM THE PAINTINGS OF
STANHOPE A. FORBES
A.R.A.

Copyright © 2018 Read Books Ltd.
This book is copyright and may not be
reproduced or copied in any way without
the express permission of the publisher in writing

British Library Cataloguing-in-Publication Data
A catalogue record for this book is available from
the British Library

CONTENTS

	PAGE
A GREAT FARMHOUSE	9
A COUNTRY CRICKET MATCH	18
A VILLAGE BEAU	35
TOM CORDERY	45
BRAMLEY MAYING	57
A COUNTRY APOTHECARY	67
THE COPSE	81
WHITSUN EVE	95
THE RAT-CATCHER	103
THE OLD GIPSY	116
THE BIRD-CATCHER	128
A VISIT TO LUCY	140
HANNAH BINT	152
DOCTOR TUBB	164
A COUNTRY BARBER	174
OUR MAYING	187
THE HARD SUMMER	199

CONTENTS

	PAGE
THE MOLE-CATCHER	212
MATTHEW SHORE	222
OLD MASTER GREEN	232
PATTY'S NEW HAT	242
NUTTING	249
A NEW MARRIED COUPLE	258
A CHRISTMAS PARTY	266
TOM HOPKINS	279
A WIDOW GENTLEWOMAN	287
MY GODFATHER	296
MY GODFATHER'S MANŒUVRING	311

REPRODUCTIONS IN COLOUR
from the Paintings of
STANHOPE A. FORBES, A.R.A.

———◆———

	PAGE
THE WOODMAN . . . . *Frontispiece*	
FEBRUARY SUNSHINE	24
HOME ALONG	40
THE POACHERS	56
THE HAYCART	72
THE VILLAGE BRIDGE	88
THE CARTER—AN EARLY START . . .	104
THE GIPSIES	120
A VILLAGE BY THE SEA	152
A VILLAGE STREET	184
BRINGING HOME THE MILK	200
THE EVENING HOUR	216
OLD CRONIES	232
MENDING	264
AN ITINERANT MUSICIAN	280
A SON OF THE SEA	296

ENGLISH LIFE AND CHARACTER

A GREAT FARMHOUSE

THESE are bad times for farmers. I am sorry for it. Independently of all questions of policy, as a mere matter of taste and of old association, it was a fine thing to witness the hearty hospitality, and to think of the social happiness of a great farmhouse. No situation in life seemed so richly privileged; none had so much power for good and so little for evil; it seemed a place where pride could not live, and poverty could not enter. These thoughts pressed on my mind the other day, in passing the green sheltered lane, overhung with trees like an avenue, that leads to the great farm at M., where, ten or twelve years ago, I used to spend so many pleasant days. I could not help advancing a few paces up the lane, and then turning to lean over the gate, seemingly gazing on the rich undulating valley, crowned with woody hills, which, as I stood under that dark and shady arch, lay bathed in the sunshine before me, but really absorbed in thoughts of other times, in recollections of the old delights of that delightful place, and of the admirable qualities of its owners. How often I had opened that gate, and how gaily—certain of meeting a smiling welcome—and what a picture of comfort it was!

Passing up the lane, we used first to encounter a thick solid suburb of ricks, of all sorts, shapes, and dimensions. Then came the farm, like a town; a magnificent series of buildings, stables, cart-houses, cow-houses, granaries, and barns, that might hold half the corn of the parish, placed at all angles towards each other, and mixed with smaller habitations for pigs, dogs, and poultry. They formed, together with the old substantial farmhouse, a sort of amphitheatre, looking over a beautiful meadow, which swept greenly and abruptly down into fertile enclosures, richly set with hedgerow timber, oak, and ash, and elm. Both the meadow and the farmyard swarmed with inhabitants of the earth and of the air; horses, oxen, cows, calves, heifers, sheep, and pigs; beautiful greyhounds, all manner of poultry, a tame goat, and a pet donkey.

The master of this land of plenty was well fitted to preside over it; a thick, stout man, of middle height, and middle age, with a healthy, ruddy, square face, all alive with intelligence and good-humour. There was a lurking jest in his eye, and a smile about the corners of his firmly closed lips, that gave assurance of good-fellowship. His voice was loud enough to have hailed a ship at sea, without the assistance of a spea   -trumpet, wonderfully rich and round in its tones, and harmonising admirably with his bluff, jovial visage. He wore his dark shining hair combed straight over his forehead, and had a trick, when particularly merry, of stroking it down with his hand. The moment his right hand approached his head, out flew a jest.

Besides his own great farm, the business of which seemed to go on like machinery, always regular, prosperous, and unfailing,—besides this and two or three constant stewardships, and a perpetual succession of arbitrations, in which, such was the influence of his acuteness, his temper, and his sturdy justice, that he was often named by both parties, and left to decide alone,—in addition to these occupations, he was a sort of standing overseer and church-warden; he ruled his own hamlet like a despotic monarch, and took a prime minister's share in the government of the large parish to which it was attached; and one of the gentlemen, whose estates he managed, being the independent member for an independent borough, he had every now and then a contested election on his shoulders. Even that did not discompose him. He had always leisure to receive his friends at home, or to visit them abroad; to take journeys to London, or make excursions to the seaside; was as punctual in pleasure as in business, and thought being happy and making happy as much the purpose of his life as getting rich. His great amusement was coursing. He kept several brace of capital greyhounds, so high-blooded, that I remember when five of them were confined in five different kennels on account of their ferocity. The greatest of living painters once called a greyhound "the line of beauty in perpetual motion." Our friend's large dogs were a fine illustration of this remark. His old dog, Hector, for instance, for whom he refused a hundred guineas,—what a superb dog was Hector!—a model of grace and symmetry, necked and crested like an Arabian, and bearing himself with a stateliness and gallantry that showed some "conscience of his worth." He was the largest dog I ever saw; but so finely proportioned, that the most determined fault-finder could call him neither too long nor too heavy. There was not an inch too much of him. His colour was the purest white, entirely unspotted, except that his head was very regularly and richly marked with black. Hector was certainly a perfect beauty. But the little bitches, on which his master piqued himself still more, were not in my poor judgment so admirable. They were pretty little round, graceful things, sleek and glossy, and for the most part milk-white, with the smallest heads, and the most dove-like eyes that were ever seen. There was a peculiar sort of innocent beauty about them, like that of a roly-poly child. They were as gentle as lambs too: all the evil spirit of the family evaporated in the gentlemen. But, to my thinking, these pretty creatures were fitter for the parlour than the field. They were strong, certainly, excellently loined,

cat-footed, and chested like a warhorse; but there
was a want of length about them—a want of room,
as the coursers say; something a little, a very little
inclining to the clumsy; a dumpiness, a pointer-
look. They went off like an arrow from a bow;
for the first hundred yards nothing could stand
against them; then they began to flag, to find
their weight too much for their speed, and to lose
ground from the shortness of the stroke. Uphill,
however, they were capital. There their compact-
ness told. They turned with the hare, and lost
neither wind nor way in the sharpest ascent. I
shall never forget one single-handed course of
our good friend's favourite little bitch Helen, on
W. Hill. All the coursers were in the valley
below, looking up to the hillside as on a moving
picture. I suppose she turned the hare twenty
times on a piece of greensward not much bigger
than an acre, and as steep as the roof of a house.
It was an old hare, a famous hare, one that had
baffled half the dogs in the county; but she killed
him; and then, though almost as large as herself,
took it up in her mouth, brought it to her master,
and laid it down at his feet. Oh, how pleased he
was! and what a pleasure it was to see his triumph!
He did not always find W. Hill so fortunate. It is
a high steep hill, of a conical shape, encircled by
a mountain road winding up to the summit like a
cork-screw,—a deep road dug out of the chalk, and
fenced by high mounds on either side. The hares
always make for this hollow way, as it is called,

because it is too wide for a leap, and the dogs lose much time in mounting and descending the sharp acclivities. Very eager dogs will sometimes dare the leap, and two of our good friend's favourite greyhounds perished in the attempt in two following years. They were found dead in the hollow way. After this he took a dislike to distant coursing meetings, and sported chiefly on his own beautiful farm.

His wife was like her husband, with a difference, as they say in heraldry. Like him in looks, only thinner and paler; like him in voice and phrase, only not so loud; like him in merriment and good-humour; like him in her talent of welcoming and making happy, and being kind; like him in cherishing an abundance of pets, and in getting through with marvellous facility an astounding quantity of business and pleasure. Perhaps the quality in which they resembled each other most completely was the happy ease and serenity of behaviour, so seldom found amongst people of the middle rank, who have usually a best manner and a worst, and whose best (that is the studied, the company manner) is so very much the worst. She was frankness itself; entirely free from prickly defiance, or bristling self-love. She never took offence or gave it; never thought of herself or of what others would think of her; had never been afflicted with the besetting sins of her station, a dread of the vulgar, or an aspiration after the genteel. Those "words of fear" had never disturbed her delightful heartiness.

A GREAT FARMHOUSE

Her pets were her cows, her poultry, her bees, and her flowers; chiefly her poultry, almost as numerous as the bees, and as various as the flowers. The farmyard swarmed with peacocks, turkeys, geese, tame and wild ducks, fowls, guinea-hens, and pigeons; besides a brood or two of favourite bantams in the green court before the door, with a little ridiculous strutter of a cock at their head, who imitated the magnificent demeanour of the great Tom of the barnyard, just as Tom in his turn copied the fierce bearing of that warlike and terrible biped the he-turkey. I am the least in the world afraid of a turkey-cock, and used to steer clear of the turkery as often as I could. Commend me to the peaceable vanity of that jewel of a bird the peacock, sweeping his gorgeous tail along the grass, or dropping it gracefully from some low-boughed tree, whilst he turns round his crested head with the air of a birthday belle, to see who admires him. What a glorious creature it is! How thoroughly content with himself and with all the world!

Next to her poultry our good farmer's wife loved her flower-garden; and indeed it was of the very first water, the only thing about the place that was fine. She was a real genuine florist; valued pinks, tulips, and auriculas, for certain qualities of shape and colour, with which beauty has nothing to do; preferred black ranunculuses, and gave into all those obliquities of a triple-refined taste by which the professed florist contrives to keep pace with the vagaries of the bibliomaniac. Of all odd fashions, that of dark, gloomy, dingy flowers, appears to me the oddest. Your true *connoisseur* now, shall prefer a deep puce hollyhock, to the gay pink blossoms which cluster round that splendid plant like a pyramid of roses. So did she. The nomenclature of her garden was more distressing still. One is never thoroughly sociable with flowers till they are naturalised as it were, christened, provided with decent, homely, well-wearing English names. Now her plants had all sorts of heathenish appellations, which—no offence to her learning—always sounded wrong. I liked the bees' garden best; the plot of ground immediately round their hives, filled with common flowers for their use, and literally " redolent of sweets." Bees are insects of great taste in every way, and seem often to select for beauty as much as for flavour. They have a better eye for colour than the florist. The butterfly is also a *dilettante*. Rover though he be, he generally prefers the blossoms that become him best. What a pretty picture it is, in a sunshiny autumn day, to see a bright spotted butterfly, made up of gold and purple and splendid brown, swinging on the rich flower of the china aster!

To come back to our farm. Within doors everything went as well as without. There were no fine misses sitting before the piano, and mixing the alloy of their new-fangled tinsel with the old sterling metal; nothing but an only son excellently brought up, a fair slim youth, whose extraordinary somewhat pensive elegance of mind and manner was thrown into fine relief by his father's loud hilarity, and harmonised delightfully with the smiling kindness of his mother. His Spensers and Thomsons, too, looked well amongst the hyacinths and geraniums that filled the windows of the little snug room in which they usually sate; a sort of afterthought, built at an angle from the house, and looking into the farmyard. It was closely packed with favourite arm-chairs, favourite sofas, favourite tables, and a sideboard decorated with the prize-cups and collars of the greyhounds, and generally loaded with substantial work-baskets, jars of flowers, great pyramids of home-made cakes, and sparkling bottles of gooseberry-wine, famous all over the country. The walls were covered with portraits of half a dozen greyhounds, a brace of spaniels, as large as life, an old pony, and the master and mistress of the house in half-length. She as unlike as possible, prim, mincing, delicate, in lace and satin; he so staringly and ridiculously like, that when the picture fixed its good-humoured eyes upon you as you entered the room, you were almost tempted to say—How d'ye do?——Alas! the portraits are gone now, and the originals. Death and distance have despoiled that pleasant home. The garden has lost its smiling mistress; the greyhounds their kind master; and new people, new manners, and new cares, have taken possession of the old abode of peace and plenty—the great farmhouse.

A COUNTRY CRICKET MATCH

I DOUBT if there be any scene in the world more animating or delightful than a cricket-match;— I do not mean a set match at Lord's Ground for money, hard money, between a certain number of gentlemen and players, as they are called— people who make a trade of that noble sport, and degrade it into an affair of bettings, and hedgings, and cheatings, it may be, like boxing or horse-racing: nor do I mean a pretty fête in a gentleman's park, where one club of cricketing dandies encounters another such club, and where they show off in graceful costume to a gay marquee of admiring belles, who condescend so to purchase admiration, and while away a long summer morning in partaking of cold collations, conversing occasionally, and seeming to understand the game; —the whole being conducted according to ball-room etiquette, so as to be exceedingly elegant and exceedingly dull. No! the cricket that I mean is a real solid, old-fashioned match between neighbouring parishes, where each attacks the other for honour and a supper, glory, and half a crown a man. If there be any gentlemen amongst them, it is well—if not, it is so much the better. Your gentleman cricketer is in general rather an anomalous character. Elderly gentlemen are obviously good for nothing; and young beaux are, for the most part, hampered and trammelled by dress and habit; the stiff cravat, the pinched-in waist, the dandy walk—oh, they will never do for cricket! Now, our country lads, accustomed to the flail or the hammer (your blacksmiths are capital hitters), have the free use of their arms; they know how to move their shoulders; and they can move their feet too—they can run; then they are so much better made, so much more athletic, and yet so much lissomer—to use a Hampshire phrase, which deserves at least to be good English. Here and there, indeed, one meets with an old Etonian, who retains his boyish love for that game which formed so considerable a branch of his education; some even preserve their boyish proficiency, but in general it wears away like the Greek, quite as certainly, and almost as fast; a few years of Oxford, or Cambridge, or the Continent, are sufficient to annihilate both the power and the inclination. No! a village match is the thing,—where our highest officer—our conductor (to borrow a musical term) is but a little farmer's second son; where a day-labourer is our bowler, and a blacksmith our long-stop; where the spectators consist of the retired cricketers, the veterans of the green, the careful mothers, the girls, and all the boys of two parishes, together with a few amateurs little above them in rank, and not at all in pretension; where laughing and shouting, and the very ecstasy of merriment and good-humour, prevail: such a match, in short, as I attended yesterday, at the expense of getting twice wet through, and as I would attend to-morrow, at the certainty of having that ducking doubled.

For the last three weeks our village has been in a state of great excitement, occasioned by a challenge from our north-western neighbours, the men of B., to contend with us at cricket. Now we have not been much in the habit of playing matches. Three or four years ago, indeed, we encountered the men of S., our neighbours south-by-east, with a sort of doubtful success, beating them on our own ground, whilst they in the second match returned the compliment on theirs. This discouraged us. Then an unnatural coalition between a high-church curate and an evangelical gentleman-farmer drove our lads from the Sunday evening practice, which, as it did not begin before both services were concluded, and as it tended to keep the young men from the ale-house, our magistrates had winked at, if not encouraged. The sport therefore had languished until the present season, when under another change of circumstances the spirit began to revive. Half a dozen fine active lads, of influence amongst their comrades, grew into men and yearned for cricket: an enterprising publican gave a set of ribands; his rival, mine host of the Rose, an out-doer by profession, gave two; and the clergyman and his lay ally, both well-disposed and good-natured men, gratified by the submission to their authority, and finding, perhaps, that no great good resulted from the substitution of public-houses for out-of-door diversions, relaxed. In short the practice recommenced, and the hill was again alive with men and boys, and innocent merriment; but further than the riband matches amongst ourselves nobody dreamed of going, till this challenge—we were modest, and doubted our own strength. The B. people, on the other hand, must have been braggers born, a whole parish of gasconaders. Never was such boasting! such crowing! such ostentatious display of practice! such mutual compliments from man to man—bowler to batter, batter to bowler! It was a wonder they did not challenge all England. It must be confessed that we were a little astounded; yet we firmly resolved not to decline the combat; and one of the most spirited of the new growth, William Grey by name, took up the glove in a style of manly courtesy that would have done honour to a knight in the days of chivalry.—" We were not professed players," he said; "being little better than schoolboys, and scarcely older; but, since they had done us the honour to challenge us, we would try our strength. It would be no discredit to be beaten by such a field."

Having accepted the wager of battle, our champion began forthwith to collect his forces.

William Grey is himself one of the finest youths that one shall see,—tall, active, slender and yet strong, with a piercing eye full of sagacity, and a smile full of good-humour,—a farmer's son by station, and used to hard work as farmers' sons are now, liked by everybody, and admitted to be an excellent cricketer. He immediately set forth to muster his men, remembering with great complacency that Samuel Long, a bowler *comme il y en a peu*, the very man who had knocked down nine wickets, had beaten us, bowled us out at the fatal return match some years ago at S., had luckily, in a remove of a quarter of a mile last Lady Day, crossed the boundaries of his old parish, and actually belonged to us. Here was a stroke of good fortune! Our captain applied to him instantly; and he agreed at a word. Indeed Samuel Long is a very civilised person. He is a middle-aged man who looks rather old amongst our young lads, and whose thickness and breadth give no token of remarkable activity; but he is very active, and so steady a player! so safe! We had half gained the match when we had secured him. He is a man of substance, too, in every way; owns one cow, two donkeys, six pigs, and geese and ducks beyond count; dresses like a farmer, and owes no man a shilling;—and all this from pure industry, sheer day-labour. Note, that your good cricketer is commonly the most industrious man in the parish; the habits that make him such are precisely those which make a good workman — steadiness, sobriety, and activity— Samuel Long might pass for the beau ideal of the two characters. Happy were we to possess him! Then we had another piece of good luck. James Brown, a journeyman blacksmith and a native, who, being of a rambling disposition, had roamed from place to place for half a dozen years, had just returned to settle with his brother at another corner of our village, bringing with him a prodigious reputation in cricket and in gallantry— the gay Lothario of the neighbourhood. He is said to have made more conquests in love and in cricket than any blacksmith in the county. To him also went the indefatigable William Grey, and he also consented to play. No end to our good fortune! Another celebrated batter, called Joseph Hearne, had likewise recently married into the parish. He worked, it is true, at the A. Mills, but slept at the house of his wife's father in our territories. He also was sought and found by our leader. But he was grand and shy; made an immense favour of the thing; courted courting and then hung back;—"Did not know that he could be spared; had partly resolved not to play again—at least not this season; thought it rash to accept the challenge; thought they might do without him——"—"Truly I think so too," said our spirited champion; "we will not trouble you, Mr. Hearne."

Having thus secured two powerful auxiliaries, and rejected a third, we began to reckon and select the regular native forces. Thus ran our list:—William Grey, 1.—Samuel Long, 2.—James Brown, 3.—George and John Simmons, one capital, the other so-so,—an uncertain hitter, but a good fieldsman, 5. — Joel Brent, excellent, 6. — Ben Appleton—Here was a little pause—Ben's abilities at cricket were not completely ascertained; but then he was so good a fellow, so full of fun and waggery! no doing without Ben. So he figured in the list, 7.—George Harris—a short halt there too! Slowish—slow but sure. I think the proverb brought him in, 8.—Tom Coper—oh, beyond the world, Tom Coper! the red-headed gardening lad, whose left-handed strokes send *her* (a cricket-ball, like that other moving thing, a ship, is always of the feminine gender), send her spinning a mile, 9.—Robert Willis, another blacksmith, 10.

We had now ten of our eleven, but the choice of the last occasioned some demur. Three young Martins, rich farmers of the neighbourhood, successively presented themselves, and were all rejected by our independent and impartial general for want of merit—*cricketal* merit. "Not good enough," was his pithy answer. Then our worthy neighbour, the half-pay lieutenant, offered his services—he, too, though with some hesitation and modesty, was refused—" Not quite young enough " was his sentence. John Strong, the exceedingly long son of our dwarfish mason, was the next candidate,—a nice youth—everybody likes John Strong,—and a willing, but so tall and so limp,

in the middle—a thread-paper, six feet high! We were all afraid tha   spite of his name, his strength would never hold out. "Wait till next year, John," quoth William Grey, with all the dignified seniority of twenty speaking to eighteen. "Coper's a year younger," said John. "Coper's a foot shorter," replied William: so John retired; and the eleventh man remained unchosen, almost till the eleventh hour. The eve of the match arrived, and the post was still vacant, when a little boy of fifteen, David Willis, brother to Robert, admitted by accident to the last practice, saw eight of them out, and was voted in by acclamation.

That Sunday evening's practice (for Monday was the important day) was a period of great anxiety, and, to say the truth, of great pleasure. There is something strangely delightful in the innocent spirit of party. To be one of a numerous body, to be authorised to say *we*, to have a rightful interest in triumph or defeat, is gratifying at once to social feeling and to personal pride. There was not a ten-year-old urchin, or a septuagenary woman in the parish, who did not feel an additional importance, a reflected consequence, in speaking of "our side." An election interests in the same way; but that feeling is less pure. Money is there, and hatred, and politics, and lies. Oh, to be a voter, or a voter's wife, comes nothing near the genuine and hearty sympathy of belonging to a parish, breathing the same air, looking on the same trees, listening to the same nightingales!

Talk of a patriotic elector!—Give me a parochial patriot, a man who loves his parish! Even we, the female partisans, may partake the common ardour. I am sure I did. I never, though tolerably eager and enthusiastic at all times, remember being in a more delicious state of excitation than on the eve of that battle. Our hopes waxed stronger and stronger. Those of our players, who were present, were excellent. William Grey got forty notches off his own bat; and that brilliant hitter Tom Coper gained eight from two successive balls. As the evening advanced, too, we had encouragement of another sort. A spy, who had been despatched to reconnoitre the enemy's quarters, returned from their practising ground, with a most consolatory report. "Really," said Charles Grover, our intelligencer—a fine old steady judge, one who had played well in his day —"they are no better than so many old women. Any five of ours would beat their eleven." This sent us to bed in high spirits.

Morning dawned less favourably. The sky promised a series of deluging showers, and kept its word, as English skies are wont to do on such occasions; and a lamentable message arrived at the headquarters from our trusty comrade Joel Brent. His master, a great farmer, had begun the hay-harvest that very morning, and Joel, being as eminent in one field as in another, could not be spared. Imagine Joel's plight! the most ardent of all our eleven! a knight held back from the tourney! a soldier from the battle! The poor swain was inconsolable. At last, one who is always ready to do a good-natured action, great or little, set forth to back his petition; and, by dint of appealing to the public spirit of our worthy neighbour, and the state of the barometer, talking alternately of the parish honour and thunder showers, of lost matches and sopped hay, he carried his point, and returned triumphantly with the delighted Joel.

In the meantime we became sensible of another defalcation. On calling over our roll, Brown was missing; and the spy of the preceding night, Charles Grover,—the universal scout and messenger of the village, a man who will run half a dozen miles for a pint of beer, who does errands for the very love of the trade, who, if he had been a lord, would have been an ambassador—was instantly despatched to summon the truant. His report spread general consternation. Brown had set off at four o'clock in the morning to play in a cricket-match at M., a little town twelve miles off, which had been his last residence. Here was desertion! Here was treachery! Here was treason against that goodly state, our parish! To send James Brown to Coventry was the immediate resolution; but even that seemed too light a punishment for such delinquency. Then how we cried him down! At ten, on Sunday night (for the rascal had actually practised with us, and never said a word of his intended disloyalty), he was our faithful mate, and the best player (take him for all in all) of the eleven. At ten in the morning he had run away, and we were well rid of him; he was no batter compared with William Grey or Tom Coper; not fit to wipe the shoes of Samuel Long, as a bowler; nothing of a scout to John Simmons; the boy David Willis was worth fifty of him—

> "I trust we have within our realm
> Five hundred good as he,"

was the universal sentiment. So we took tall John Strong, who, with an incurable hankering after the honour of being admitted, had kept constantly with the players, to take the chance of some such accident—we took John for our *pis-aller*. I never saw any one prouder than the good-humoured lad was of this not very flattering piece of preferment.

John Strong was elected, and Brown sent to Coventry; and, when I first heard of his delinquency, I thought the punishment only too mild for the crime. But I have since learned the secret history of the offence (if we could know the secret histories of all offences, how much better the world would seem than it does now!); and really my wrath is much abated. It was a piece of gallantry, of devotion to the sex, or rather a chivalrous obedience to one chosen fair. I must tell my readers the story. Mary Allen, the prettiest girl of M., had, it seems, revenged upon our blacksmith the numberless inconstancies of which he stood accused. He was in love over head and ears, but the nymph was cruel. She said no, and no, and no, and poor Brown, three times rejected, at last resolved to leave the place, partly in despair, and partly in that hope which often mingles strangely with a lover's despair, the hope that when he was gone he should be missed. He came home to his brother's accordingly; but for five weeks he heard nothing from or of the inexorable Mary, and was glad to beguile his own "vexing thoughts" by endeavouring to create in his mind an artificial and factitious interest in our cricket-match—all unimportant as such a trifle must have seemed to a man in love. Poor James, however, is a social and warm-hearted person, not likely to resist a contagious sympathy. As the time for the play advanced, the interest which he had at first affected became genuine and sincere: and he was really, when he left the ground on Sunday night, almost as enthusiastically absorbed in the event of the next day as Joel Brent himself. He little foresaw the new and delightful interest which awaited him at home, where, on the moment of his arrival, his sister-in-law and confidante presented him with a billet from the lady of his heart. It had, with the usual delay of letters sent by private hands, in that rank of life, loitered on the road in a degree inconceivable to those who are accustomed to the punctual speed of the post, and had taken ten days for its twelve-miles' journey. Have my readers any wish to see this *billet-doux*? I can show them (but in strict confidence) a literal copy. It was addressed,

> "For mistur jem browne
> "blaxmith by
> "S."

The inside ran thus :—" Mistur browne this is to Inform yew that oure parish playes bramley men next monday is a week, i think we shall lose without yew. from your humbell servant to command MARY ALLEN."

Was there ever a prettier relenting? a summons more flattering, more delicate, more irresistible? The precious epistle was undated ; but, having ascertained who brought it, and found, by cross-examining the messenger, that the Monday in question was the very next day, we were not surprised to find that *Mistur browne* forgot his engagement to us, forgot all but Mary and Mary's letter, and set off at four o'clock the next morning to walk twelve miles, and play for her parish and in her sight. Really we must not send James Brown to Coventry —must we? Though if, as his sister-in-law tells our damsel Harriet he hopes to do, he should bring the fair Mary home as his bride, he will not greatly care how little we say to him. But he must not be sent to Coventry—True-love forbid !

At last we were all assembled, and marched down to H. Common, the appointed ground, which, though in our dominions according to the map, was the constant practising place of our opponents, and *terra incognita* to us. We found our adversaries on the ground as we expected, for our various delays had hindered us from taking the field so early as we wished; and, as soon as we had settled all preliminaries, the match began.

But, alas! I have been so long settling my preliminaries that I have left myself no room for the detail of our victory, and must squeeze the account of our grand achievements into as little compass as Cowley, when he crammed the names of eleven of his mistresses into the narrow space of four eight-syllable lines. *They* began the warfare—these boastful men of B. And what think you, gentle reader, was the amount of their innings? These challengers—the famous eleven—how many did they get? Think! imagine! guess!—You cannot? —Well!—they got twenty-two, or rather they got twenty; for two of theirs were short notches, and would never have been allowed, only that, seeing what they were made of, we and our umpire were not particular.—They should have had twenty more, if they had chosen to claim them. Oh, how well we fielded! and how well we bowled! our good play had quite as much to do with their miserable failure as their bad. Samuel Long is a slow bowler, George Simmons a fast one, and the change from Long's lobbing to Simmons's fast balls posed them completely. Poor simpletons! they were always wrong, expecting the slow for the quick, and the quick for the slow. Well, we went in. And what were our innings? Guess again!—guess! A hundred and sixty-nine! in spite of soaking showers, and wretched ground, where the ball would not run a yard, we headed them by a hundred and forty-seven; and then they gave in, as well they might. William Grey pressed them much to try another innings. "There was so much chance," as he courteously observed, "in cricket, that, advantageous as our position seemed, we might, very possibly, be overtaken. The B. men had better try." But they were beaten sulky, and would not move—to my great disappointment; I wanted to prolong the pleasure of success. What a glorious sensation it is to be for five hours together winning—winning—winning! always feeling what a whist-player feels when he takes up four honours, seven trumps! Who would think that a little bit of leather, and two pieces of wood, had such a delightful and delighting power?

The only drawback on my enjoyment, was the failure of the pretty boy, David Willis, who injudiciously put in first, and playing for the first time in a match amongst men and strangers, who talked to him, and stared at him, was seized with such a fit of shame-faced shyness, that he could scarcely hold his bat, and was bowled out, without a stroke, from actual nervousness. "He will come of that," Tom Coper says.—I am afraid he will. I wonder whether Tom had ever any modesty to lose. Our other modest lad, John Strong, did very well; his length told in fielding, and he got good fame. Joel Brent,

rescued mower, got into a scrape, and out of it
; his fortune for the day. He ran out his
mate, Samuel Long; who, I do believe, but for the
excess of Joel's eagerness, would have stayed in till
this time, by which exploit he got into sad disgrace;
and then he himself got thirty-seven runs, which
redeemed his reputation. William Grey made a
hit which actually lost the cricket-ball. We think
she lodged in a hedge, a quarter of a mile off, but
nobody could find her. And George Simmons had
nearly lost his shoe, which he tossed away in a
passion, for having been caught out, owing to the
ball glancing against it. These, together with a very
complete somerset of Ben Appleton, our long-stop,
who floundered about in the mud, making faces
and attitudes as laughable as Grimaldi, none could
tell whether by accident or design, were the chief
incidents of the scene of action. Amongst the
spectators nothing remarkable occurred, beyond the
general calamity of two or three drenchings, except
that a form, placed by the side of a hedge, under
a very insufficient shelter, was knocked into the
ditch, in a sudden rush of the cricketers to escape
a pelting shower, by which means all parties shared
the fate of Ben Appleton, some on land and some
by water; and that, amidst the scramble, a saucy
gipsy of a girl contrived to steal, from the knee of
the demure and well-apparelled Samuel Long, a
smart handkerchief, which his careful dame had tied
around it to preserve his new (what is the mincing,
feminine word?), his new—inexpressibles; thus

3

reversing the story of Desdemona, and causing the new Othello to call aloud for his handkerchief, to the great diversion of the company. And so we parted; the players retired to their supper, and we to our homes; all wet through, all good-humoured, and all happy—except the losers.

To-day we are happy too. Hats, with ribands in them, go glancing up and down; and William Grey says, with a proud humility, "We do not challenge any parish; but, if we be challenged, we are ready."

A VILLAGE BEAU

THE finest young man in our village is undoubtedly Joel Brent, half-brother to my Lizzy. They are alike too; as much alike as a grown-up person and a little child of different sexes well can be; alike in a vigorous uprightness of form, light, firm, and compact as possible; alike in the bright, sparkling, triumphant blue eye, the short-curled upper lip, the brown wavy hair, the white forehead and sunburnt cheeks, and, above all, in the singular spirit and gaiety of their countenance and demeanour, the constant expression of life and glee, to which they owe the best and rarest part of their attractiveness. They seem, and they are, two of the happiest and merriest creatures that ever trode on the greensward. Really, to see Joel walking by the side of his team (for this enviable mortal, the pride of our village, is by calling a carter), to see him walking, on a fine sunny morning, by the side of his bell-team, the fore-horse decked with ribbons and flowers like a countess on the birthday, as consciously handsome as his driver, the long whip poised gracefully on his shoulder, his little sister in his hand, and his dog Ranger (a beautiful red-and-white spaniel—everything that belongs to Joel is beautiful) frisking about them;—to see this group, and to hear the merry clatter formed by Lizzy's tongue, Joel's whistling, and Ranger's delighted bark, is enough to put an amateur of pleasant sounds and happy faces in good humour for the day.

It is a grateful sight in other respects, for Joel is a very picturesque person, just such an one as a painter would select for the foreground of some English landscape, where nature is shewn in all her loveliness. His costume is the very perfection of rustic coquetry, of that grace, which all admire and few practise, the grace of adaptation, the beauty of fitness. No one ever saw Joel in that wretched piece of deformity a coat, or that still wretcheder apology for a coat a dock-tailed jacket. Broadcloth, the "common stale" of peer and peasant, approaches him not; neither does "the poor creature" fustian. His upper garment consists of that prettier jacket without skirts, call it for the more grace a doublet, of dark velveteen, hanging open over his waistcoat, giving a Spanish or an Italian air to his whole appearance, and setting off to great advantage his trim yet manly shape. To this he adds a silk handkerchief, tied very loosely round his neck, a shirt collar open so as to shew his throat, as you commonly see in the portraits of artists, very loose trousers, and a straw hat. Sometimes in cold weather he throws over all a smock-frock, and last winter brought up a fashion amongst our lads, by assuming one of that blue hight Waterloo, such as butchers wear. As soon as all his comrades had provided themselves with a similar piece of rustic finery, he abandoned his, and indeed generally sticks to his velveteen jacket, which, by some magical influence of cleanliness and neatness, always looks new. I cannot imagine how he contrives it, but dirt never hangs upon Joel; even a fall at cricket in the summer, or a tumble on the ice in the winter, fails to soil him; and he is so ardent in his diversions, and so little disposed to let his coxcombry interfere with his sports, that both have been pretty often tried; the former especially.

Ever since William Grey's secession, which took place shortly after our great match, for no cause assigned, Joel has been the leader and chief of our cricketers. Perhaps, indeed, Joel's rapid improvement might be one cause of William's withdrawal; for, without attributing anything like envy or jealousy to these fine young men, we all know that "two stars keep not their motion in one sphere," and so forth, and if it were absolutely necessary that either our "Harry Hotspur, or the Prince of Wales," should abdicate that fair kingdom the cricket-ground, I must say that I am content to retain our present champion. 'Joel is in my mind the better player, joining to William's agility, and certainty of hand and eye, all the ardour, force, and gaiety of his own quick and lively spirit. The whole man is in the game, mind and body; and his success is such as dexterity and enthusiasm united must always command. To be sure he is a *leetle* over eager, *that* I must confess, and does occasionally run out a slow mate; but he is sure to make up for it by his own exertions, and after all what a delightful fault zeal is! Now that we are on the subject of faults, it must be said, not that Joel has his share, which is of course, but that they are exceedingly venial, little shades that become him, and arise out of his brighter qualities as smoke from the flame. Thus, if he sometimes steals one of his active holidays for a revel or a cricket-match, he is sure to make up the loss to his master by a double portion of labour the next day; and if now and then at tide-times he loiters in the chimney-corner of the Rose, rather longer than strict prudence might warrant, no one can hear his laugh and his song pouring through the open door, like the very voice of "jest and youthful jollity," without feeling certain that it is good fellowship, and not good liquor, that detains him. Indeed, so much is he the delight of the country lads, who frequent that well-accustomed inn, so much is his company sought after in all rustic junketings, that I am only astonished at the strength of resolution, and power of resisting temptation, which he displays in going thither so seldom.

If our village lads be so fond of him, it is not to be doubted but our village maidens like him too. The pretty brunette, Sally Wheeler, who left a good service at B., to take in needlework, and come home to her grandmother, she being, to use Sally's phrase, "unked for want of company" (*N.B.*—Dame Wheeler is as deaf as a post, a cannon would not rouse her), is thought, in our little world, to have had an eye to Joel in this excess of dutifulness. Miss Phœbe, the lass of the Rose, she also, before her late splendid marriage to the patten-maker, is said to have becurled and beflounced herself at least two tiers higher on club-nights, and Sundays, and holidays, and whenever there was a probable chance of meeting him. The gay recruiting serjeant, and all other beaux were abandoned the instant he appeared; nay, it is even hinted that the patten-maker owes his fair bride partly to pique at Joel's indifference. Then Miss Sophia Matthews, the schoolmistress on the Lea, to whom in point of dignity Miss Phœbe was as nothing, who wears a muff and a veil, walks mincingly, and tosses her head in the air, keeps a maid,—a poor little drab of ten years old; follows, as she says, a genteel profession,—I think she may have twenty scholars at eightpence a week; and when she goes to dine with her brother, the collar-maker, hires a boy for a penny to carry her clogs; —Miss Sophia, it is well known, hath pretermitted her dignity in the matter of Joel; hath invited the whole family to tea (only think of Joel at a tea-party!), hath spoken of him as "a person above the common; a respectable young man; one, who with a discreet and accomplished wife, a woman of reading and education" (Miss Sophia, in the days of her father, the late collar-maker of happy memory, before she "taught the young idea how to shoot," had herself drunk deeply at that well of knowledge, the circulating library of B.), "not too young" (Miss Sophia calls herself twenty-eight—I wonder what the register says!), "no brazen-faced gipsey, like Sally Wheeler" (Miss Sophia's cast of countenance is altogether different from Sally's dark and sparkling beauty, she being pink-eyed, red-haired, lean, pale and freckled), "or the jill-flirt Phœbe"—— But to cut short an oration which, in spite of the lady's gentility, began to grow rather scurrilous, one fact was certain,—that Joel might, had he so chosen, have worn the crown matrimonial in Miss Sophia's territories, consisting of a freehold-cottage, a little the worse for wear, a good garden, a capital orchard, and an extensive right of common; to say nothing of the fair damsel and her school, or, as she is accustomed to call it, her seminary.

Joel's proud bright eye glanced, however, carelessly over all. There was little perceptible difference of feeling in the gay, distant smile with which he regarded the coquettish advances of the pretty brunette, Sally Wheeler, or the respectful bow with which he retreated from the dignified condescension of Miss Sophia. He fluttered about our village belles like a butterfly over a bed of tulips; sometimes approaching them for a moment, and seeming ready to fix, but oftener above and out of reach, a creature of a sprightlier element,

buoyant and volatile to light on an earthly
At last, however, the rover was caught;
our damsel, Harriet, had the glory of winning
indomitable heart.

Now Harriet is in all things Lucy's successor;
post, and favour, and beauty, and lovers. In
my eye she is still prettier than Lucy; there is
something so feminine and so attractive in her
loveliness. She is a tall young woman, finely,
though, for eighteen, rather fully formed; with a
sweet child-like face, a fair blooming complexion,
a soft innocent smile, and the eye of a dove. Add
to this a gentle voice, a quiet, modest manner, and
a natural gentility of appearance, and no wonder
that Harriet might vie with her predecessor in the
number of her admirers. She inherited also a
spice of her coquetry, although it was shewn in so
different a way that we did not immediately find
it out. Lucy was a flirt active; Harriet was a flirt
passive; Lucy talked to her beaux; Harriet only
listened to hers; Lucy, when challenged on the
number of her conquests, denied the thing, and
blushed, and laughed, and liked to be laughed at;
Harriet, on a similar charge, gave no token of
liking or denial, but said quietly that she could not
help it, and went on winning hearts by dozens,
prodigal of smiles but chary of love, till Joel came
"pleased her by manners most unlike her own,"
and gave to her delicate womanly beauty the only
charms it wanted—sensibility and consciousness.

The manner in which we discovered this new

flirtation, which, unlike her others, was concealed with the pretty reserve and mystery that wait on true love, was sufficiently curious. We had noted Joel more frequently than common about the house: sometimes he came for Lizzy; sometimes to bring news of a cricket-match; sometimes to ask questions about bats and balls; sometimes to see if his dog Ranger had followed my May; sometimes to bring me a nosegay. All this occasioned no suspicion; we were too glad to see Joel to think of enquiring why he came. But when the days shortened, and evening closed in dark and cold before his work was done, and cricket and flowers were over, and May and Lizzy safe in their own warm beds, and poor Joel's excuses fairly at an end; then it was, that in the after-dinner pause about seven, when the clatter of plates and dishes was over, that the ornithological ear of the master of the house, a dabbler in natural history, was struck by a regular and melodious call, the note, as he averred, of a skylark. That a skylark should sing in front of our house, at seven o'clock, in a December evening, seemed, to say the least, rather startling. But our ornithologist happening to agree with Mr. White, of Selborne, in the opinion that many more birds sing by night than is commonly supposed, and becoming more and more confident of the identity of the note, thought the thing possible; and not being able to discover any previous notice of the fact, had nearly inserted it, as an original observation, in the *Naturalist's*

Calendar, when running out suddenly one moonlight night, to try for a peep at the nocturnal songster, he caught our friend Joel, whose accomplishments in this line we had never dreamt of, in the act of whistling a summons to his lady-love.

For some weeks our demure coquette listened to none but this bird-like wooing; partly from pride in the conquest; partly from real preference; and partly, I believe, from a lurking consciousness that Joel was by no means a lover to be trifled with. Indeed he used to threaten, between jest and earnest, a ducking in the goose-pond opposite, to whoever should presume to approach his fair intended; and the waters being high and muddy, and he at all points a formidable rival, most of her former admirers were content to stay away. At last, however, she relapsed into her old sin of listening. A neighbouring farmer gave a ball in his barn, to which both our lovers were invited and went. Now Harriet loves dancing, and Joel, though arrayed in a new jacket, and thin cricketing-pumps, would not dance; he said he could not, but that, as Harriet observes, is incredible. I agree with her that the gentleman was too fine. He chose to stand and look on, and laugh, and make laugh, the whole evening. In the meantime his fair betrothed picked up a new partner, and a new beau, in the shape of a freshly arrived carpenter, a grand martial-looking figure, as tall as a grenadier, who was recently engaged as foreman to our civil Wheeler, and who, even if he had heard of the denunciation, was of a size and spirit to set Joel and the goose-pond at defiance,— David might as well have attempted to goose-pond Goliath! He danced the whole evening with his pretty partner, and afterwards saw her home; all of which Joel bore with great philosophy. But the next night he came again; and Joel approaching to give his own skylark signal, was startled at seeing another lover leaning over the wicket, and his faithless mistress standing at the half-open door, listening to the tall carpenter, just as complacently as she was wont to do to himself. He passed on without speaking, turned down the little lane that leads to Dame Wheeler's cottage, and in less than two minutes Harriet heard the love-call sounded at Sally's gate. The effect was instantaneous; she discarded the tall carpenter at once and for ever, locked and bolted the door, and sate down to work or to cry in the kitchen. She did not cry long. The next night we again heard the note of the skylark louder and more brilliant than ever, echoing across our court, and the lovers, the better friends for their little quarrel, have been as constant as turtle-doves ever since.

TOM CORDERY

THERE are certain things and persons that seem as if they could never die: things of such vigour and hardiness, that they seem constituted for an interminable duration, a sort of immortality. An old pollard oak of my acquaintance used to give me this impression. Never was tree so gnarled, so knotted, so full of crooked life. Garlanded with ivy and woodbine, almost bending under the weight of its own rich leaves and acorns, tough, vigorous, lusty, concentrating as it were the very spirit of vitality into its own curtailed proportions,—could that tree ever die? I have asked myself twenty times, as I stood looking on the deep water over which it hung, and in which it seemed to live again—would that strong dwarf ever fall? Alas! the question is answered. Walking by the spot to-day—this very day—there it lay prostrate; the ivy still clinging about it, the twigs swelling with sap, and putting forth already the early buds. There it lay a victim to the taste and skill of some admirer of British woods, who with the tact of Ugo Foscolo (that prince of amateurs) has discovered in the knots and gnarls of the exterior coat the leopard-like beauty which is concealed within the trunk. There it lies, a type of sylvan instability, fallen like an emperor. Another piece of strong nature in a human form used to convey to me exactly the same feeling —and he is gone too! Tom Cordery is dead. The bell is tolling for him at this very moment. Tom Cordery dead! the words seem almost a contradiction. One is tempted to send for the sexton and the undertaker, to undig the grave, to force open the coffin-lid — there must be some mistake. But, alas! it is too true; the typhus fever, that axe which levels the strong as the weak, has hewed him down at a blow. Poor Tom Cordery!

This human oak grew on the wild North-of-Hampshire country, of which I have before made honourable mention; a country of heath, and hill, and forest, partly reclaimed, enclosed, and planted by some of the greater proprietors, but for the most part uncultivated and uncivilised; a proper refuge for wild animals of every species. Of these the most notable was my friend Tom Cordery, who presented in his own person no unfit emblem of the district in which he lived—the gentlest of savages, the wildest of civilised men. He was by calling rat-catcher, hare-finder, and broom-maker; a triad of trades which he has substituted for the one grand profession of poaching, which he had followed in his younger days with unrivalled talent and success, and would, undoubtedly, have pursued till his death, had not the bursting of an overloaded gun unluckily shot off his left hand. As it was, he still contrived to mingle a little of his old unlawful occupation with his honest callings; was a reference of high authority amongst the young aspirants, an adviser of undoubted honour and secrecy—suspected, and more than suspected, as being one "who, though he played no more, o'erlooked the cards." Yet he kept to windward of the law, and indeed contrived to be on such terms of social and even friendly intercourse with the guardians of the game on M. Common, as may be said to prevail between reputed thieves and the myrmidons of justice in the neighbourhood of Bow Street. Indeed his especial crony, the head-keeper, used sometimes to hint, when Tom, elevated by ale, had provoked him by overcrowing, "that a stump was no bad shield, and that to shoot off a hand and a bit of an arm for a blind, would be nothing to so daring a chap as Tom Cordery." This conjecture, never broached till the keeper was warm with wrath and liquor, and Tom fairly out of hearing, always seemed to me a little super-subtle; but it is certain that Tom's new professions did bear rather a suspicious analogy to the old, and the ferrets, and terriers, and mongrels by whom he was surrounded, "did really look," as the worthy keeper observed, "fitter to find Christian hares and pheasants, than rats and such vermin." So in good truth did Tom himself. Never did any human being look more like that sort of sportsman commonly called a poacher. He was a tall, finely-built man, with a prodigious stride, that cleared the ground like a horse, and a power of continuing his slow and steady speed, that seemed nothing less than miraculous. Neither man, nor horse, nor dog could out-tire him. He had a bold, undaunted presence, and an evident strength and power of bone and muscle. You might see by looking at him that he did not know what fear meant. In his youth he had fought more battles than any man in the forest. He was as if born without nerves, totally insensible to the recoils and disgusts of humanity. I have known him take up a huge adder, cut off its head, and then deposit the living and writhing body in his brimless hat, and walking with it coiling and wreathing about his head, like another Medusa, till the sport of the day was over, and he carried it home to secure the fat. With all this iron stubbornness of nature, he was of a most mild and gentle demeanour, had a fine placidity of countenance, and a quick blue eye beaming with good-humour. His face was sunburnt into one general pale vermilion hue that overspread all his features; his very hair was sunburnt too. His costume was generally a smock-frock of no doubtful complexion, dirt-coloured, which hung round him in tatters like fringe, rather augmenting than diminishing the freedom, and, if I may so say, the gallantry of his bearing. This frock was furnished with a huge inside pocket, in which to deposit the game killed by his patrons—for of his three employments, that which consisted of finding hares for the great farmers and small gentry, who were wont to course on the common, was by far the most profitable and most pleasing to him, and to them. Everybody liked Tom Cordery. He had himself an aptness to like, which is almost certain to be repaid in kind —the very dogs knew him, and loved him, and would beat for him almost as soon as for their master. Even May, the most sagacious of greyhounds, appreciated his talents, and would almost as soon listen to Tom sohoing as to old Tray giving tongue.

Nor was his conversation less agreeable to the other part of the company. Servants and masters were equally desirous to secure Tom. Besides his general and professional familiarity with beasts and birds, their ways and doings, a knowledge so minute and accurate that it might have put to shame many a professed naturalist, he had no small acquaintance with the goings-on of that unfeathered biped called man ; in short, he was, next after Lucy, who recognised his rivalry by hating, decrying, and undervaluing him, by far the best news-gatherer of the country-side. His news he of course picked up on the civilised side of the parish (there is no gossiping in the forest), partly at that well-frequented inn the Red Lion, of which Tom was a regular and noted supporter—partly amongst his several employers, and partly by his own sagacity. In the matter of marriages (pairings he was won't to call them), he relied chiefly on his own skill in noting certain preliminary indications; and certainly for a guesser by profession, and a very bold one, he was astonishingly often right. At the alehouse especially, he was of the first authority. An air of mild importance, a diplomatic reserve on some points, great smoothness of speech, and that gentleness which is so often the result of conscious power, made him there an absolute ruler. Perhaps the effect of these causes might be a little aided by the latent dread which that power inspired in others. Many an exploit had proved that Tom Cordery's one arm was fairly worth any two on the common. The pommelling of Bob Arlott, and the levelling of Jem Serle to the earth by one swing of a huge old hare (which unusual weapon was, by the way, the first-slain of Mayflower, on its way home to us in that walking cupboard, his pocket, when the unlucky rencontre with Jem Serle broke two heads, the dead and the living), arguments such as these might have some cogency at the Red Lion.

But he managed everybody, as your gentle-mannered person is apt to do. Even the rude 'squires and rough farmers, his temporary masters, he managed, particularly as far as concerned the beat, and was sure to bring them round to his own peculiar fancies or prejudices, however strongly their own wishes might turn them aside from the direction indicated, and however often Tom's sagacity in that instance might have been found at fault. Two spots in the large wild enclosures into which the heath had been divided were his especial favourites; the Hundred Acres, alias the Poor Allotment, alias the Burnt Common—(Do any or all of these titles convey any notion of the real destination of that many-named place? a piece of moorland portioned out to serve for fuel to the poor of the parish)—this was one. Oh, the barrenness of this miserable moor! Flat, marshy, dingy, bare. Here that piece of green treachery, a bog; there parched, and bared, and shrivelled, and black with smoke and ashes; utterly desolate and wretched everywhere, except where amidst the desolation blossomed, as in mockery, the enamelled gentianella. No hares ever came there; they had too much taste. Yet thither would Tom lead his unwary employers; thither, however warned, or cautioned, or experienced, would he by reasoning or induction, or gentle persuasion, or actual fraud, entice the hapless gentlemen; and then to see him with his rabble of finders pacing up and down this precious "sitting-ground" (for so was Tom, thriftless liar, wont to call it), pretending to look for game, counterfeiting a meuse; forging a form; and telling a story some ten years old of a famous hare once killed in that spot by his honour's favourite bitch Marygold. I never could thoroughly understand whether it were design, a fear that too many hares might be killed, or a real and honest mistake, a genuine prejudice in favour of the place, that influenced Tom Cordery in this point. Half the one, perhaps, and half the other. Mixed motives, let Pope and his disciples say what they will, are by far the commonest in this parti-coloured world. Or he had shared the fate of greater men, and lied till he believed—a coursing Cromwell, beginning in hypocrisy and ending in fanaticism. Another pet spot was the Gallows-piece, an enclosure almost as large as the Hundred Acres, where a gibbet had once borne the bodies of two murderers, with the chains and bones, even in my remembrance, clanking and creaking in the wind. The gibbet was gone now; but the name remained, and the feeling, deep, sad, and shuddering. The place, too, was wild, awful, fearful; a heathy, furzy spot, sinking into broken hollows, where murderers might lurk; a few withered pines at the upper end, and amongst them, half hidden by the brambles, the stone in which the gallows had been fixed;—the bones must have been mouldering beneath. All Tom's eloquence, seconded by two capital courses, failed to drag me thither a second time.

Tom was not, however, without that strong sense of natural beauty which they who live amongst the wildernesses and fastnesses of nature so often exhibit. One spot, where the common trenches on the civilised world, was scarcely less his admiration than mine. It is a high hill, half covered with furze and heath and broom, and sinking abruptly down to a large pond, almost a lake, covered with wild waterfowl. The ground, richly clothed with wood, oak, and beech, and elm, rises on the other side with equal abruptness, as if shutting in those glassy awters from all but the sky, which shines so brightly in their clear bosom : just in the bottom peeps a small sheltered farm, whose wreaths of light smoke and the white, glancing wings of the wild-ducks, as they flit across the lake, are all that give token of motion or of life. I have stood there in utter oblivion of greyhound or of hare, till moments have swelled to minutes, and minutes to hours; and so has Tom, conveying, by his exclamations of delight at its "pleasantness," exactly the same feeling which a poet or a painter (for it breathes the very spirit of calm and sunshiny beauty that a master-painter loves) would express by different but not truer praise. He called his own home "pleasant" too; and there, though one loves to hear any home so called—there, I must confess, that favourite phrase, which I like almost as well as they who have no other, did seem rather misapplied. And yet it was finely placed, very finely. It stood in a sort of defile, where a road almost perpendicular wound from the top of a steep, abrupt hill, crowned with a tuft of old Scottish firs, into a dingle of fern and wild brushwood. A shallow, sullen stream oozed from the bank on one side, and, after forming a rude channel across the road, sank into a dark, deep pool, half hidden amongst the sallows. Behind these sallows, in a nook between them and the hill, rose the uncouth and shapeless cottage of Tom Cordery. It is a scene which hangs upon the eye and the memory, striking, grand, almost sublime, and above all, eminently foreign. No English painter would choose such a subject for an English landscape; no one in a picture would take it for English. It might pass for one of those scenes which have furnished models to Salvator Rosa. Tom's cottage was, however, very thoroughly national and characteristic; a low, ruinous hovel, the door of which was fastened with a sedulous attention to security, that contrasted strangely with the tattered thatch of the roof, and the half-broken windows. No garden, no pig-sty, no pens for geese, none of the usual signs of cottage habitation:—yet the house was covered with nondescript dwellings, and the very walls were animate with their extraordinary tenants; pheasants, partridges, rabbits, tame wild-ducks, half-tame hares, and their enemies by nature and education, the ferrets, terriers, and mongrels, of whom his retinue consisted. Great ingenuity had been evinced in keeping separate these jarring elements; and by dint of hutches, cages, fences, kennel, and half a dozen little hurdled enclosures resembling the sort of courts which children are apt to build round their card-houses, peace was in general tolerably well preserved. Frequent sounds, however, of fear or of anger, as their several instincts were aroused, gave token that it was but a forced and hollow truce, and at such times the clamour was prodigious. Tom had the remarkable tenderness for animals when domesticated, which is so often found in those whose sole vocation seems to be their destruction in the field; and the one long, straggling, unceiled, barn-like room, which served for kitchen, bed-chamber, and hall, was cumbered with bipeds and quadrupeds of all kinds and descriptions—the sick, the delicate, the newly caught, the lying-in. In the midst of this menagerie sate Tom's wife (for he was married, though without a family—married to a woman lame of a leg as he himself was minus an arm), now trying to quiet her noisy inmates, now to outscold them. How long his friend the keeper would have continued to wink at this den of live game, none can say: the roof fairly fell in during the deep snow of last winter, killing, as poor Tom observed, two as fine litters of rabbits as ever were kittened. Remotely, I have no doubt that he himself fell a sacrifice to this misadventure. The overseer, to whom he applied to reinstate his beloved habitation, decided that the walls would never bear another roof, and removed him and his wife, as an especial favour, to a tidy, snug, comfortable room in the workhouse. The workhouse! From that hour poor Tom visibly altered. He lost his hilarity and independence. It was a change such as he had himself often inflicted, a complete change of habits, a transition from the wild to the tame. No labour was demanded of him; he went about as before, finding hares, killing rats, selling brooms, but the spirit of the man was departed. He talked of the quiet of his old abode, and the noise of the new; complained of children and other bad company; and looked down on his neighbours with the sort of contempt with which a cock-pheasant might regard a barn-door fowl. Most of all did he, braced into a gipsy-like defiance of wet and cold, grumble at the warmth and dryness of his apartment. He used to foretell that it would kill him, and assuredly it did so. Never could the typhus fever have found out that wild hillside, or have lurked under that broken roof. The free touch of the air would have chased the dæmon. Alas, poor Tom! warmth, and snugness, and comfort, whole windows, and an entire ceiling, were the death of him. Alas, poor Tom!

BRAMLEY MAYING

MR. GEOFFREY CRAYON has, in his delightful but somewhat fanciful writings, brought into general view many old sports and customs, some of which, indeed, still linger about the remote counties, familiar as local peculiarities to their inhabitants, whilst the greater part lie buried in books of the Elizabethan age, known only to the curious in English literature. One rural custom, which would have enchanted him, and which prevails in the north of Hampshire, he has not noticed, and probably does not know. Did any of my readers ever hear of a Maying? Let not any notions of chimney-sweepers soil the imagination of the gay Londoner! A country Maying is altogether a different affair from the street exhibitions which mix so much pity with our mirth, and do the heart good, perhaps, but not by gladdening it. A country Maying is a meeting of the lads and lasses of two or three parishes, who assemble in certain erections of green boughs called May-houses, to dance and—— But I am going to tell all about it in due order, and must not forestall my description.

Last year we went to Bramley Maying. There had been two or three such merry-makings before in that inaccessible neighbourhood, where the distance from large towns, the absence of great houses, and the consequent want of all decent roads, together with a country of peculiar wildness and beauty, combine to produce a sort of modern Arcadia. We had intended to assist at a Maying in the forest of Pamber, thinking that the deep glades of that fine woodland scenery would be more congenial to the spirit of old English merriment, as it breathed more of Robin Hood and Maid Marian than a mere village green—to say nothing of its being, of the two, more accessible by four-footed and two-wheeled conveyances. But the Pamber day had been suffered to pass, and Bramley was the last Maying of the season. So to Bramley we went.

As we had a considerable distance to go, we set out about noon, intending to return to dinner at six. Never was a day more congenial to a happy purpose! It was a day made for country weddings and dances on the green—a day of dazzling light, of ardent sunshine falling on hedgerows and meadows fresh with spring showers. You might almost see the grass grow and the leaves expand under the influence of that vivifying warmth; and we passed through the well-known and beautiful scenery of W. Park, and the pretty village of M., with a feeling of new admiration, as if we had never before felt their charms; so gloriously did the trees in their young leaves, the grass springing beneath them, the patches of golden broom and deeper furze, the cottages covered with roses, the blooming orchards, and the light snowy sprays of the cherry-trees tossing their fair blossoms across the deep blue sky, pour upon the eye the full magic of colour. On we passed gaily and happily as far as we knew our way—perhaps a little farther, for the place of our destination was new to both of us, when we had the luck, good or bad, to meet with a director in the person of the butcher of M. My companion is known to most people within a circuit of ten miles; so we had ready attention and most civil guidance from the man of beef and mutton—a prodigious person, almost as big as a prize ox, as rosy and jovial-looking as Falstaff himself, who was standing in the road with a slender, shrewd-looking boy, apt and ready enough to have passed for the page. He soon gave us the proper, customary, and unintelligible directions as to lanes and turnings—first to the right, then to the left, then round Farmer Jennings's close, then across the Holy Brook, then to the right again—till at last, seeing us completely bewildered, he offered to send the page, who was going our way for half a mile to carry out a shoulder of veal, to attend us to that distance as a guide; an offer gratefully accepted by all parties, especially the boy, whom we relieved of his burthen and took up behind, where he swang in an odd but apparently satisfactory posture, between running and riding. Whilst he continued with us, we fell into no mistakes; but at last he and the shoulder of veal reached their place of destination; and, after listening to a repetition, or perhaps a variation, of the turns right and left which were to conduct us to Bramley Green, we and our little guide parted.

On we went, twisting and turning through a labyrinth of lanes, getting deeper and deeper every moment, till at last, after many doubtings, we became fairly convinced that we had lost our way. Not a soul was in the fields; not a passenger in the road; not a cottage by the roadside: so on we went—I am afraid to say how far (for when people have lost their way, they are not the most accurate measurers of distance)—till we came suddenly on a small farmhouse, and saw at once that the road we had trodden led to that farm, and thither only. The solitary farmhouse had one solitary inmate, a smiling, middle-aged woman, who came to us and offered her services with the most alert civility: —" All her boys and girls were gone to the Maying," she said, "and she remained to keep house." —" The Maying! We were near Bramley then?" —Only two miles the nearest way across the fields —were we going?—she would see to the horse—we should soon be there, only over that stile and then across that field, and then turn to the right, and then take the next turning——no! the next but one to the left."—Right and left again for two miles over those deserted fields!—Right and left! we shuddered at the words. " Is there no carriage-road?—Where are we?"—"At Silchester, close to the walls, only half a mile from the church."—"At Silchester!" and in ten minutes we had said a thankful farewell to our kind informant, had retraced our steps a little, had turned up another lane, and found ourselves at the foot of that commanding spot which antiquaries call the amphitheatre, close under the walls of the Roman city, and in full view of an old acquaintance, the schoolmaster of Silchester, who happened to be there in his full glory, playing the part of cicerone to a party of ladies, and explaining far more than he knows, or than any one knows of streets, and gates, and sites of temples, which, by the bye, the worthy pedagogue usually calls parish-churches. I never was so glad to see him in my life, never thought he could have spoken with so much sense and eloquence as were comprised in the two words "straight forward," by which he answered our inquiry as to the road to Bramley.

And forward we went by a way beautiful beyond description: a road bounded on one side by every variety of meadow, and cornfield, and rich woodland; on the other by the rock-like walls of the old city, crowning an abrupt, magnificent bank of turf, broken by fragments, crags as it were, detached from the ruin, and young trees, principally ash, with silver stems standing out in picturesque relief from the green slope, and itself crowned with every sort of vegetation, from the rich festoons of briar and ivy, which garlanded its side, to the venerable oaks and beeches which nodded on its summit. I never saw anything so fine in my life. To be sure, we nearly broke our necks. Even I, who, having been overset astonishingly often, without any harm happening, have acquired, from frequency of escape, the confidence of escaping, and the habit of not caring for that particular danger, which is, I suppose, what in a man and in battle would be called courage; even I was glad enough to get out, and do all I could towards wriggling the gig round the rock-like stones, or sometimes helping to lift a wheel over the smaller impediments. We escaped that danger, and left the venerable walls behind us.—But I am losing my way here, too; I must loiter on the road no longer. Our other delays of a broken bridge—a bog—another wrong turning—and a meeting with a loaded waggon in a lane too narrow to pass—all this must remain untold.

At last we reached a large farmhouse at Bramley; another mile remained to the Green, but that was impassable. Nobody thinks of riding at Bramley. The late lady of the manor, when at rare and uncertain intervals she resided for a few weeks at her house of B. R., used, in visiting her only neighbour, to drive her coach and four through her farmers' ploughed fields. We must walk: but the appearance of gay crowds of rustics, all passing along one path, gave assurance that this time we should not lose our way. Oh, what a pretty path it was! along one sunny sloping field, up and down, dotted with trees like a park; then across a deep shady lane, with cows loitering and cropping grass from the banks; then up a long narrow meadow, in the very pride and vigour of its greenness, richly bordered by hedgerow timber, and terminating in the churchyard, and a little country church.

Bramley Church is well worth seeing. It contains that rare thing, a monument fine in itself and finer in its situation. We had heard of it, and, in spite of the many delays we had experienced, could not resist the temptation of sending one of the loiterers, who seemed to stand in the churchyard as a sort of out-guard to the Maying, to the vicar's house for the key. Prepared as we had been to see something unusual, we were very much struck. The church is small, simple, decaying, almost ruinous; but as you turn from the entrance into the centre aisle, and advance up to the altar, your eye falls on a lofty recess, branching out like a chapel on one side, and seen through a Gothic arch. It is almost paved with monumental brasses of the proud family of B., who have possessed the surrounding property from the time of the Conqueror; and in the centre of the large open space stands a large monument, surrounded by steps, on which reclines a figure of a dying man, with a beautiful woman leaning over him, full of a lovely look of anxiety and tenderness. The figures are very fine; but that which makes the grace and glory of this remarkable piece of sculpture is its being backed by an immense Gothic window, nearly the whole size of the recess, entirely composed of old stained glass. I do not know the story which the artist, in the series of pictures, intended to represent; but there they are, the gorgeous, glorious colours—reds, and purples, and greens, glowing like an anemone bed in the sunshine, or like one of the windows made of amethysts and rubies in the Arabian Tales, and throwing out the monumental figures with an effect almost magical. The parish clerk was at the Maying, and we had only an unlettered rustic to conduct us, so that I do not even know the name of the sculptor—he must have a strange, mingled feeling if ever he saw his work in its present home—delight that it looks so well, and regret that there is no one to look at it. That monument alone was worth losing our way for.

But cross two fields more, and up a quiet lane, and we are at the Maying, announced afar off by the merry sound of music, and the merrier clatter of childish voices. Here we are at the Green; a little turfy spot, where three roads meet, close shut in by hedgerows, with a pretty white cottage, and its long slip of a garden at one angle. I had no expectation of scenery so compact, so like a glade in a forest; it is quite a cabinet picture, with green trees for the frame. In the midst grows a superb horse-chesnut, in the full glory of its flowery pyramids, and from the trunk of the chesnut the May-houses commence. They are covered alleys built of green boughs, decorated with garlands and great bunches of flowers, the gayest that blow—lilacs,

Guelder-roses, peonies, tulips, stocks—hanging down like chandeliers among the dancers; for of dancers—gay, dark-eyed young girls in straw bonnets and white gowns, and their lovers in their Sunday attire,—the May-houses were full. The girls had mostly the look of extreme youth, and danced well and quietly like ladies—too much so; I should have been glad to see less elegance and more enjoyment; and their partners, though not altogether so graceful, were as decorous and as indifferent as real gentlemen. It was quite like a ballroom, as pretty and almost as dull. Outside was the fun. It is the outside, the upper gallery of the world, that has that good thing. There were children laughing, eating, trying to cheat, and being cheated, round an ancient and practised vendor of oranges and gingerbread; and on the other side of the tree lay a merry group of old men, in coats almost as old as themselves, and young ones in no coats at all, excluded from the dance by the disgrace of a smock-frock. Who would have thought of etiquette finding its way into the May-houses! That group would have suited Teniers; it smoked and drank a little, but it laughed a great deal more. There were a few decent, matronly looking women, too, sitting in a cluster; and young mothers strolling about with infants in their arms; and ragged boys peeping through the boughs at the dancers; and the bright sun shining gloriously on all this innocent happiness. Oh, what a pretty sight it was!—worth losing our way for—worth losing our dinner—both which events happened; whilst a party of friends, who were to have joined us, were far more unlucky; for they not only lost their way and their dinner, but rambled all day about the country, and never reached Bramley Maying.

A COUNTRY APOTHECARY

ONE of the most important personages in a small country town is the apothecary. He takes rank next after the rector and the attorney, and before the curate; and could be much less easily dispensed with than either of those worthies, not merely as holding "fate and physic" in his hand, but as the general, and as it were official, associate, adviser, comforter, and friend, of all ranks and all ages, of high and low, rich and poor, sick and well. I am no despiser of dignities; but twenty emperors shall be less intensely missed in their wide dominions than such a man as my friend John Hallett in his own small sphere.

The spot which was favoured with the residence of this excellent person was the small town of Hazelby, in Dorsetshire; a pretty little place, where everything seems at a standstill. It was originally built in the shape of the letter T; a long, broad market-place (still so called, although the market be gone) serving for the perpendicular stem, traversed by a straight, narrow, horizontal street, to answer for the top line. Not one addition has occurred to interrupt this architectural regularity since; fifty years ago, a rich London tradesman built, at the west end of the horizontal street, a wide-fronted single house, with two low wings, iron palisades before, and a fish-pond opposite, which still goes by the name of New Place, and is balanced, at the east end of the street, by an erection of nearly the same date, a large, square, dingy mansion enclosed within high walls, inhabited by three maiden sisters, and called, probably by way of nickname, the Nunnery. New Place being on the left of the road, and the Nunnery on the right, the T has now something the air of the Italic capital *T*, turned up at one end and down on the other. The latest improvements are the bow-window in the market-place, commanding the pavement both ways, which the late brewer, Andrews, threw out in his snug parlour some twenty years back, and where he used to sit smoking, with the sash up, in summer afternoons, enjoying himself, good man; and the great room at the Swan, originally built by the speculative publican, Joseph Allwright, for an assembly-room. That speculation did not answer. The assembly, in spite of canvassing and patronage, and the active exertions of all the young ladies in the neighbourhood, dwindled away and died at the end of two winters: then it became a club-room for the hunt; but the hunt quarrelled with Joseph's cookery: then a market-room for the farmers; but the farmers (it was in the high-price time) quarrelled with Joseph's wine: then it was converted into the magistrates'-room—the bench; but the bench and the market went away together, and there was an end of justicing: then Joseph tried the novel attraction (to borrow a theatrical phrase) of a billiard-table; but, alas! that novelty succeeded as ill as if it had been theatrical; there were not customers enough to pay the marker: at last, it has merged finally in that unconscious receptacle of pleasure and pain, a post-office; although Hazelby has so little to do with traffic of any sort—even the traffic of correspondence—that a saucy mail-coach will often carry on its small bag, and as often forget to call for the London bag in return.

In short, Hazelby is an insignificant place;—my readers will look for it in vain in the map of Dorsetshire;—it is omitted, poor dear town!—left out by the map-maker with as little remorse as a dropped letter!—and it is also an old-fashioned place. It has not even a cheap shop for female gear. Everything in the one store which it boasts, kept by Martha Deane, linen-draper and haberdasher, is dear and good, as things were wont to be. You may actually get there thread made of flax, from the gouty, uneven, clumsy, shiny fabric, yclept whited-brown, to the delicate commodity of Lisle, used for darning muslin. I think I was never more astonished than when, on asking, from the mere force of habit, for thread, I was presented, instead of the pretty lattice-wound balls or snowy reels of cotton, with which that demand is usually answered, with a whole drawerful of skeins, peeping from their blue papers—such skeins as in my youth a thrifty maiden would draw into the nicely stitched compartments of that silken repository, a housewife, or fold into a congeries of graduated thread-papers, "fine by degrees, and beautifully less." The very literature of Hazelby is doled out at the pastry-cook's, in a little one-windowed shop, kept by Matthew Wise. Tarts occupy one end of the counter, and reviews the other; whilst the shelves are parcelled out between books, and dolls, and gingerbread. It is a question, by which of his trades poor Matthew gains least; he is so shabby, so threadbare, and so starved.

Such a town would hardly have known what to do with a highly informed and educated surgeon, such as one now generally sees in that most liberal profession. My friend, John Hallett, suited it exactly. His predecessor, Mr. Simon Shuter, had been a small, wrinkled, spare old gentleman, with a short cough and a thin voice, who always seemed as if he needed an apothecary himself. He wore generally a full suit of drab, a flaxen wig of the sort called a Bob Jerom, and a very tight muslin stock; a costume which he had adopted in his younger days in imitation of the most eminent physician of the next city, and continued to the time of his death. Perhaps the cough might have been originally an imitation also, ingrafted on the system by habit. It had a most unsatisfactory sound, and seemed more like a trick than a real effect of nature. His talk was civil, prosy, and fidgety, much addicted to small scandal, and that kind of news which passes under the denomination of tittle-tattle. He was sure to tell one half of the town where the other drank tea, and recollected the blancmangers and jellies on a supper-table, or described a new gown, with as much science and unction as if he had been used to make jellies and wear gowns in his own person. Certain professional peculiarities might have favoured the supposition. His mode of practice was exactly that popularly attributed to old women. He delighted in innocent remedies—manna, magnesia, and camphor julep; never put on a blister in his life; and would sooner, from pure complaisance, let a patient die than administer an unpalatable prescription.

So qualified, to say nothing of his gifts in tea-drinking, casino, and quadrille (whist was too many for him), his popularity could not be questioned. When he expired all Hazelby mourned. The lamentation was general. The women of every degree (to borrow a phrase from that great phrase-monger, Horace Walpole) "cried quarts"; and the procession to the churchyard—that very churchyard to which he had himself followed so many of his patients—was now attended by all of them that remained alive.

It was felt that the successor of Mr. Simon Shuter would have many difficulties to encounter. My friend, John Hallett, "came, and saw, and overcame." John was what is usually called a rough diamond. Imagine a short, clumsy, stout-built figure, almost as broad as it is long, crowned by a bullet head, covered with shaggy brown hair sticking out in every direction; the face round and solid, with a complexion originally fair, but dyed one red by exposure to all sorts of weather; open, good-humoured eyes of a greenish cast, his admirers called them hazel; a wide mouth, full of large white teeth; a cocked-up nose, and a double chin; bearing altogether a strong resemblance to a print which I once saw hanging up in an alehouse parlour, of "the celebrated divine" (to use the identical words of the legend) "Doctor Martin Luther."

The condition of a country apothecary being peculiarly liable to the inclemency of the season, John's dress was generally such as might bid defiance to wind or rain, or snow or hail. If anything, he wrapt up most in the summer, having a theory that people were never so apt to take cold as in hot weather. He usually wore a bearskin greatcoat, a silk handkerchief over his cravat, top-boots on those sturdy pillars his legs, a huge pair of overalls, and a hat, which, from the day in which it first came into his possession to that in which it was thrown aside, never knew the comfort of being freed from its oilskin—never was allowed to display the glossy freshness of its sable youth. Poor dear hat! how its vanity (if hats have vanity) must have suffered! For certain its owner had none, unless a lurking pride in his own bluffness and bluntness may be termed such. He piqued

himself on being a plain, downright Englishman, and on a voice and address pretty much like his apparel, rough, strong, and warm, and fit for all weathers. A heartier person never lived.

In his profession he was eminently skilful, bold, confident, and successful. The neighbouring physicians liked to come after Mr. Hallett; they were sure to find nothing to undo. And blunt and abrupt as was his general manner, he was kind and gentle in a sick-room; only nervous disorders, the pet diseases of Mr. Simon Shuter, he could not abide. He made short work with them; frightened them away, as one does by children when they have the hiccough; or if the malady were pertinacious and would not go, he fairly turned off the patient. Once or twice, indeed, on such occasions, the patient got the start, and turned him off; Mrs. Emery, for instance, the lady's-maid at New Place, most delicate and mincing of waiting-gentlewomen, motioned him from her presence; and Miss Deane, daughter of Martha Deane, haberdasher, who, after completing her education at a boarding-school, kept a closet full of millinery in a little den behind her mamma's shop, and was by many degrees the finest lady in Hazelby, was so provoked at being told by him that nothing ailed her, that, to prove her weakly condition, she pushed him by main force out of doors.

With these exceptions Mr. Hallett was the delight of the whole town, as well as of all the farmhouses within six miles round. He just suited the rich yeomanry, cured their diseases, and partook of their feasts; was constant at christenings, and a man of prime importance at weddings. A country merry-making was nothing without "the Doctor." He was "the very prince of good fellows"; had a touch of epicurism, which, without causing any distaste of his own homely fare, made dainties acceptable when they fell in his way; was a most absolute carver; prided himself upon a sauce of his own invention, for fish and game—"Hazelby sauce" he called it; and was universally admitted to be the best compounder of a bowl of punch in the country.

Besides these rare convivial accomplishments, his gay and jovial temper rendered him the life of the table. There was no resisting his droll faces, his droll stories, his jokes, his tricks, or his laugh—the most contagious cachinnation that ever was heard. Nothing in the shape of fun came amiss to him. He would join in a catch or roar out a solo, which mght be heard a mile off; would play at hunt the slipper, or blindman's-buff; was a great man in a country dance, and upon very extraordinary occasions would treat the company to a certain remarkable hornpipe, which put the walls in danger of tumbling about their ears, and belonged to him as exclusively as the Hazelby sauce. It was a sort of parody on a *pas seul* which he had once seen at the Opera House, in which his face, his figure, his costume, his rich humour, and his strange, awkward, unexpected activity told amazingly. "The force of frolic could no further go" than "the Doctor's hornpipe." It was the climax of jollity.

But the chief scene of Mr. Hallett's gaiety lay out of doors, in a very beautiful spot, called the Down, a sloping upland, about a mile from Hazelby; a side view of which, with its gardens and orchards, its pretty church peeping from amongst lime- and yew-trees, and the fine piece of water called Hazelby Pond, it commanded. The Down itself was an extensive tract of land covered with the finest verdure, backed by a range of hills, and surrounded by coppice-woods, large patches of which were scattered over the turf, like so many islands on an emerald sea. Nothing could be more beautiful or more impenetrable than these thickets; they were principally composed of birch, holly, hawthorn, and maple, woven together by garlands of woodbine, interwreathed and intertwisted by bramble and brier, till even the sheep, although the bits of their snowy fleece left on the bushes bore witness to the attempt, could make no way in the leafy mass. Here and there a huge oak or beech rose towering above the rich underwood; and all around, as far as the eye could pierce, the borders of this natural shrubbery were studded with a countless variety of woodland flowers. When the old thorns were in blossom, or when they were succeeded by the fragrant woodbine and the delicate briar-rose, it was like a garden, if it were possible to fancy any garden so peopled with birds.

The only human habitation on this charming spot

was the cottage of the shepherd, old Thomas Tolfrey, who with his granddaughter Jemima, a light, pretty maiden of fourteen, tended the flocks on the Down; and the rustic carols of this little lass and the tinkling of the sheep-bells were usually the only sounds that mingled with the sweet songs of the feathered tribes. On May-days and holidays, however, the thickets resounded with other notes of glee than those of the linnet and the wood-lark. Fairs, revels, May-games, and cricket-matches—all were holden on the Down; and there would John Hallett sit, in his glory, universal umpire and referee of cricketer, wrestler, or back-sword player, the happiest and greatest man in the field. Little Jemima never failed to bring her grandfather's arm-chair, and place it under the old oak for the good doctor; I question whether John would have exchanged his throne for that of the King of England.

On these occasions he certainly would have been the better for that convenience, which he piqued himself on not needing—a partner. Generally speaking, he really, as he used to boast, did the business of three men; but when a sickly season and a Maying happened to come together, I cannot help suspecting that the patients had the worst of it. Perhaps, however, a partner might not have suited him. He was sturdy and independent to the verge of a fault, and would not have brooked being called to account, or brought to a reckoning by any man under the sun; still less would he endure the thought of that more important and durable co-partnery—marriage. He was a most determined bachelor; and so afraid of being mistaken for a wooer, or incurring the reputation of a gay deceiver, that he was as uncivil as his good-nature would permit to every unwedded female from sixteen to sixty, and had nearly fallen into some scrapes on that account with the spinsters of the town, accustomed to the soft silkiness of Mr. Simon Shuter; but they got used to it—it was the man's way; and there was an indirect flattery in his fear of their charms which the maiden ladies, especially the elder ones, found very mollifying; so he was forgiven.

In his shop and his household he had no need either of partner or of wife: the one was excellently managed by an old rheumatic journeyman, slow in speech and of vinegar aspect, who had been a pedagogue in his youth, and now used to limp about with his Livy in his pocket, and growl as he compounded the medicines over the bad latinity of the prescriptions; the other was equally well conducted by an equally ancient housekeeper and a cherry-cheeked niece, the orphan daughter of his only sister, who kept everything within doors in the bright and shining order in which he delighted. John Hallett, notwithstanding the roughness of his aspect, was rather knick-knacky in his tastes; a great patron of small inventions, such as the improved *ne plus ultra* corkscrew, and the latest patent snuffers. He also trifled with horticulture, dabbled in tulips, was a connoisseur in pinks, and had gained a prize for polyanthuses. The garden was under the especial care of his pretty niece, Miss Margaret, a grateful, warm-hearted girl, who thought she never could do enough to please her good uncle, and prove her sense of his kindness. He was indeed as fond of her as if he had been her father, and as kind.

Perhaps there was nothing very extraordinary in his goodness to the gentle and cheerful little girl who kept his walks so trim and his parlour so neat, who always met him with a smile, and who (last and strongest tie to a generous mind) was wholly dependent on him—had no friend on earth but himself. There was nothing very uncommon in that. But John Hallett was kind to every one, even where the sturdy old English prejudices, which he cherished as virtues, might seem most likely to counteract his gentler feelings. One instance of his benevolence and of his delicacy shall conclude this sketch.

Several years ago an old French *emigré* came to reside at Hazelby. He lodged at Matthew Wise's, of whose twofold shop for cakes and novels I have before made honourable mention, in the low three-cornered room, with a closet behind it, which Matthew had the impudence to call his first floor. Little was known of him but that he was a thin, pale, foreign-looking gentleman, who shrugged his shoulders in speaking, took a great deal of snuff, and made a remarkably low bow. The few persons with whom he had any communication spoke with amusement of his bad English, and with admiration of his good-humour, and it soon appeared, from a written paper placed in a conspicuous part of Matthew's shop, that he was an Abbé, and that he would do himself the honour of teaching French to any of the nobility or gentry of Hazelby who might think fit to employ him. Pupils dropped in rather slowly. The curate's daughters, and the attorney's son, and Miss Deane the milliner—but she found the language difficult, and left off, asserting that M. l'Abbé's snuff made her nervous. At last poor M. l'Abbé fell ill himself, really ill, dangerously ill, and Matthew Wise went in all haste to summon Mr. Hallett. Now Mr. Hallett had such an aversion to a Frenchman, in general, as a cat has to a dog; and was wont to erect himself into an attitude of defiance and wrath at the mere sight of the object of his antipathy. He hated and despised the whole nation, abhorred the language, and "would as lief," he assured Matthew, "have been called in to a toad." He went, however, grew interested in the case, which was difficult and complicated; exerted all his skill, and in about a month accomplished a cure.

By this time he had also become interested in his patient, whose piety, meekness, and resignation had won upon him in an extraordinary degree. The disease was gone, but a languor and lowness remained, which Mr. Hallett soon traced to a less curable disorder, poverty: the thought of the debt to himself evidently weighed on the poor Abbé's spirits, and our good apothecary at last determined to learn French purely to liquidate his own long bill. It was the drollest thing in the world to see this pupil of fifty, whose habits were so entirely unfitted for a learner, conning his task; or to hear him conjugating the verb *avoir*, or blundering through the first phrases of the easy dialogues. He was a most unpromising scholar, shuffled the syllables together in a manner that would seem incredible, and stumbled at every step of the pronunciation, against which his English tongue rebelled amain. Every now and then he solaced himself with a fluent volley of execrations in his own language, which the Abbé understood well enough to return, after rather a politer fashion, in French. It was a most amusing scene. But the motive! the generous, noble motive! M. l'Abbé, after a few lessons, detected this delicate artifice, and, touched almost to tears, insisted on dismissing his pupil, who, on his side, declared that nothing should induce him to abandon his studies. At last they came to a compromise. The cherry-cheeked Margaret took her uncle's post as a learner, which she filled in a manner much more satisfactory; and the good old Frenchman not only allowed Mr. Hallett to administer gratis to his ailments, but partook of his Sunday dinner as long as he lived.

THE COPSE

APRIL 18th.—Sad wintery weather; a north-east wind; a sun that puts out one's eyes, without affording the slightest warmth; dryness that chaps lips and hands like a frost in December; rain that comes chilling and arrowy like hail in January; nature at a dead pause; no seeds up in the garden; no leaves out in the hedgerows; no cowslips swinging their pretty bells in the fields; no nightingales in the dingles; no swallows skimming round the great pond; no cuckoos (that ever I should miss that rascally sonneteer!) in any part! Nevertheless there is something of a charm in this wintery spring, this putting-back of the seasons. If the flower-clock must stand still for a month or two, could it choose a better time than that of the primroses and violets? I never remember (and for such gauds my memory, if not very good for aught of wise or useful, may be trusted) such an affluence of the one or such a duration of the other. Primrosy is the epithet which this year will retain in my recollection. Hedge, ditch, meadow, field, even the very paths and highways, are set with them; but their chief *habitat* is a certain copse, about a mile off, where they are spread like a carpet, and where I go to visit them rather oftener than quite comports with the dignity of a lady of mature age. I am going thither this very afternoon, and May and her company are going too.

This Mayflower of mine is a strange animal. Instinct and imitation make in her an approach to reason which is sometimes almost startling. She mimics all that she sees us do, with the dexterity of a monkey and far more of gravity and apparent purpose; cracks nuts and eats them; gathers currants and severs them from the stalk with the most delicate nicety; filches and munches apples and pears; is as dangerous in an orchard as a schoolboy; smells to flowers; smiles at meeting; answers in a pretty lively voice when spoken to (sad pity that the language should be unknown!), and has greatly the advantage of us in a conversation, inasmuch as our meaning is certainly clear to her;—all this and a thousand amusing prettinesses (to say nothing of her canine feat of bringing her game straight to her master's feet, and refusing to resign it to any hand but his) does my beautiful greyhound perform untaught, by the mere effect of imitation and sagacity. Well, May, at the end of the coursing season, having lost Brush, our old spaniel, her great friend, and the blue greyhound Mariette, her comrade and rival, both of which four-footed worthies were sent out to keep for the summer, began to find solitude a weary condition, and to look abroad for company. Now it so happened that the same suspension of sport which had reduced our little establishment from three dogs to one, had also dispersed the splendid kennel of a celebrated courser in our neighbourhood, three of whose finest young dogs came home to "their walk" (as the sporting phrase goes) at the collar-maker's in our village. May, accordingly, on the first morning of her solitude (she had never taken the slightest notice of her neighbours before, although they had sojourned in our street upwards of a fortnight), bethought herself of the timely resource offered to her by the vicinity of these canine *beaux*, and went up boldly and knocked at their stable door, which was already very commodiously on the half-latch. The three dogs came out with much alertness and gallantry, and May, declining apparently to enter their territories, brought them off to her own. This manœuvre has been repeated every day, with one variation: of the three dogs, the first a brindle, the second a yellow, and the third a black, the two first only are now admitted to walk or consort with her, and the last, poor fellow, for no fault that I can discover except May's caprice, is driven away not only by the fair lady, but even by his old companions—is, so to say, sent to Coventry. Of her two permitted followers, the yellow gentleman, Saladin by name, is decidedly the favourite. He is, indeed, May's shadow, and will walk with me whether I choose or not. It is quite impossible to get rid of him unless by discarding Miss May also;—and to accomplish a walk in the country without her would be like an adventure of Don Quixote without his faithful 'squire Sancho.

So forth we set, May and I, and Saladin and the brindle; May and myself walking with the sedateness and decorum befitting our sex and age (she is five years old this grass, rising six)—the young things, for the soldan and the brindle are (not meaning any disrespect) little better than puppies, frisking and frolicking as best pleased them.

Our route lay for the first part along the sheltered, quiet lanes which lead to our old habitation; a way never trodden by me without peculiar and home-like feelings, full of the recollections, the pains and pleasures of other days. But we are not to talk sentiment now;—even May would not understand that maudlin language. We must get on. What a wintery hedgerow this is for the eighteenth of April! Primrosy, to be sure, abundantly spangled with those stars of the earth, —but so bare, so leafless, so cold! The wind whistles through the brown boughs as in winter. Even the early elder shoots, which do make an approach to springiness, look brown, and the small leaves of the woodbine, which have also ventured to peep forth, are of a sad purple, frost-bitten, like a dairy-maid's elbows on a snowy morning. The very birds, in this season of pairing and building, look chilly and uncomfortable, and their nests!——"Oh, Saladin! come away from the hedge! Don't you see that what puzzles you and makes you leap up in the air is a redbreast's nest? Don't you see the pretty speckled eggs? Don't you hear the poor hen calling as it were for help? Come here this moment, sir!" And by good luck Saladin (who for a paynim has tolerable qualities) comes, before he has touched the nest, or before his playmate the brindle, the less manageable of the two, has espied it.

Now we go round the corner and cross the bridge, where the common, with its clear stream winding between clumps of elms, assumes so park-like an appearance. Who is this approaching so slowly and majestically, this square bundle of petticoat and cloak, this road-waggon of a woman? It is, it must be Mrs. Sally Mearing, the completest specimen within my knowledge of farmeresses (may I be allowed that innovation in language?) as they were. It can be nobody else.

Mrs. Sally Mearing, when I first became acquainted with her, occupied, together with her father (a superannuated man of ninety), a large farm very near our former habitation. It had been anciently a great manor-farm or court-house, and was still a stately, substantial building, whose lofty halls and spacious chambers gave an air of grandeur to the common offices to which they were applied. Traces of gilding might yet be seen on the panels which covered the walls, and on the huge carved chimney-pieces which rose almost to the ceilings; and the marble tables and the inlaid oak staircase still spoke of the former grandeur of the court. Mrs. Sally corresponded well with the date of her mansion, although she troubled herself little with its dignity. She was thoroughly of the old school, and had a most comfortable contempt for the new; rose at four in winter and summer, breakfasted at six, dined at eleven in the forenoon, supped at five, and was regularly in bed before eight, except when the hay-time or the harvest imperiously required her to sit up till sunset,—a necessity to which she submitted with no very good grace. To a deviation from these hours, and to the modern iniquities of white aprons, cotton stockings, and muslin handkerchiefs (Mrs. Sally herself always wore check, black worsted, and a sort of yellow compound which she was wont to call *susy*), together with the invention of drill ploughs and threshing-machines, and other agricultural novelties, she failed not to attribute all the mishaps or misdoings of the whole parish. The last-mentioned discovery especially aroused her indignation. Oh, to hear her descant on the merits of the flail, wielded by a stout right arm, such as she had known in her youth (for by her account there was as great a deterioration in bones and sinews as in the other implements of husbandry), was enough to make the very inventor break his machine. She would even take up her favourite instrument, and thrash the air herself by way of illustrating her argument, and, to say truth, few men in these degenerate days could have matched the stout, brawny, muscular limb which Mrs. Sally displayed at sixty-five.

In spite of this contumacious rejection of agricultural improvements, the world went well with her at Court Farm. A good landlord, an easy rent, incessant labour, unremitting frugality, and excellent times, ensured a regular though moderate profit; and she lived on, grumbling and prospering, flourishing and complaining, till two misfortunes befell her at once—her father died, and her lease expired. The loss of her father, although a bedridden man, turned of ninety, who could not in the course of nature have been expected to live long, was a terrible shock to a daughter who was not so much younger as to be without fears for her own life, and who had besides been so used to nursing the good old man, and looking to his little comforts, that she missed him as a mother would miss an ailing child. The expiration of the lease was a grievance and a puzzle of a different nature. Her landlord would have willingly retained his excellent tenant, but not on the terms on which she then held the land, which had not varied for fifty years: so that poor Mrs. Sally had the misfortune to find rent rising and prices sinking both at the same moment—a terrible solecism in political economy. Even this, however, I believe she would have endured rather than have quitted the house where she was born, and to which all her ways and notions were adapted, had not a priggish steward, as much addicted to improvement and reform as she was to precedent and established usages, insisted on binding her by lease to spread a certain number of loads of chalk on every field. This tremendous innovation, for never had that novelty in manure whitened the crofts and pightles of Court Farm, decided her at once. She threw the proposals into the fire, and left the place in a week.

Her choice of a habitation occasioned some wonder and much amusement in our village world. To be sure, upon the verge of seventy, an old maid may be permitted to dispense with the more rigid punctilio of her class, but Mrs. Sally had always been so tenacious on the score of character, so very a prude, so determined an avoider of the "men folk" (as she was wont contemptuously to call them), that we all were conscious of something like astonishment on finding that she and her little handmaiden had taken up their abode in one end of a spacious farmhouse belonging to the bluff old bachelor, George Robinson of the Lea. Now Farmer Robinson was quite as notorious for his aversion to petticoated things as Mrs. Sally for her hatred to the unfeathered bipeds who wear doublet and hose, so that there was a little astonishment in that quarter too, and plenty of jests, which the honest farmer speedily silenced, by telling all who joked on the subject that he had given his lodger fair warning that, let people say what they would, he was quite determined not to

marry her; so that, if she had any views that way, it would be better for her to go elsewhere. This declaration, which must be admitted to have been more remarkable for frankness than civility, made, however, no ill impression on Mrs. Sally. To the farmer's she went, and at his house she lives still, with her little maid, her tabby cat, a decrepit sheep-dog, and much of the lumber of Court Farm, which she could not find in her heart to part from. There she follows her old ways and her old hours, untempted by matrimony, and unassailed (as far as I hear) by love or by scandal, with no other grievance than an occasional dearth of employment for herself and her young lass (even pewter dishes do not always want scouring), and now and then a twinge of the rheumatism.

Here she is, that good relique of the olden time —for, in spite of her whims and prejudices, a better and a kinder woman never lived—here she is, with the hood of her red cloak pulled over her close black bonnet of that silk which once (it may be presumed) was fashionable, since it is still called mode, and her whole stout figure huddled up in a miscellaneous and most substantial covering of thick petticoats, gowns, aprons, shawls, and cloaks, —a weight which it requires the strength of a thresher to walk under—here she is with her square honest visage and her loud frank voice;—and we hold a pleasant disjointed chat of rheumatisms and early chickens, bad weather, and hats with feathers in them;—the last exceedingly sore subject being introduced by poor Jane Davies a cousin of Mrs. Sally), who, passing us in a beaver bonnet on her road from school, stopped to drop her little curtsy, and was soundly scolded for her civility. Jane, who is a gentle, humble, smiling lass, about twelve years old, receives so many rebukes from her worthy relative, and bears them so meekly, that I should not wonder if they were to be followed by a legacy: I sincerely wish they may. Well, at last we said good-bye; when, on inquiring my destination, and hearing that I was bent to the ten-acre copse (part of the farm which she ruled so long), she stopped me to tell a dismal story of two sheep-stealers who sixty years ago were found hidden in that copse, and only taken after great difficulty and resistance, and the maiming of a peace-officer.—" Pray don't go there, Miss! For mercy's sake don't be so venturesome! Think if they should kill you!" were the last words of Mrs. Sally.

Many thanks for her care and kindness! But without being at all fool-hardy in general, I have no great fear of the sheep-stealers of sixty years ago. Even if they escaped hanging for that exploit, I should greatly doubt their being in case to attempt another. So on we go: down the short shady lane, and out on the pretty retired green, shut in by fields and hedgerows, which we must cross to reach the copse. How lively this green nook is to-day, half covered with cows and horses and sheep! And how glad these frolicsome greyhounds are to exchange the hard gravel of the high road for this pleasant short turf, which seems made for their gambols! How beautifully they are at play, chasing each other round and round in lessening circles, darting off at all kinds of angles, crossing and recrossing May, and trying to win her sedateness into a game at romps, turning round on each other with gay defiance, pursuing the cows and the colts, leaping up as if to catch the crows in their flight;—all in their harmless and innocent—— "Ah, wretches! villains! rascals! four-footed mischiefs! canine plagues! Saladin! Brindle!"—They are after the sheep—"Saladin, I say!"—They have actually singled out that pretty spotted lamb —"Brutes, if I catch you! Saladin, Brindle!" We shall be taken up for sheep-stealing presently ourselves. They have chased the poor little lamb into a ditch, and are mounting guard over it, standing at bay—"Ah, wretches, I have you now! For shame, Saladin! Get away, Brindle! See how good May is. Off with you, brutes! For shame! 'For shame!" and brandishing a handkerchief, which could hardly be an efficient instrument of correction, I succeeded in driving away the two puppies, who after all meant nothing more than play, although it was somewhat rough, and rather too much in the style of the old fable of the boys and the frogs. May is gone after them, perhaps to scold them; for she has been as grave as a judge during the whole proceeding, keeping ostentatiously close to me, and taking no part whatever in the mischief.

The poor little pretty lamb! here it lies on the bank quite motionless, frightened I believe to death, for certainly those villains never touched it. It does not stir. Does it breathe? Oh yes, it does! It is alive, safe enough. Look, it opens its eyes, and, finding the coast clear and its enemies far away, it springs up in a moment and gallops to its dam, who has stood bleating the whole time at a most respectful distance. Who would suspect a lamb of so much simple cunning? I really thought the pretty thing was dead—and now how glad the ewe is to recover her curling spotted little one! How fluttered they look! Well! this adventure has flurried me too: between fright and running, I warrant you, my heart beats as fast as the lamb's.

Ah! here is the shameless villain Saladin, the cause of the commotion, thrusting his slender nose into my hand to beg pardon and make up! "Oh wickedest of soldans! Most iniquitous pagan! Soul of a Turk!"—but there is no resisting the good-humoured creature's penitence. I must pat him. "There! there! Now we will go to the copse, I am sure we shall find no worse malefactors than ourselves—shall we, May?—and the sooner we get out of sight of the sheep the better; for Brindle seems meditating another attack. *Allons, messieurs*, over this gate, across this meadow, and here is the copse."

How boldly that superb ash-tree with its fine silver bark rises from the bank, and what a fine entrance it makes with the holly beside it, which also deserves to be called a tree! But here we are in the copse. Ah! only one half of the underwood was cut last year, and the other is at its full growth; hazel, briar, woodbine, bramble, forming one impenetrable thicket, and almost uniting with the lower branches of the elms, and oaks, and beeches, which rise at regular distances overhead. No foot can penetrate that dense and thorny entanglement; but there is a walk all round by the side of the wide sloping bank, walk and bank and copse carpeted with primroses, whose fresh and balmy odour impregnates the very air. Oh how exquisitely beautiful! and it is not the primroses only, those gems of flowers, but the natural mosaic of which they form a part:—that network of ground ivy, with its lilac blossoms and the subdued tint of its purplish leaves, those rich mosses, those enamelled wild hyacinths, those spotted arums, and above all those wreaths of ivy linking all the flowers together with chains of leaves more beautiful than blossoms, whose white veins seem swelling amidst the deep green or splendid brown;—it is the whole earth that is so beautiful. Never surely were primroses so richly set, and never did primroses better deserve such a setting. There they are of their own lovely yellow, the hue to which they have given a name, the exact tint of the butterfly that overhangs them (the first I have seen this year! can spring really be coming at last?)—sprinkled here and there with tufts of a reddish purple, and others of the purest white, as some accident of soil affects that strange and inscrutable operation of nature, the colouring of flowers. Oh, how fragrant they are, and how pleasant it is to sit in this sheltered copse listening to the fine creaking of the wind amongst the branches, the most unearthly of sounds, with this gay tapestry under our feet, and the wood-pigeons flitting from tree to tree, and mixing their deep note of love with the elemental music.

Yes! spring is coming. Wood-pigeons, butterflies, and sweet flowers, all give token of the sweetest of the seasons. Spring is coming. The hazel stalks are swelling and putting forth their pale tassels; the satin palms, with their honeyed odours, are out on the willow, and the last lingering winter berries are dropping from the hawthorn, and making way for the bright and blossomy leaves.

WHITSUN EVE

THE pride of my heart and the delight of my eyes is my garden. Our house, which is in dimensions very much like a bird-cage, and might, with almost equal convenience, be laid on a shelf, or hung up in a tree, would be utterly unbearable in warm weather were it not that we have a retreat out of doors,—and a very pleasant retreat it is. To make my readers fully comprehend it, I must describe our whole territories.

Fancy a small plot of ground, with a pretty, low, irregular cottage at one end; a large granary, divided from the dwelling by a little court running along one side; and a long, thatched shed open towards the garden, and supported by wooden pillars on the other. The bottom is bounded, half by an old wall, and half by an old paling, over which we see a pretty distance of woody hills. The house, granary, wall, and paling are covered with vines, cherry-trees, roses, honeysuckles, and jessamines, with great clusters of tall hollyhocks running up between them; a large elder overhanging the little gate, and a magnificent bay-tree, such a tree as shall scarcely be matched in these parts, breaking with its beautiful conical form the horizontal lines of the buildings. This is my garden; and the long pillared shed, the sort of rustic arcade which runs along one side, parted from the flower-beds by a row of rich geraniums, is our out-of-door drawing-room.

I know nothing so pleasant as to sit there on a summer afternoon, with the western sun flickering through the great elder-tree, and lighting up our gay parterres, where flowers and flowering shrubs are set as thick as grass in a field, a wilderness of blossom, interwoven, intertwined, wreathy, garlandy, profuse beyond all profusion, where we may guess that there is such a thing as mould but never see it. I know nothing so pleasant as to sit in the shade of that dark bower, with the eye resting on that bright piece of colour, lighted so gloriously by the evening sun, now catching a glimpse of the little birds as they fly rapidly in and out of their nests—for there are always two or three birds'-nests in the thick tapestry of cherry-trees, honeysuckles, and China-roses, which cover our walls—now tracing the gay gambols of the common butterflies as they sport around the dahlias; now watching that rarer moth, which the country people, fertile in pretty names, call the bee-bird; that bird-like insect, which flutters in the hottest days over the sweetest flowers, inserting its long proboscis into the small tube of the jessamine, and hovering over the scarlet blossoms of the geranium, whose bright colour seems reflected on its own feathery breast; that insect which seems so thoroughly a creature of the air, never at rest; always, even when feeding, self-poised and self-supported, and whose wings, in their ceaseless motion, have a sound so deep, so full, so lulling, so musical. Nothing so pleasant as to sit amid that mixture of the flower and the leaf, watching the bee-bird! Nothing so pretty to look at as my garden! It is quite a picture; only unluckily it resembles a picture in more qualities than one,—it is fit for nothing but to look at. One might as well think of walking in a bit of framed canvass. There are walks to be sure—tiny paths of smooth gravel, by courtesy called such—but they are so overhung by roses and lilies, and such gay encroachers—so over-run by convolvulus, and heart's-ease, and mignonette, and other sweet stragglers, that, except to edge through them occasionally, for the purposes of planting, or weeding, or watering, there might as well be no paths at all. Nobody thinks of walking in my garden. Even May glides along with a delicate and trackless step, like a swan through the water; and we, its two-footed denizens, are fain to treat it as if it were really a saloon, and go out for a walk towards sunset, just as if we had not been sitting in the open air all day.

What a contrast from the quiet garden to the lively street! Saturday night is always a time of stir and bustle in our village, and this is Whitsun Eve, the pleasantest Saturday of all the year, when London journeymen and servant lads and lasses snatch a short holiday to visit their families. A short and precious holiday, the happiest and liveliest of any; for even the gambols and merry-makings of Christmas offer but a poor enjoyment compared with the rural diversions, the Mayings, revels, and cricket-matches of Whitsuntide.

We ourselves are to have a cricket-match on Monday, not played by the men, who, since a certain misadventure with the Beech-Hillers, are, I am sorry to say, rather chap-fallen, but by the boys, who, zealous for the honour of their parish, and headed by their bold leader, Ben Kirby, marched in a body to our antagonists' ground the Sunday after our melancholy defeat, challenged the boys of that proud hamlet, and beat them out and out on the spot. Never was a more signal victory. Our boys enjoyed this triumph with so little moderation that it had like to have produced a very tragical catastrophe. The captain of the Beech-Hill youngsters, a capital bowler, by name Amos Stone, enraged past all bearing by the crowing of his adversaries, flung the ball at Ben Kirby with so true an aim, that if that sagacious leader had not warily ducked his head when he saw it coming, there would probably have been a coroner's inquest on the case, and Amos Stone would have been tried for manslaughter. He let fly with such vengeance, that the cricket-ball was found embedded in a bank of clay five hundred yards off, as if it had been a cannon shot. Tom Coper and Farmer Thackum, the umpires, both say that they never saw so tremendous a ball. If Amos Stone live to be a man (I mean to say, if he be not hanged first) he'll be a pretty player. He is coming here on Monday with his party to play the return match, the umpires having respectively engaged Farmer Thackum that Amos shall keep the peace, Tom Coper that Ben shall give no unnecessary or wanton provocation—a nicely worded and lawyer-like clause, and one that proves that Tom Coper hath his doubts of the young gentleman's discretion; and, of a truth, so have I. I would not be Ben Kirby's surety, cautiously as the security is worded,—no! not for a white double dahlia, the present object of my ambition.

This village of ours is swarming to-night like a hive of bees, and all the church bells round are pouring out their merriest peals, as if to call them together. I must try to give some notion of the various figures.

First there is a group suited to Teniers, a cluster of out-of-door customers of the Rose, old benchers of the inn, who sit round a table smoking and drinking in high solemnity to the sound of Timothy's fiddle. Next, a mass of eager boys, the combatants of Monday, who are surrounding the shoemaker's shop, where an invisible hole in their ball is mending by Master Keep himself, under the joint superintendence of Ben Kirby and Tom Coper. Ben showing much verbal respect and outward deference for his umpire's judgment and experience, but managing to get the ball done his own way after all; whilst outside the shop, the rest of the eleven, the less-trusted commons, are shouting and bawling round Joel Brent, who is twisting the waxed twine round the handles of the bats—the poor bats, which please nobody, which the taller youths are despising as too little and too light, and the smaller are abusing as too heavy and too large. Happy critics! winning their match can hardly be a greater delight—even if to win it they be doomed! Farther down the street is the pretty black-eyed girl, Sally Wheeler, come home for a day's holiday from B., escorted by a tall footman in a dashing livery, whom she is trying to curtsy off before her deaf grandmother sees him. I wonder whether she will succeed!

Ascending the hill are two couples of a different description. Daniel Tubb and his fair Valentine, walking boldly along like licensed lovers; they have been asked twice in church, and are to be married on Tuesday; and closely following that happy pair, near each other, but not together, come Jem Tanner and Mabel Green, the poor culprits of the wheat-hoeing. Ah! the little clerk hath not relented! The course of true love doth not yet run smooth in that quarter. Jem dodges along, whistling "cherry-ripe," pretending to walk by himself, and to be thinking of nobody; but every now and then he pauses in his negligent saunter, and turns round outright to steal a glance at Mabel, who, on her part, is making believe to walk with poor Olive Hathaway, the lame mantua-maker, and even affecting to talk and to listen to that gentle, humble creature, as she points to the wild-flowers on the common, and the lambs and children disporting amongst the gorse, but whose thoughts and eyes are evidently fixed on Jem Tanner, as she meets his backward glance with a blushing smile, and half springs forward to meet him; whilst Olive has broken off the conversation as soon as she perceived the preoccupation of her companion, and begun humming, perhaps unconsciously, two or three lines of Burns, whose "Whistle and I'll come to thee, my love," and "Gi'e me a glance of thy bonnie black ee," were never better exemplified than in the couple before her. Really it is curious to watch them, and to see how gradually the attraction of this tantalising vicinity becomes irresistible, and the rustic lover rushes to his pretty mistress like the needle to the magnet. On they go, trusting to the deepening twilight, to the little clerk's absence, to the good-humour of the happy lads and lasses, who are passing and repassing on all sides—or rather, perhaps, in a happy oblivion of the cross uncle, the kind villagers, the squinting lover, and the whole world. On they trip, linked arm-in-arm, he trying to catch a glimpse of her glowing face under her bonnet, and she hanging down her head and avoiding his gaze with a mixture of modesty and coquetry, which well becomes the rural beauty. On they go, with a reality and intensity of affection which must overcome all obstacles; and poor Olive follows with an evident sympathy in their happiness, which makes her almost as enviable as they; and we pursue our walk amidst the moonshine and the nightingales, with Jacob Frost's cart looming in the distance, and the merry sounds of Whitsuntide, the shout, the laugh, and the song echoing all around us, like "noises of the air."

THE RAT-CATCHER

BEAUTIFULLY situated on a steep knoll, overhanging a sharp angle in the turnpike road, which leads through our village of Aberleigh, stands a fantastic rustic building, with a large yew-tree on one side, a superb weeping ash hanging over it on the other, a clump of elms forming a noble background behind, and all the prettinesses of porches garlanded with clematis, windows mantled with jessamine, and chimneys wreathed with luxuriant ivy, adding grace to the picture. To form a picture, most assuredly, it was originally built,—a point of view, as it is called, from Allonby Park, to which the by-road that winds round this inland cape, or headland, directly leads; and most probably it was also copied from some book of tasteful designs for lodges or ornamented cottages, since not only the building itself, but the winding path that leads up the acclivity, and the gate which gives entrance to the little garden, smack of the pencil and the graver.

For a picture certainly, and probably from a picture, was that cottage erected, although its ostensible purpose was merely that of a receiving-house for letter and parcels for the Park; to which the present inhabitant, a jolly, bustling, managing dame, of great activity and enterprise in her own peculiar line, has added the profitable occupation of a thriving and well-accustomed village-shop; contaminating the picturesque, old-fashioned bay-window of the fancy letter-house by the vulgarities of red-herrings, tobacco, onions, and salt-butter; a sight which must have made the projector of her elegant dwelling stare again,—and forcing her customers to climb up and down an ascent almost as steep as the roof of a house, whenever they wanted a penny-worth of needles, or a half-penny-worth of snuff; a toil whereat some of our poor old dames groaned aloud. Sir Henry threatened to turn her out, and her customers threatened to turn her off; but neither of these events happened. Dinah Forde appeased her landlord and managed her customers: for Dinah Forde was a notable woman; and it is really surprising what great things, in a small way, your notable woman will compass.

Besides Mrs. Dinah Forde, and her apprentice, a girl of ten years old, the letter-house had lately acquired another occupant, in the shape of Dinah's tenant or lodger,—I don't know which word best expresses the nature of the arrangement,—my old friend, Sam Page, the Rat-catcher; who, together with his implements of office, two ferrets, and four mongrels, inhabited a sort of shed or outhouse at the back of the premises,—serving, "especially the curs," as Mrs. Forde was wont to express herself,

of guard and protection to a lone woman's

Page was, as I have said, an old acquaint-
of ours, although neither as a resident of
, nor in his capacity of rat-catcher, both
were recent assumptions. It was, indeed,
to see Sam Page as a resident anywhere.
abode seemed to be the highway. One should
soon have expected to find a gipsy within stone
, as soon have looked for a hare in her last
form, or a bird in her old nest, as for Sam Page
the same place a month together: so completely
he belong to that order which the lawyers call
grants, and the common people designate by the
nificant name of trampers; and so entirely of
all rovers did he seem the most roving, of all
wanderers the most unsettled. The winds, the
clouds, even our English weather, were but a type
of his mutability.
Our acquaintance with him had commenced
above twenty years ago, when, a lad of some
fifteen or thereaway, he carried muffins and cakes
about the country. The whole house was caught
by his intelligence and animation, his light active
figure, his keen grey eye, and the singular mixture
of shrewdness and good-humour in his sharp but
pleasant features. Nobody's muffins could go
down but Sam Page's. We turned off our old,
stupid, deaf cakeman, Simon Brown, and appointed
Sam on the instant. (*N.B.*—This happened at the
period of a general election, and Sam wore the

right colour, and Simon the wrong.) Three times a week he was to call. Faithless wretch!—he never called again! He took to selling election ballads, and carrying about hand-bills. We waited for him a fortnight, went muffinless for fourteen days, and then, our candidate being fairly elected, and blue and yellow returned to their original non-importance, were fain to put up once more with poor old deaf Simon Brown.

Sam's next appearance was in the character of a letter-boy, when he and a donkey set up a most spirited opposition to Thomas Hearne and the post-cart. Everybody was dissatisfied with Thomas Hearne, who had committed more sins than I can remember, of forgetfulness, irregularity, and all manner of postman-like faults; and Sam, when applying for employers, made a most successful canvass, and for a week performed miracles of punctuality. At the end of that time he began to commit, with far greater vigour than his predecessor, Thomas Hearne, the several sins for which that worthy had been discarded. On Tuesday he forgot to call for the bag in the evening; on Wednesday he omitted to bring it in the morning; on Thursday he never made his appearance at all; on Friday his employers gave him warning; and on Saturday they turned him off. So ended this hopeful experiment.

Still, however, he continued to travel the country in various capacities. First, he carried a tray of casts; then a basket of Staffordshire ware; then he cried cherries; then he joined a troop of ruddle-men, and came about redder than a red Indian; then he sported a barrel-organ, a piece of mechanism of no small pretensions, having two sets of puppets on the top, one of girls waltzing, the other of soldiers at drill; then he drove a knife-grinder's wheel; then he led a bear and a very accomplished monkey; then he escorted a celebrated company of dancing dogs; and then, for a considerable time, during which he took a trip to India and back, we lost sight of him.

He reappeared, however, at B. Fair, where one year he was showman to the Living Skeleton, and the next a performer in the tragedy of the Edinburgh Murders, as exhibited every half-hour at the price of a penny to each person. Sam showed so much talent for melodrama, that we fully expected to find him following his new profession, which offered all the advantage of the change of place and of character which his habits required; and on his being again, for several months, an absentee, had little doubt but he had been promoted from a booth to a barn, and even looked for his name amongst a party of five strollers, three men and two women, who issued play-bills at Aberleigh, and performed tragedy, comedy, opera, farce, and pantomime, with all the degrees and compounds thereof described by Polonius, in the great room at the Rose, divided for the occasion into a row of chairs called the Boxes, at a shilling per seat, and two of benches called the Pit, at sixpence. I even suspected that a Mr. Theodore Fitzhugh, the genius of the company, might be Sam Page fresh christened. But I was mistaken. Sam, when I saw him again, and mentioned my suspicion, pleaded guilty to a turn for the drama; he confessed that he liked acting of all things, especially tragedy, "it was such fun." But there was a small obstacle to his pursuit of the more regular branches of the histrionic art—the written drama: our poor friend could not read. To use his own words, "he was no scholar"; and on recollecting certain small aberrations which had occurred during the three days that he carried the letter-bag, and professed to transact errands, such as the mis-delivery of notes, and the non-performance of written commissions, we were fain to conclude that, instead of having, as he expressed it, "somehow or other got rid of his learning," learning was a blessing which Sam had never possessed, and that a great luminary was lost to the stage simply from the accident of not knowing his alphabet.

Instead of being, as we had imagined, ranting in Richard, or raving in Lear, our unlucky hero had been amusing himself by making a voyage to the West Indies, and home by the way of America, having had some thoughts of honouring the New World by making it the scene of his residence, or rather of his peregrinations; and a country where the whole population seems movable would, probably, have suited him: but the yellow fever seized him, and pinned him fast at the very beginning of his North American travels; and, sick and weary, he returned to England, determined, as he said, "to take a room and live respectably."

The apartment on which he fixed was, as I have intimated, an outhouse belonging to Mrs. Dinah Forde, in which he took up his abode the beginning of last summer, with his two ferrets, harmless, foreign-looking things (no native English animal has so outlandish an appearance as the ferret, with its long limber body, its short legs, red eyes, and ermine-looking fur), of whose venom, gentle as they looked, he was wont to boast amain; four little dogs, of every variety of mongrel ugliness, whose eminence in the same quality nobody could doubt, for one had lost an eye in battle, and one an ear, the third halted in his fore-quarters, and the fourth limped behind; and a jay of great talent and beauty, who turned his pretty head this way and that, and bent and bowed most courteously when addressed, and then responded in words equally apt and courteous to all that was said to him. Mrs. Dinah Forde fell in love with that jay at first sight; borrowed him of his master, and hung him at one side of her door, where he soon became as famous all through the parish as the talking bird in the Arabian Tales, or the parrot Vert-vert, immortalised by Gresset.

Sam's own appearance was as rat-catcher-like, I had almost said as venomous, as that of his retinue. His features sharper than ever, thin, and worn, and sallow, yet arch and good-humoured withal; his keen eye and knowing smile, his pliant active figure, and the whole turn of his equipment, from the shabby straw hat to the equally shabby long gaiters, told his calling almost as plainly as the sharp heads of the ferrets, which were generally protruded from the pockets of his dirty jean jacket, or the bunch of dead rats with which he was wont to parade the streets of B. on a market-day. He seemed, at last, to have found his proper vocation; and having stuck to it for four or five months, with great success and reputation, there seemed every chance of his becoming stationary at Aberleigh.

In his own profession his celebrity was, as I have said, deservedly great. The usual complaint against rat-catchers, that they take care not to ruin the stock, that they are sure to leave breeders enough, could not be applied to Sam; who, poor fellow, never was suspected of forethought in his life; and who, in this case, had evidently too much delight in the chase himself, to dream of checking or stopping it whilst there was a rat left unslain. On the contrary, so strong was the feeling of his sportsmanship, and that of his poor curs, that one of his grand operations, on the taking in of a wheat-rick, for instance, or the clearing out of a barn, was sure to be attended by all the idle boys and unemployed men in the village,—by all, in short, who, under the pretence of helping, could make an excuse to their wives, their consciences, or the parish-officers. The grand battue, on emptying

Farmer Brookes's great barn, will be long remembered in Aberleigh; there was more noise made, and more beer drunk, than on any occasion since the happy marriage of Miss Phœbe and the pattenmaker; it even emulated the shouts and the tipsiness of the B. election—and that's a bold word! The rats killed were in proportion to the din—and that is a bold word too! I am really afraid to name the number, it seemed to myself, and would appear to my readers, so incredible. Sam and Farmer Brookes were so proud of the achievement, that they hung the dead game on the lower branches of the great oak outside the gate, after the fashion practised by mole-catchers, to the unspeakable consternation of a cockney cousin of the good farmer's, a very fine lady, who had never in her life before been out of the sound of Bow-bell, and who, happening to catch sight of this portentous crop of acorns in passing under the tree, caused her husband, who was driving her, to turn the gig round, and, notwithstanding remonstrance and persuasion, and a most faithful promise that the boughs should be dismantled before night, could not be induced to set foot in a place where the trees were, to use her own words, "so heathenish," and betook herself back to her own domicile at Holborn Bars, in great and evident perplexity as to the animal or vegetable quality of the oak in question.

Another cause of the large assemblage at Sam's rat-hunts was, besides the certainty of good sport the eminent popularity of the leader of the chase.

Sam was an universal favourite. He had goodfellowship enough to conciliate the dissipated, and yet stopped short of the licence which would have disgusted the sober,—was pleasant-spoken, quick, lively, and intelligent,—sang a good song, told a good story, and had a kindness of temper, and a lightness of heart, which rendered him a most exhilarating and coveted companion to all in his own station. He was, moreover, a proficient in country games; and so eminent at cricket especially, that the men of Aberleigh were no sooner able, from his residence in the parish, to count him amongst their eleven, than they challenged their old rivals, the men of Hinton, and beat them forthwith.

Two nights before the return match, Sam, shabbier even than usual, and unusually out of spirits, made his appearance at the house of an old Aberleigh cricketer, still a patron and promoter of that noble game, and the following dialogue took place between them:

"Well, Sam, we are to win this match."

"I hope so, please your honour. But I'm sorry to say I shan't be at the winning of it."

"Not here, Sam! What, after rattling the stumps about so gloriously last time, won't you stay to finish them now? Only think how those Hinton fellows will crow! You must stay over Wednesday."

"I can't, your honour. 'Tis not my fault. But, here I've had a lawyer's letter on the part of Mrs. Forde, about the trifle of rent, and a bill that I owe her; and if I'm not off to-night Heaven knows what she'll do with me!"

"The rent—that can't be much. Let's see if we can't manage——"

"Ay, but there's a longish bill, sir," interrupted Sam. "Consider, we are seven in family."

"Seven!" interrupted, in his turn, the other interlocutor.

"Ay, sir, counting the dogs and the ferrets, poor beasts! for I suppose she has not charged for the jay's board, though 'twas that unlucky bird made the mischief."

"The jay! What could he have to do with the matter? Dinah used to be as fond of him as if he had been her own child! and I always thought Dinah Forde a good-natured woman."

"So she is, in the main, your honour," replied Sam, twirling his hat, and looking half shy and half sly, at once knowing and ashamed. "So she is, in the main; but this, somehow, is a particular sort of an affair. You must know, sir," continued Sam, gathering courage as he went on, "that at first the widow and I were very good friends, and several of these articles which are charged in the bill, such as milk for the ferrets, and tea and lump-sugar, and young onions for myself, I verily thought were meant as presents; and so I do believe at the time she did mean them. But, howsoever, Jenny Dobbs, the nursery-maid at the Park (a pretty black-eyed lass—perhaps your honour may have noticed her walking with the children), she used to come out of an evening like to see us play cricket, and then she praised my bowling, and then I talked to her, and so at last we began to keep company; and the jay, owing, I suppose, to hearing me say so sometimes, began to cry out, 'Pretty Jenny Dobbs!'"

"Well, and this affronted the widow?".

"Past all count, your honour. You never saw a woman in such a tantrum. She declared I had taught the bird to insult her, and posted off to Lawyer Latitat. And here I have got this letter, threatening to turn me out, and put me in gaol, and what not, from the lawyer; and Jenny, a false-hearted jade, finding how badly matters are going with me, turns round and says, that she never meant to have me, and is going to marry the French Mounseer (Sir Henry's French valet), a foreigner and a papist, who may have a dozen wives before for anything she can tell. These women are enough to drive a man out of his senses!" And poor Sam gave his hat a mighty swing, and looked likely to cry from a mixture of grief, anger, and vexation. "These women are enough to drive a man mad!" reiterated Sam, with increased energy.

"So they are, Sam," replied his host, administering a very efficient dose of consolation, in the shape of a large glass of Cognac brandy; which, in spite of its coming from his rival's country, Sam swallowed with hearty goodwill. "So they are. But Jenny's not worth fretting about: she's a poor feckless thing after all, fitter for a Frenchman than an Englishman. If I were you, I would make up to the widow: she's a person of property, and a fine comely woman into the bargain. Make up to the widow, Sam; and drink another glass of brandy to your success!"

And Sam followed both pieces of advice. He drank the brandy, and he made up to the widow, the former part of the prescription probably inspiring him with courage to attempt the latter; and the lady was propitious, and the wedding speedy: and the last that I heard of them was, the jay's publishing the banns of marriage, under a somewhat abridged form, from his cage at the door of Mrs. Dinah's shop (a proceeding at which she seemed, outwardly, scandalised; but over which, it may be suspected, she chuckled inwardly, or why not have taken in the cage?), and the French valet's desertion of Jenny Dobbs, whom he, in his turn, jilted; and the dilemma of Lawyer Latitat, who found himself obliged to send in his bill for the threatening letter to the identical gentleman to whom it was addressed. For the rest, the cricket-match was won triumphantly, the wedding went off with great *éclat*, and our accomplished rat-catcher is, we trust, permanently fixed in our good village of Aberleigh.

THE OLD GIPSY

WE have few gipsies in our neighbourhood. In spite of our tempting green lanes, our woody dells and heathy commons, the rogues don't take to us. I am afraid that we are too civilised, too cautious; that our sheep-folds are too closely watched; our barn-yards too well guarded; our geese and ducks too fastly penned; our chickens too securely locked up; our little pigs too safe in their sty; our game too scarce; our laundresses too careful. In short, we are too little primitive: we have a snug brood of vagabonds and poachers of our own, to say nothing of their regular followers, constables and justices of the peace:—we have stocks in the village, and a treadmill in the next town; and therefore we go gipsyless—a misfortune of which every landscape painter, and every lover of that living landscape, the country, can appreciate the extent. There is nothing under the sun that harmonises so well with Nature, especially in her woodland recesses, as that picturesque people, who are, so to say, the wild genus—the pheasants and roebucks of the human race.

Sometimes, indeed, we used to see a gipsy procession passing along the common, like an Eastern caravan, men, women, and children, donkeys and dogs; and sometimes a patch of bare earth, strewed with ashes and surrounded by scathed turf, on the broad green margin of some cross-road, would give token of a gipsy halt; but a regular gipsy encampment has always been so rare an event, that I was equally suprised and delighted to meet with one in the course of my walks last autumn, particularly as the party was of the most innocent description, quite free from those tall, dark, lean, Spanish-looking men, who it must be confessed, with all my predilection for the caste, are rather startling to meet when alone in an unfrequented path; and a path more solitary than that into which the beauty of a bright October morning had tempted me could not well be imagined.

Branching off from the high road, a little below our village, runs a wide green lane, bordered on either side by a row of young oaks and beeches just within the hedge, forming an avenue, in which, on a summer afternoon, you may see the squirrels disporting from tree to tree, whilst the rooks, their fellow-denizens, are wheeling in noisy circles over their heads. The fields sink gently down on each side, so that, being the bottom of a natural winding valley, and crossed by many little rills and rivulets, the turf exhibits even in the driest summers an emerald verdure. Scarcely any one passes the end of that lane without wishing to turn into it; but the way is in some sort dangerous and difficult for foot-passengers, because the brooklets which intersect it are in many instances bridgeless, and in others bestridden by planks so decayed that it were rashness to pass them; and the nature of the ground, treacherous and boggy, and in many places as unstable as water, renders it for carriages wholly impracticable.

I, however, who do not dislike a little difficulty where there is no absolute danger, and who am, moreover, almost as familiar with the one only safe track as the heifers who graze there, sometimes venture along this seldom-trodden path, which terminates, at the end of a mile and a half, in a spot of singular beauty. The hills become abrupt and woody, the cultivated enclosures cease, and the long narrow valley ends in a little green, bordered on one side by a fine old park, whose mossy paling, overhung with thorns and hollies, comes sweeping round it, to meet the rich coppices which clothe the opposite acclivity. Just under the high and irregular paling, shaded by the birches and sycamores of the park, and by the venerable oaks which are scattered irregularly on the green, is a dark deep pool, whose broken banks, crowned with fern and wreathed with briar and bramble, have an air of wildness and grandeur that might have suited the pencil of Salvator Rosa.

In this lonely place (for the mansion to which the park belongs has long been uninhabited) I first saw our gipsies. They had pitched their little tent under one of the oak trees, perhaps from a certain dim sense of natural beauty, which those who live with nature in the fields are seldom totally without; perhaps because the neighbourhood of the coppices, and of the deserted Hall, was favourable to the acquisition of game, and of the little fuel which their hardy habits required. The party consisted only of four—an old crone, in a tattered red cloak and black bonnet, who was stooping over a kettle, of which the contents were probably as savoury as that of Meg Merrilies, renowned in story; a pretty, black-eyed girl, at work under the trees; a sunburnt urchin of eight or nine, collecting sticks and dead leaves to feed their out-of-door fire, and a slender lad two or three years older, who lay basking in the sun, with a couple of shabby dogs of the sort called mongrel, in all the joy of idleness, whilst a grave, patient donkey stood grazing hard by. It was a pretty picture, with its soft autumnal sky, its rich woodiness, its sunshine, its verdure, the light smoke curling from the fire, and the group disposed around it so harmless, poor outcasts! and so happy—a beautiful picture! I stood gazing on it till I was half ashamed to look longer, and came away half afraid that they should depart before I could see them again.

This fear I soon found to be groundless. The old gipsy was a celebrated fortune-teller, and the post having been so long vacant, she could not have brought her talents to a better market. The whole village rang with the predictions of this modern Cassandra—unlike her Trojan predecessor inasmuch as her prophecies were never of evil. I myself could not help admiring the real cleverness, the genuine gipsy tact, with which she adapted her foretellings to the age, the habits, and the known desires and circumstances of her clients.

To our little pet Lizzy, for instance, a damsel of seven, she predicted a fairing; to Ben Kirby, a youth of thirteen, head batter of the boys, a new cricket-ball; to Ben's sister Lucy, a girl some three years his senior, and just promoted to that ensign of womanhood a cap, she promised a pink top-knot; whilst for Miss Sophia Matthews, our old-maidish schoolmistress, who would be heartily glad to be a girl again, she foresaw one handsome husband, and for the smart Widow Simmons, two. These were the least of her triumphs. George Davis, the dashing young farmer of the hill-house, a gay sportsman, who scoffed at fortune-tellers and matrimony, consulted her as to whose greyhound would win the courser's cup at the beacon meeting; to which she replied, that she did not know to whom the dog would belong, but that the winner of the cup would be a white greyhound, with one blue ear, and a spot on its side, being an exact description of Mr. George Davis's favourite Helen, who followed her master's steps like his shadow, and was standing behind him at this very instant. This prediction gained our gipsy half a crown; and Master Welles—the thriving, thrifty yeoman of the lea—she managed to win sixpence from his hard, honest, frugal hand, by a prophecy that his old

brood mare, called Blackfoot, should bring forth twins; and Ned the blacksmith, who was known to court the tall nursemaid at the mill—she got a shilling from Ned, simply by assuring him that his wife should have the longest coffin that ever was made in our wheelwright's shop. A most tempting prediction! ingeniously combining the prospect of winning and of surviving the lady of his heart—a promise equally adapted to the hot and cold fits of that ague, called love; lightening the fetters of wedlock; uniting in a breath the bridegroom and the widower. Ned was the best pleased of all her customers, and enforced his suit with such vigour, that he and the fair giantess were asked in church the next Sunday, and married at the fortnight's end.

No wonder that all the world—that is to say, all our world—were crazy to have their fortunes told—to enjoy the pleasure of hearing from such undoubted authority that what they wished to be should be. Amongst the most eager to take a peep into futurity, was our pretty maid Harriet, although her desire took the not unusual form of disclamation,—"nothing should induce her to have her fortune told, nothing upon earth!" "She never thought of the gipsy, not she!" and to prove the fact, she said so at least twenty times a day. Now Harriet's fortune seemed told already; her destiny was fixed. She, the belle of the village, was engaged, as everybody knows, to our village beau, Joel Brent; they were only waiting for a little more money to marry; and as Joel was already head carter to our head farmer, and had some prospect of a bailiff's place, their union did not appear very distant. But Harriet, besides being a beauty, was a coquette, and her affection for her betrothed did not interfere with certain flirtations which came in like Isabella, "by the bye," and occasionally cast a shadow of coolness between the lovers, which, however, Joel's cleverness and good-humour generally contrived to chase away. There had probably been a little fracas in the present instance, for at the end of one of her daily professions of unfaith in gipsies and their predictions, she added, "that none but fools did believe them; that Joel had had his fortune told, and wanted to treat her to a prophecy—but she was not such a simpleton."

About half an hour after the delivery of this speech I happened, in tying up a chrysanthemum, to go to our woodyard for a stick of proper dimensions, and there, enclosed between the faggot-pile and the coal-shed, stood the gipsy, in the very act of palmistry, conning the lines of fate in Harriet's hand. Never was a stronger contrast than that between the old withered sybil, dark as an Egyptian, with bright, laughing eyes, and an expression of keen humour under all her affected solemnity, and our village beauty, tall, and plump, and fair, blooming as a rose, and simple as a dove. She was listening too intently to see me, but the fortune-teller did, and stopped so suddenly that her attention was awakened and the intruder discovered.

Harriet at first meditated a denial. She called up a pretty, innocent, unconcerned look; answered my silence (for I never spoke a word) by muttering something about "coals for the parlour"; and catching up my new-painted, green watering-pot, instead of the coal-scuttle, began filling it with all her might, to the unspeakable discomfiture of that useful utensil, on which the dingy dust stuck like birdlime —and of her own clean apron, which exhibited a curious interchange of black and green on a white ground. During the process of filling the watering-pot, Harriet made divers signs to the gipsy to decamp. The old sybil, however, budged not a foot, influenced probably by two reasons: one, the hope of securing a customer in the new-comer, whose appearance is generally, I am afraid, the very reverse of dignified, rather merry than wise; the other, a genuine fear of passing through the yard-gate, on the outside of which a much more imposing person, my greyhound Mayflower, who has a sort of beadle instinct anent drunkards and pilferers, and disorderly persons of all sorts, stood barking most furiously.

This instinct is one of May's remarkable qualities. Dogs are all, more or less, physiognomists, and commonly pretty determined aristocrats, fond of the fine and averse to the shabby, distinguishing, with a nice accuracy, the master castes from the pariahs of the world. But May's power of perception is another matter, more, as it were, moral. She has no objection to honest rags; can away with dirt, or age, or ugliness, or any such accident, and, except just at home, makes no distinction between kitchen and parlour. Her intuition points entirely to the race of people commonly called suspicious, on whom she pounces at a glance. What a constable she would have made! What a jewel of a thief-taker! Pity that those four feet should stand in the way of her preferment! she might have risen to be a Bow Street officer. As it is we make the gift useful in a small way. In the matter of hiring and marketing the whole village likes to consult May. Many a chap has stared when she has been whistled up to give her opinion as to his honesty; and many a pig bargain has gone off on her veto. Our neighbour, mine host of the Rose, used constantly to follow her judgment in the selection of his lodgers. His house was never so orderly as when under her government. At last he found out that she abhorred tipplers as well as thieves—indeed, she actually barked away three of his best customers: and he left off appealing to her sagacity, since which he has, at different times, lost three silver spoons and a leg of mutton. With every one else May is an oracle. Not only in the case of wayfarers and vagrants, but amongst our own people, her fancies are quite a touchstone. A certain hump-backed cobbler, for instance—May cannot abide him, and I don't think he has had so much as a job of heel-piecing to do since her dislike became public. She really took away his character.

Longer than I have taken to relate Mayflower's

accomplishments stood we, like the folks in the Critic, at a dead-lock; May, who probably regarded the gipsy as a sort of rival, an interloper on her oracular domain, barking with the voice of a lioness —the gipsy trying to persuade me into having my fortune told—and I endeavouring to prevail on May to let the gipsy pass. Both attempts were unsuccessful: and the fair consulter of destiny, who had by this time recovered from the shame of her detection, extricated us from our dilemma by smuggling the old woman away through the house.

Of course Harriet was exposed to some raillery, and a good deal of questioning about her future fate, as to which she preserved an obstinate, but evidently satisfied, silence. At the end of three days, however—my readers are, I hope, learned enough in gipsy lore to know that, unless kept secret for three entire days, no prediction can come true —at the end of three days, when all the family except herself had forgotten the story, our pretty soubrette, half bursting with the long retention, took the opportunity of lacing on my new half-boots to reveal the prophecy. "She was to see within the week, and this was Saturday, the young man, the real young man, whom she was to marry." "Why, Harriet, you know poor Joel." "Joel, indeed! the gipsy said that the young man, the real young man, was to ride up to the house drest in a dark greatcoat (and Joel never wore a greatcoat in his life— all the world knew that he wore smock-frocks and jackets), and mounted on a white horse—and where should Joel get a white horse?" "Had this real young man made his appearance yet?" "No; there had not been a white horse passed the place since Tuesday: so it must certainly be to-day."

A good look-out did Harriet keep for white horses during this fateful Saturday, and plenty did she see. It was the market-day at B., and team after team came by with one, two, and three white horses; cart after cart, and gig after gig, each with a white steed: Colonel M.'s carriage, with its prancing pair —but still no horseman. At length one appeared; but he had a greatcoat whiter than the animal he rode; another, but he was old Farmer Lewington, a married man; a third, but he was little Lord L., a schoolboy, on his Arabian pony. Besides, they all passed the house; and as the day wore on, Harriet began, alternately, to profess her old infidelity on the score of fortune-telling, and to let out certain apprehensions that, if the gipsy did really possess the power of foreseeing events, and no such horseman arrived, she might possibly be unlucky enough to die an old maid—a fate for which, although the proper destiny of a coquette, our village beauty seemed to entertain a very decided aversion.

At last, just at dusk, just as Harriet, making believe to close our casement shutters, was taking her last peep up the road, something white appeared in the distance coming leisurely down the hill. Was it really a horse? Was it not rather Titus Strong's cow driving home to milking? A minute or two dissipated that fear: it certainly was a horse, and as certainly it had a dark rider. Very slowly he descended the hill, pausing most provokingly at the end of the village, as if about to turn up the Vicarage lane. He came on, however, and after another short stop at the Rose, rode full up to our little gate, and catching Harriet's hand as she was opening the wicket, displayed to the half-pleased, half-angry damsel the smiling, triumphant face of her own Joel Brent, equipped in a new greatcoat, and mounted on his master's newly purchased market nag. Oh Joel! Joel! The gipsy! the gipsy!

THE BIRD-CATCHER

A LONDON fog is a sad thing, as every inhabitant of London knows full well: dingy, dusky, dirty, damp; an atmosphere black as smoke and wet as steam, that wraps round you like a blanket; a cloud reaching from earth to heaven; a "palpable obscure," which not only turns day into night, but threatens to extinguish the lamps and lanthorns, with which the poor street-wanderers strive to illumine their darkness, dimming and paling the "ineffectual fires," until the volume of gas at a shop-door cuts no better figure than a hedge glow-worm, and a duchess's flambeau would veil its glories to a Will-o'-the-wisp. A London fog is, not to speak profanely, a sort of renewal and reversal of Joshua's miracle; the sun seems to stand still as on that occasion, only that now it stands in the wrong place, and gives light to the Antipodes. The very noises of the street come stifled and smothered through that suffocating medium; din is at a pause; the town is silenced; and the whole population, biped and quadruped, sympathise with the dead and chilling weight of the out-of-door world. Dogs and cats just look up from their slumbers, turn round, and go to sleep again; the little birds open their pretty eyes, stare about them, wonder that the night is so long, and settle themselves afresh on their perches. Silks lose their gloss, cravats their stiffness, hackney-coachmen their way; young ladies fall out of curl, and mammas out of temper; masters scold; servants grumble; and the whole city, from Hyde Park Corner to Wapping, looks sleepy and cross, like a fine gentleman roused before his time, and forced to get up by candle-light. Of all detestable things, a London fog is the most detestable.

Now a country fog is quite another matter. To say nothing of its rarity, and in this dry and healthy midland county few of the many variations of our variable English climate are rarer; to say nothing of its unfrequent recurrence, there is about it much of the peculiar and characteristic beauty which almost all natural phenomena exhibit to those who have themselves that faculty, oftener perhaps claimed than possessed, a genuine feeling of nature. This last lovely autumn, when the flowers of all seasons seemed mingling as one sometimes sees them in a painter's garland—the violets and primroses reblossoming, and new crops of sweetpeas and mignonette blending with the chrysanthemum, the Michaelmas daisy, and the dahlia, the latest blossoms of the year—when the very leaves clung to the trees with a freshness so vigorous and so youthful, that they seemed to have determined, in spite of their old bad habit, that for once they would not fall—this last lovely autumn has given us more foggy mornings, or rather more foggy days, than I ever remember to have seen in Berkshire: days beginning in a soft and vapoury mistiness, enveloping the whole country in a veil, snowy, fleecy, and light, as the smoke which one often sees circling in the distance from some cottage chimney, or as the still whiter clouds which float around the moon; and finishing in sunsets of a surprising richness and beauty, when the mist is lifted up from the earth, and turned into a canopy of unrivalled gorgeousness, purple, rosy, and golden, disclosing the splendid autumn landscape, with its shining rivulets, its varied and mellow woodland tints, and its deep emerald pasture lands, every blade and leaf covered with a thousand little drops, as pure as crystal, glittering and sparkling in the sunbeams like the dew on a summer morning, or the still more brilliant scintillations of frost.

It was in one of these days, early in November, that we set out about noon to pay a visit to a friend at some distance. The fog was yet on the earth, only some brightening in the south-west gave token that it was likely to clear away. As yet, however, the mist held complete possession—a much prettier, lighter, and cleaner vapour than that which is defiled with London smoke, but every whit as powerful and as delusive. We could not see the shoemaker's shop across the road—no! nor our chaise when it drew up before our door; were fain to guess at our own laburnum tree; and found the sign of the Rose invisible, even when we ran against the sign-post. Our little maid, a kind and careful lass, who, perceiving the dreariness of the weather, followed us across the court with extra wraps, had well-nigh tied my veil round her master's hat, and enveloped me in his bearskin; and my dog Mayflower, a white greyhound of the largest size, who had a mind to give us the undesired honour of her company, carried her point, in spite of the united efforts of half a dozen active pursuers, simply because the fog was so thick that nobody could see her. It was a complete game at bo-peep. Even mine host of the Rose, one of the most alert of her followers, remained invisible, although we heard his voice close beside us.

A misty world it was, and a watery; and I that had been praising the beauty of the fleecy white fog every day for a week before, began to sigh, and shiver, and quake, as much from dread of an overturn as from damp and chilliness, whilst my careful driver and his sagacious steed went on groping their way through the woody lanes that lead to the Loddon. Nothing but the fear of confessing my fear, that feeling which makes so many cowards brave, prevented me from begging to turn back again. On, however, we went, the fog becoming every moment heavier as we approached that beautiful and brimming river, which always, even in the midst of summer, brings with it such images of coolness and freshness as haunt the fancy after reading Undine; and where on the present occasion we seemed literally to breathe water—as Dr. Clarke said in passing the Danube. My companion, nevertheless, continued to assure me that the day would clear—nay, that it was already clearing: and I soon found that he was right. As we left the river we seemed to leave the fog; and before we had reached the pretty village of Barkham the mist had almost disappeared; and I began to lose at once my silent fears and my shivering chilliness, and to resume my cheerfulness and my admiration.

It was curious to observe how object after object glanced out of the vapour. First of all, the huge oak, at the corner of Farmer Locke's field, which juts out into the lane like a crag into the sea, forcing the road to wind around it, stood forth like a hoary giant, with its head lost in the clouds; then Farmer Hewitt's great barn—the house, ricks, and stables still invisible; then a gate, and half a cow, her head being projected over it in strong relief, whilst the hinder part of her body remained in the haze; then, more and more distinctly, hedgerows, cottages, trees, and fields, until, as we reached the top of Barkham Hill, the glorious sun broke forth, and the lovely picture lay before our eyes in its soft and calm beauty, emerging gradually from the vapour that overhung it, in such manner as the image of his sleeping Geraldine is said to have been revealed to Surrey in the magic glass. A beautiful picture it forms at all times that valley of Barkham. Fancy a road winding down a hill between high banks, richly studded with huge forest trees, oak and beech, to a sparkling stream, with a foot-bridge thrown across, which runs gurgling along the bottom; then turning abruptly, and ascending the opposite hill, whilst the rich plantations and old paling of a great park "come cranking in" on one side, and two or three irregular cottages go straggling up on the other; the whole bathed in the dewy sunshine, and glowing with the vivid colouring of autumn. The picture had, at the moment of which I speak, an additional interest, by presenting to our eyes the first human being whom we had seen during our drive (we had heard several); one, too, who, although he bore little resemblance to the fair mistress of Lord Surrey, was yet sufficiently picturesque, and in excellent keeping with the surrounding scene.

It was a robust, sturdy old man, his long grey hair appearing between his well-worn hat and his warm but weather-beaten coat, with a large package at his back, covered with oilskin, a bundle of short regular poles in one hand, and a large bunch of thistles in the other; and even before Mayflower, who now made her appearance, and was endeavouring to satisfy her curiosity by pawing and poking the knapsack, thereby awakening the noisy fears of two call-birds, who, together with a large bird-net, formed its contents,—before this audible testimony of his vocation, or the still stronger assurance of his hearty, good-humoured visage, my companion, himself somewhat of an amateur in the art, had recognised his friend and acquaintance Old Robin, the bird-catcher of B.

We soon overtook the old man, and after apologising for Mayflower's misdemeanour, who, by the way, seemed sufficiently disposed to renew the assault, we proceeded at the same slow pace up the hill, holding disjointed chat on the badness of the weather these foggy mornings, and the little chance there was of doing much good with the nets so late in the afternoon. To which Robin gave a doleful assent. He was, however, going, he said, to try for a few linnets on the common beyond the Great House, and was in hopes to get a couple of woodlarks from the plantations. He wanted the woodlarks, above all things, for Mrs. Bennet, the alderman's lady of B., whose husband had left the old shop in the Market-place, and built a fine white cottage just beyond the turnpike-gate—so madam had set her heart on a couple of woodlarks, to hang up in her new shrubbery, and make the place look rural.

"Hang up, Robin! Why there is not a tree a foot high in the whole plantation! Woodlarks! Why, they'll be dead before Christmas."

"That's sure enough, your honour," rejoined Robin.

"A soft-billed bird, that requires as much care as a nightingale!" continued my companion. "By the way, Robin, have you any nightingales now?"

"Two, sir; a hen——"

"A hen! That's something remarkable!"

"A great curiosity, sir; for your honour knows that we always set the trap for nightingales by ear like; the creature is so shy that one can seldom see it, so one is forced to put the mealworm near where one hears the song; and it's the most uncommon thing that can be to catch a hen; but I have one, and a fine cock too, that I caught last spring just afore building time. Two as healthy birds as ever were seen.

"Is the cock in song still?"

"Ay, sir, in full song; piping away, jug, jug, jug, all the day, and half the night. I wish your honour would come and hear it." And, with a promise to that effect, we parted, each our several ways; we to visit our friend, he to catch, if catch he could, a couple of woodlarks to make Mrs. Bennet's villa look rural.

Old Robin had not always been a bird-catcher. He had, what is called, fallen in the world. His father had been the best-accustomed and most fashionable shoemaker in the town of B., and Robin succeeded, in right of eldership, to his house, his business, his customers, and his debts. No one was ever less fitted for the craft. Birds had been his passion from the time that he could find a nest or string an egg: and the amusement of the boy became the pursuit of the man. No sooner was he his own master than his whole house became an aviary, and his whole time was devoted to breeding, taming, and teaching the feathered race; an employment that did not greatly serve to promote his success as a cordwainer. He married; and an extravagant wife, and a neglected, and, therefore, unprosperous business, drove him more and more into the society of the pretty creatures whose company he had always so greatly preferred to that of the two-legged, unfeathered animal, called man. Things grew worse and worse; and at length poor Robin appeared in the *Gazette*—ruined, as his wife and his customers said, by birds: or, as he himself said, by his customers and his wife. Perhaps there was some truth on either side; at least, a thousand pounds of bad debts on his books, and a whole pile of milliners and mantua-makers' bills, went nigh to prove the correctness of his assertion. Ruined, however, he was; and a happy day it was for him, since his stock being sold, his customers gone, and his prospects in trade fairly at an end, his wife (they had no family) deserted him also, and Robin, thus left a free man, determined to follow the bent of his genius, and devote the remainder of his life to the breeding, catching, and selling of birds.

For this purpose he hired an apartment in the ruinous quarter of B., called the Soak, a high, spacious attic, not unlike a barn, which came recommended to him by its cheapness, its airiness, and its extensive cage-room; and his creditors having liberally presented him with all the inhabitants of his aviary, some of which were very rare and curious, as well as a large assortment of cages, nets, traps, and seeds, he began his new business with great spirit, and has continued it ever since with various success, but with unabating perseverance, zeal, and good-humour—a very poor and a very happy man. His garret in the Soak is one of the boasts of B.; all strangers go to see the birds and the bird-catcher, and most of his visitors are induced to become purchasers, for there is no talking with Robin on his favourite subject without catching a little of his contagious enthusiasm. His room is quite a menagerie, something like what the feathered department of the ark must have been—as crowded, as numerous, and as noisy.

The din is really astounding. To say nothing of the twitter of whole legions of linnets, goldfinches, and canaries, the latter of all ages; the chattering and piping of magpies, parrots, jackdaws, and bullfinches, in every stage of their education; the deeper tones of blackbirds, thrushes, larks, and nightingales, never fail to swell the chorus, aided by the cooing of doves, the screechings of owls, the squeakings of guinea-pigs, and the eternal grinding of a barrel-organ, which a little damsel of eight years old, who officiates under Robin as feeder and cleaner, turns round, with melancholy monotony, to the loyal and patriotic tunes of " Rule Britannia " and " God save the King," the only airs, as her master observes, which are sure not to go out of fashion.

Except this young damsel and her music, the apartment exhibits but few signs of human habitation. A macaw is perched on the little table, and a cockatoo chained to the only chair; the roof is tenanted by a choice breed of tumbler pigeons, and the floor cumbered by a brood of curious bantams, unrivalled for ugliness.

Here Robin dwells, in the midst of the feathered population, except when he sallies forth at morning or evening to spread his nets for goldfinches or bullfinches on the neighbouring commons, or to place his trap-cages for the larger birds. Once or twice a year, indeed, he wanders into Oxfordshire, to meet the great flocks of linnets, six or seven hundred together, which congregate on those hills, and may be taken by dozens; and he has had ambitious thoughts of trying the great market of Covent Garden for the sale of his live stock. But in general he remains quietly at home. That nest in the Soak is too precious a deposit to leave long; and he is seldom without some especial favourite to tend and fondle. At present, the hen-nightingale seems his pet; the last was a white blackbird; and once he had a whole brood of gorgeous kingfishers, seven glorious creatures, for whose behoof he took up a new trade and turned fisherman, dabbling all day with a hand-net in the waters of the Soak. It was the prettiest sight in the world to see them snatch the minnows from his hand, with a shy, mistrustful tameness, glancing their bright heads from side to side, and then darting off like bits of the rainbow. I had an entire sympathy with Robin's delight in his kingfishers. He sold them to his chief patron, Mr. Jay, a little, fidgety old bachelor, with a sharp face, a hooked nose, a brown complexion, and a full suit of snuff-colour, not much unlike a bird himself; and that worthy gentleman's mismanagement and a frosty winter killed the kingfishers every one. It was quite affecting to hear poor Robin talk of their death. But Robin has store of tender anecdotes; and any one who has a mind to cry over the sorrows of a widowed turtle-dove, and to hear described to the life her vermilion-eye, black gorget, soft plumage, and plaintive note, cannot do better than pay a visit to the garret in the Soak, and listen for half an hour to my friend the birdcatcher.

A VISIT TO LUCY

LUCY, who in her single state bore so striking a resemblance to Jenny Dennison in the number and variety of her lovers, continues to imitate that illustrious original in her married life by her dexterous and excellent management, of which I have been lately an amused and admiring witness. Not having seen her for a long time, tempted by the fineness of the day, the first day of summer, and by the pleasure of carrying to her a little housewifely present from her some time mistress, we resolved to take a substantial luncheon at two o'clock, and drive over to drink tea with her at five, such being, as we well knew, the fashionable visiting hour at S.

The day was one glow of sunshine, and the road wound through a beautiful mixture of hill and dale and rich woodland, clothed in the brightest foliage, and thickly studded with gentlemen's seats, and prettier cottages, their gardens gay with the blossoms of the plum and the cherry, tossing their snowy garlands across the deep blue sky. So we journeyed on through pleasant villages and shady lanes till we emerged into the opener and totally different scenery of M. Common; a wild district, always picturesque and romantic, but now peculiarly brilliant, and glowing with the luxuriant orange flowers of the furze in its height of bloom, stretching around us like a sea of gold, and loading the very air with its rich almond odour. Who would have believed that this brown, barren, shaggy heath could have assumed such splendour, such majesty? The farther we proceeded, the more beautiful it appeared, the more gorgeous, the more brilliant. Whether climbing up the steep bank, and mixing with the thick plantation of dark firs; or checkered with brown heath and green turf on the open plain, where the sheep and lambs were straying; or circling round the pool covered with its bright white flowers; or edging the dark morass inlaid with the silky tufts of the cotton grass; or creeping down the deep dell where the alders grow; or mixing by the roadside with the shining and varied bark, now white, now purplish, and the light tremulous leaves of the feathery birch-tree;—in every form or variety this furze was beauty itself. We almost lamented to leave it, as we wound down the steep hill of M. West End, that most picturesque village, with its long open sheds for broom and faggot-making; its little country inn, the Red Lion; its pretty school just in the bottom, where the clear stream comes bubbling over the road, and the romantic foot-bridge is flung across; and with cottages straggling up the hill on the opposite ascent, orchards backed by meadows, and the light wreaths of smoke sailing along the green hillside, the road winding amidst all, beside another streamlet whose deep rust-coloured scum gives token of a chalybeate spring.

Even this sweet and favourite scene, which, when I would think of the perfection of village landscape, of a spot to live and die in, rises unbidden before my eyes,—this dear and cherished picture which I generally leave so reluctantly,—was hurried over now, so glad were we to emerge once more from its colder colouring into the full glory of the waving furze on S. Common, brighter even than that of M. which we left behind us. Even Lucy's house was unheeded till we drove up to the door, and found, to our great satisfaction, that she was at home.

The three years that have elapsed since her marriage have changed the style of her beauty. She is grown very fat, and rather coarse; and having, moreover, taken to loud speaking (as I apprehend a village schoolmistress must do in pure self-defence, that her voice may be heard in the *mêlée*), our airy sparkling soubrette, although still handsome, has been transmuted somewhat suddenly into a bustling, merry country dame, looking her full age, if not a little older. It is such a transition as a rosebud experiences when turned into a rose, such as might befall the pretty coquette Mistress Anne Page when she wedded Master Fenton and became one of the Merry Wives of Windsor. Lucy, however, in her dark gown and plain cap (for her dress hath undergone as much alteration as her person), her smiles and her rosiness, is still as fair a specimen of country comeliness as heart can desire.

We found her very busy, superintending the operations of a certain she-tailor, a lame woman famous for buttonholes, who travels from house to house in that primitive district, making and repairing men's gear, and who was at that moment endeavouring to extract a smart waistcoat for our friend the schoolmaster out of a remnant of calico and a blemished waistcoat-piece, which had been purchased at half-price for his behoof by his frugal helpmate. The more material parts of the cutting out had been effected before my arrival, considerably at the expense of the worthy pedagogue's comfort, although to the probable improvement of his shape ; for certainly the new fabric promised to be at least an inch smaller than the pattern ;—that point, however, had been by dint of great ingenuity satisfactorily adjusted, and I found the lady of the shears and the lady of the rod in the midst of a dispute on the question of buttons, which the tailoress insisted must be composed of metal or mother-of-pearl, or anything but covered moulds, inasmuch as there would be no stuff left to cover them ; whilst Lucy, on her side, insisted that there was plenty, that anything (as all the world knew) would suffice to cover buttons if people were clever and careful, and that certain most diminutive and irregular scraps, which she gathered from the table and under it, and displayed with great ostentation, were amply sufficient for the purpose. "If the pieces are not big enough," continued she, "you have nothing to do but to join them." And as Lucy had greatly the advantage both in loudness of voice and fluency of thought and word, over the itinerant seamstress, who was a woman of slow, quiet speech, she carried her point in the argument most triumphantly, although whether the unlucky waistcoat-maker will succeed in stretching her materials so as to do the impossible remains to be proved, the button question being still undecided when I left S.

Her adversary being fairly silenced, Lucy laid aside her careful thoughts and busy looks; and leaving the poor woman to her sewing and stitching, and a little tidy lass (a sort of half-boarder, who acts half as servant, half as pupil), to get all things ready for tea, she prepared to accompany me to a pleasant coppice in the neighbourhood, famous for wild lilies-of-the-valley, to the love of which delicate flower, she, not perhaps quite unjustly, partly attributed my visit.

Nothing could be more beautiful than the wood where they are found, which we reached by crossing first the open common, with its golden waves of furze, and then a clover field intensely green, deliciously fresh and cool to the eye and the tread. The copse was just in its pleasantest state, having luckily been cut last year, and being too thinly clothed with timber to obstruct the view. It goes sloping down a hill, till it is lost in the green depths of P. Forest, with an abruptness of descent which resembles a series of terraces, or rather ledges, so narrow that it is sometimes difficult to find a space on which to walk. The footing is the more precarious, as even the broader paths are intersected and broken by hollows and caves, where the ground has given way and been undermined by fox earths. On the steepest and highest of these banks, in a very dry, unsheltered situation, the lily of the valley grows so profusely that the plants almost cover the ground with their beautiful broad leaves, and the snowy white bells, which envelop the most delicate of odours. All around grow the fragile wind-flowers, pink as well as white; the coral blossoms of the whortle-berry; the graceful wood-sorrel; the pendent drops of the stately Solomon's seal, which hang like waxen tassels under the full and regular leaves; the bright wood-vetch; the unobtrusive woodruff, whose scent is like new hay, and which retains and communicates it when dried; and, lastly, those strange freaks of nature the orchises, where the portrait of an insect is so quaintly depicted in a flower. The bee orchis abounds also in the Maple Durham woods—those woods where whilom flourished the two stately but unlovely flowers Martha and Teresa Blount of *Popish* fame, and which are still in the possession of their family. But, although it is found at Maple Durham as well as in these copses of North Hampshire, yet, in the little slip of Berks which divides Hants from

Oxfordshire, I have never been able to discover it. The locality of flowers is a curious puzzle. The field tulip, for instance, through whose superb pendent blossoms, checkered with puce and lilac, the sun shines as gloriously as through stained glass, and which, blended with a still more elegant white variety, covers whole acres of the Kennet meadows, can by no process be coaxed into another habitation, however apparently similar in situation and soil. Treat them as you may, they pine and die and disappear. The Duke of Marlborough only succeeded in naturalizing them at White Knights by the magnificent operation of transplanting half an acre of meadow, grass and earth and all, to the depth of two feet! and even there they seem dwindling. The wood-sorrel, which I was ambitious of fixing in the shrubberies of our old place, served me the provoking trick of living a year or two, and bearing leaves, but never flowers; and that far rarer but less beautiful plant, the field-star of Bethlehem,—a sort of large hyacinth of the hue of the mistletoe, which, in its pale and shadowy stalk and blossom has something to me awful, unearthly, ghastly, mystical, druidical,—used me still worse, not only refusing to grow in a corner of our orchard where I planted it, but vanishing from the spot where I procured the roots, although I left at least twenty times as many as I took.

Nothing is so difficult to tame as a wild-flower; and wisely so, for they generally lose much of their characteristic beauty by any change of soil or situation. That very wood-sorrel now, which I coveted so much, I saw the other day in a green-house! By what chance my fellow amateur persuaded that swamp-loving, cold-braving, shade-seeking plant to blossom in the very region of light, and heat, and dryness, I cannot imagine; but there it was in full bloom, as ugly a little abortion as ever showed its poor face, smaller far than in its native woods, the flowers unveined and colourless, and bolt upright, the leaves full spread and stiff,—no umbrella fold! no pendent grace! no changing hue! none but a lover's eye would have recognised the poor beauty of the woods in the faded prisoner of the green-house. No caged bird ever underwent such a change. I will never try to domesticate that pretty blossom again—content to visit it in its own lovely haunts, the bed of moss or the beech-root sofa.

The lily-of-the-valley we may perhaps try to transplant. The garden is its proper home; it seems thrown here by accident; we cannot help thinking it an abasement, a condescension. The lily must be transportable. For the present, however, we were content to carry away a basket of blossoms, reserving till the autumn our design of peopling a shady border in our own small territories, the identical border where in summer our geraniums flourish, with that simplest and sweetest of flowers.

We then trudged back to Lucy's to tea, talking by the way of old stories, old neighbours, and old friends—mixed on her part with a few notices of her new acquaintance, lively,' shrewd, and good-humoured as usual. She is indeed a most agreeable and delightful person; I think the lately developed quality at which I hinted in my opening remarks, the slight tinge of Jenny-Dennison-ism, only renders her conversation more piquant and individualised, and throws her merits into sharper relief. We talked of old stories and new, and soon found she had lost none of her good gift in gossipry; of her thousand and one lovers, about whom, although she has quite left off coquetry, she inquired with a kindly interest; of our domestic affairs, and above all of her own. She has no children—a circumstance which I sometimes think she regrets; I do not know why, except that my dear mother having given her on her marriage, amongst a variety of parting gifts, a considerable quantity of baby things, she probably thinks it a pity that they should not be used. And yet the expensiveness of children might console her on the one hand, and the superabundance of them with which she is blest in school-time on the other. Indeed she has now the care of a charity Sunday school in addition to her work-day labours—a circumstance which has by no means altered her opinion of the inefficacy and inexpediency of general education.

I suspect that the irregularity of payment is one cause of her dislike to the business; and yet she is so ingenious a contriver in the matter of extracting money's worth from those who have no money, that we can hardly think her unreasonable in requiring the *hen-tailor* to cover buttons out of nothing. Where she can get no cash, she takes the debt in kind; and, as most of her employers are in that predicament, she lives in this respect like the Loochooans, who never heard of a currency. She accommodates herself to this state of things with admirable facility. She has sold her cow, because she found she could be served with milk and butter by the wife of a small farmer who has four children at her school; and has parted with her poultry and pigs, and left off making bread, because the people of both shops are customers to her husband in his capacity of shoemaker, and she gets bread, and eggs, and bacon for nothing. On the same principle she has commenced brewing, because the maltster's son and daughter attend her seminary, and she procured three new barrels, coolers, tubs, etc., from a cooper who was in debt to her husband for shoes. "Shoes," or "children," is indeed the constant answer to the civil notice which one is accustomed to take of any novelty in the house. "Shoes" produced the commodious dressing-table and washing-stand, coloured like rosewood, which adorn her bed-chamber; "children" were the source of the good-as-new roller and wheelbarrow which stand in the court; and to "shoes and children" united are they indebted for the excellent double hedge-row of grubbed wood which she took me to see in returning from the copse—"a brand (as she observed) snatched out of the fire; for the poor man who owed them the money must break, and had nothing useful to give them, except this wood, which was useless to him, as he had not money to get it grubbed up.—If he holds on till the autumn," continued Lucy, "we shall have a good crop of potatoes from the hedgerow. We have planted them on the chance." The ornamental part of her territory comes from the same fertile source. Even the thrift which adorns the garden (fit emblem of its mistress!) was a present from the drunken gardener of a gentleman in the neighbourhood. "He does not pay his little girl's schooling very regularly," quoth she; "but then he is so civil, poor man! anything in the garden is at our service."

"Shoes and children" are the burden of the song. The united professions react on each other in a remarkable manner;—shoes bring scholars, and scholars consume shoes. The very charity school before mentioned, a profitable concern, of which the payment depends on rich people and not on poor, springs indirectly from a certain pair of purple kid boots, a capital fit (I must do our friend, the pedagogue, the justice to say that he understands the use of his awl, no man better!) which so pleased the vicar's lady, who is remarkable for a neat ankle, that she not only gave a magnificent order for herself, and caused him to measure her children, but actually prevailed on her husband to give the appointment of Sunday schoolmaster to this matchless cordwainer. I should not wonder if, through her powerful patronage, he should one day rise to be parish-clerk.

Well, the tea and the bread-and-butter were discussed with the appetite produced by a two hours' ride and a three hours' walk—to say nothing of the relish communicated to her viands by the hearty hospitality of our hostess, who "gaily pressed and smiled." And then the present, our ostensible errand, a patch-work quilt, long the object of Lucy's admiration, was given with due courtesy, and received with abundance of pleased and blushing thanks.

At last the evening began to draw in, her husband, who had been absent, returned, and we were compelled to set out homewards, and rode back with our basket of lilies through a beautiful twilight world, inhaling the fragrance of the blossomed furze, listening to the nightingales, and talking of Lucy's good management.

HANNAH BINT

THE Shaw, leading to Hannah Bint's habitation, is, as I perhaps have said before, a very pretty mixture of wood and coppice; that is to say, a track of thirty or forty acres covered with fine growing timber—ash, and oak, and elm—very regularly planted; and interspersed here and there with large patches of underwood, hazel, maple, birch, holly, and hawthorn, woven into almost impenetrable thickets by long wreaths of the bramble, the briony, and the briar-rose, or by the pliant and twisting garlands of the wild honeysuckle. In other parts, the Shaw is quite clear of its bosky undergrowth, and clothed only with large beds of feathery fern, or carpets of flowers, primroses, orchises, cowslips, ground-ivy, crane's-bill, cottongrass, Solomon's seal, and forget-me-not, crowded together with a profusion and brilliancy of colour such as I have rarely seen equalled even in a garden. Here the wild hyacinth really enamels the ground with its fresh and lovely purple; there,

"On aged roots, with bright green mosses clad,
Dwells the wood-sorrel, with its bright thin leaves

Heart-shaped and triply folded, and its root
Creeping like beaded coral ; whilst around
Flourish the copse's pride, anemones,
With rays like golden studs on ivory laid
Most delicate ; but touched with purple clouds,
Fit crown for April's fair but changeful brow."

The variety is much greater than I have enumerated; for the ground is so unequal, now swelling in gentle ascents, now dimpling into dells and hollows, and the soil so different in different parts, that the sylvan flora is unusually extensive and complete.

The season is, however, now too late for this floweriness; and except the tufted woodbines, which have continued in bloom during the whole of this lovely autumn, and some lingering garlands of the purple wild-vetch, wreathing round the thickets, and uniting with the ruddy leaves of the bramble, and the pale festoons of the briony, there is little to call one's attention from the grander beauties of the trees—the sycamore, its broad leaves already spotted — the oak, heavy with acorns—and the delicate shining rind of the weeping birch, "the lady of the woods," thrown out in strong relief from a background of holly and hawthorn, each studded with coral berries, and backed with old beeches, beginning to assume the rich, tawny hue which makes them perhaps the most picturesque of autumnal trees, as the transparent freshness of their young foliage is undoubtedly the choicest ornament of the forest in spring.

A sudden turn round one of these magnificent beeches brings us to the boundary of the Shaw, and, leaning upon a rude gate, we look over an open space of about ten acres of ground, still more varied and broken than that which we have passed, and surrounded on all sides by thick woodland. As a piece of colour, nothing can well be finer. The ruddy glow of the heath-flower, contrasting, on the one hand, with the golden-blossomed furze,—on the other, with a patch of buckwheat, of which the bloom is not past, although the grain be ripening, the beautiful buckwheat, whose transparent leaves and stalks are so brightly tinged with vermilion, while the delicate pink-white of the flower, a paler persicaria, has a feathery fall, at once so rich and so graceful, and a fresh and reviving odour, like that of birch-trees in the dew of a May evening. The bank that surmounts this attempt at cultivation is crowned with the late fox-glove and the stately mullein; the pasture, of which so great a part of the waste consists, looks as green as an emerald; a clear pond, with the bright sky reflected in it, lets light into the picture: the white cottage of the keeper peeps from the opposite coppice; and the vine-covered dwelling of Hannah Bint rises from amidst the pretty garden, which lies bathed in the sunshine around it.

The living and moving accessories are all in keeping with the cheerfulness and repose of the landscape. Hannah's cow grazing quietly beside keeper's pony: a brace of fat pointer puppies holding amicable intercourse with a litter of young pigs; ducks, geese, cocks, hens, and chickens scattered over the turf; Hannah herself sallying forth from the cottage-door, with her milk-bucket in her hand, and her little brother following with the milking-stool.

My friend, Hannah Bint, is by no means an ordinary person. Her father, Jack Bint (for in all his life he never arrived at the dignity of being called John, indeed, in our parts he was commonly known by the cognomen of London Jack), was a drover of high repute in his profession. No man, between Salisbury Plain and Smithfield, was thought to conduct a flock of sheep so skilfully through all the difficulties of lanes and commons, streets and high roads, as Jack Bint, aided by Jack Bint's famous dog, Watch; for Watch's rough, honest face, black, with a little white about the muzzle, and one white ear, was as well known at fairs and markets, as his master's equally honest and weather-beaten visage. Lucky was the dealer that could secure their services; Watch being renowned for keeping a flock together better than any shepherd's dog on the road—Jack, for delivering them more punctually, and in better condition. No man had a more thorough knowledge of the proper night-stations, where good feed might be procured for his charge, and good liquor for Watch and himself; Watch, like other sheep-dogs, being accustomed to live chiefly on bread and beer. His master, although not averse to a pot of good double X, preferred gin; and they who plod slowly along, through wet and weary ways, in frost and in fog, have undoubtedly a stronger temptation to indulge in that cordial and reviving stimulus, than we water-drinkers, sitting in warm and comfortable rooms, can readily imagine. For certain, our drover could never resist the gentle seduction of the gin-bottle, and being of a free, merry, jovial temperament, one of those persons commonly called good fellows, who like to see others happy in the same way with themselves, he was apt to circulate it at his own expense, to the great improvement of his popularity and the great detriment of his finances.

All this did vastly well whilst his earnings continued proportionate to his spendings, and the little family at home were comfortably supported by his industry: but when a rheumatic fever came on, one hard winter, and finally settled in his limbs, reducing the most active and hardy man in the parish to the state of a confirmed cripple, then his reckless improvidence stared him in the face; and poor Jack, a thoughtless, but kind creature, and a most affectionate father, looked at his three motherless children with the acute misery of a parent who has brought those whom he loves best in the world to abject destitution. He found help, where he probably least expected it, in the sense and spirit of his young daughter, a girl of twelve years old.

Hannah was the eldest of the family, and had ever since her mother's death, which event had occurred two or three years before, been accustomed to take the direction of their domestic concerns, to manage her two brothers, to feed the pigs and the poultry, and to keep house during the almost constant absence of her father. She was a quick, clever lass, of a high spirit, a firm temper, some pride, and a horror of accepting parochial relief, which is every day becoming rarer amongst the peasantry; but which forms the surest safeguard to the sturdy independence of the English character. Our little damsel possessed this quality in perfection; and when her father talked of giving up their comfortable cottage, and removing to the workhouse, whilst she and her brothers must go to service, Hannah formed a bold resolution, and, without disturbing the sick man by any participation of her hopes and fears, proceeded after settling their trifling affairs to act at once on her own plans and designs.

Careless of the future as the poor drover had seemed, he had yet kept clear of debt, and by subscribing constantly to a benefit club had secured a pittance that might at least assist in supporting him during the long years of sickness and helplessness to which he was doomed to look forward. This his daughter knew. She knew, also, that the employer in whose service his health had suffered so severely was a rich and liberal cattle-dealer in the neighbourhood, who would willingly aid an old and faithful servant, and had, indeed, come forward with offers of money. To assistance from such a quarter Hannah saw no objection. Farmer Oakley and the parish were quite distinct things. Of him, accordingly, she asked, not money, but something much more in his own way—"a cow! any cow! old or lame, or what not, so that it were a cow! she would be bound to keep it well; if she did not, he might take it back again. She even hoped to pay for it by and by, by instalments, but that she would not promise!" and partly amused, partly interested by the child's earnestness, the wealthy yeoman gave her, not as a purchase, but as a present, a very fine young Alderney. She then went to the lord of the manor, and, with equal knowledge of character, begged his permission to keep her cow on the Shaw common. "Farmer Oakley had given her a fine Alderney, and she would be bound to pay the rent, and keep her father off the parish, if he would only let it graze on the waste"; and he, too, half from real good nature—half, not to be outdone in liberality by his tenant, not only granted the requested permission, but reduced the rent so much that the produce of the vine seldom fails to satisfy their kind landlord.

Now, Hannah shewed great judgment in setting up as a dairy-woman. She could not have chosen an occupation more completely unoccupied, or more loudly called for. One of the most provoking of the petty difficulties which beset people with a small establishment, in this neighbourhood, is the trouble, almost the impossibility, of procuring the pastoral luxuries of milk, eggs, and butter, which rank, unfortunately, amongst the indispensable necessaries of housekeeping. To your thoroughbred Londoner, who, whilst grumbling over his own breakfast, is apt to fancy that thick cream, and fresh butter, and new-laid eggs, grow, so to say, in the country—form an actual part of its natural produce—it may be some comfort to learn, that in this great grazing district, however the calves and the farmers may be the better for cows, nobody else is; that farmers' wives have ceased to keep poultry; and that we unlucky villagers sit down often to our first meal in a state of destitution, which may well make him content with his thin milk and his Cambridge butter, when compared to our imputed pastoralities.

Hannah's Alderney restored us to one rural privilege. Never was so cleanly a little milkmaid. She changed away some of the cottage finery, which, in his prosperous days, poor Jack had pleased himself with bringing home; the china tea-service, the gilded mugs, and the painted waiters, for the more useful utensils of the dairy, and speedily established a regular and gainful trade in milk, eggs, butter, honey and poultry—for poultry they had always kept.

Her domestic management prospered equally. Her father, who retained the perfect use of his hands, began a manufacture of mats and baskets, which he constructed with great nicety and adroitness; the eldest boy, a sharp and clever lad, cut for him his rushes and osiers; erected, under his sister's direction, a shed for the cow, and enlarged and cultivated the garden (always with the good leave of her kind patron the lord of the manor) until it became so ample that the produce not only kept the pig, and half kept the family, but afforded another branch of merchandise to the indefatigable directress of the establishment. For the younger boy, less quick and active, Hannah contrived to obtain an admission to the charity-school, where he made great progress—retaining him at home, however, in the hay-making and leasing season, or whenever his services could be made available, to the great annoyance of the schoolmaster, whose favourite he is, and who piques himself so much on George's scholarship (your heavy sluggish boy at country work often turns out quick at his book), that it is the general opinion that this much-vaunted pupil will, in process of time, be promoted to the post of assistant, and may, possibly, in course of years rise to the dignity of a parish pedagogue in his own person; so that his sister, although still making him useful at odd times, now considers George as pretty well off her hands, whilst his elder brother, Tom, could take an under-gardener's place directly, if he were not too important at home to be spared even for a day.

In short, during the five years that she has ruled at the Shaw cottage, the world has gone well with Hannah Bint. Her cow, her calves, her pigs, her bees, her poultry, have each, in their several ways, thriven and prospered. She has even brought Watch to like buttermilk as well as strong beer, and has nearly persuaded her father (to whose wants and wishes she is most anxiously attentive) to accept of milk as a substitute for gin. Not but Hannah hath had her enemies as well as her betters. Why should she not? The old woman at the lodge, who always piqued herself on being spiteful, and crying down new ways, foretold from the first she would come to no good, and could not forgive her for falsifying her prediction; and Betty Barnes, the slatternly widow of a tippling farmer, who rented a field, and set up a cow herself, and was universally discarded for insufferable dirt, said all that the wit of an envious woman could devise against Hannah and her Alderney; nay, even Ned Myles, the keeper, her next neighbour, who had, whilom, held entire sway over the Shaw common, as well as its coppices, grumbled as much as so good-natured and genial a person could grumble, when he found a little girl sharing his dominion, a cow grazing beside his pony, and vulgar cocks and hens hovering around the buckwheat destined to feed his noble pheasants. Nobody that had been accustomed to see that paragon of keepers, so tall and manly and pleasant looking, with his merry eye, and his knowing smile, striding gaily along, in his green coat and his gold-laced hat, with Neptune, his noble Newfoundland dog (a retriever is the sporting word), and his beautiful spaniel Flirt at his heels, could conceive how askew he looked, when he first found Hannah and Watch holding equal reign over his old territory, the Shaw common.

Yes! Hannah hath had her enemies; but they are passing away. The old woman at the lodge is dead, poor creature; and Betty Barnes, having herself taken to tippling, has lost the few friends she once possessed, and looks, luckless wretch, as if she would soon die, too!—and the keeper?—why, he is not dead, or like to die; but the change that has taken place there is the most astonishing of all — except, perhaps, the change in Hannah herself.

Few damsels of twelve years old, generally a very pretty age, were less pretty than Hannah Bint. Short and stunted in her figure, thin in face, sharp in feature, with a muddled complexion, wild, sunburnt hair, and eyes whose very brightness had in them something startling, over-informed, super-subtle, too clever for her age,—at twelve years old she had quite the air of a little old fairy. Now, at seventeen, matters are mended. Her complexion has cleared: her countenance has developed itself; her figure has shot up into height and lightness, and a sort of rustic grace; her bright, acute eye is softened and sweetened by the womanly wish to please; her hair is trimmed, and curled and brushed, with exquisite neatness; and her whole dress arranged with that nice attention to the becoming, the suitable both in form and texture, which would be called the highest degree of coquetry, if it did not deserve the better name of propriety. Never was such a transmogrification beheld. The lass is really pretty, and Ned Myles has discovered that she is so. There he stands, the rogue, close at her side (for he hath joined her whilst we have been telling her little story, and the milking is over!)—there he stands—holding her milk-pail in one hand, and stroking Watch with the other; whilst she is returning the compliment, by patting Neptune's magnificent head. There they stand, as much like lovers as may be; he smiling, and she blushing—he never looking so handsome, nor she so pretty in all their lives. There they stand, in blessed forgetfulness of all except each other; as happy a couple as ever trod the earth. There they stand, and one would not disturb them for all the milk and butter in Christendom. I should not wonder if they were fixing the wedding day.

DOCTOR TUBB

EVERY country village has its doctor. I allude to that particular department of the medical world which is neither physician, nor surgeon, nor apothecary, although it unites the offices of all three; which is sometimes an old man, and sometimes an old woman, but generally an oracle, and always (with reverence be it spoken) a quack. Our village, which is remarkably rich in functionaries adorned with the true official qualities, could hardly be without so essential a personage. Accordingly we have a quack of the highest and most extended reputation in the person of Doctor Tubb, inventor and compounder of medicines, bleeder, shaver, and physicker of man and beast.

How this accomplished barber-surgeon came by his fame I do not very well know; his skill he inherited (as I have been told) in the female line, from his great-aunt Bridget, who was herself the first practitioner of the day, the wise woman of the village, and bequeathed to this favourite nephew her blessing, Culpepper's Herbal, a famous salve for cuts and chilblains, and a still. This legacy decided his fate. A man who possessed a herbal and could read it without much spelling, who had a still and could use it, had already the great requisites for his calling. He was also blest with a natural endowment, which I take to be at least equally essential to the success of quackery of any sort, especially of medical quackery; namely, a prodigious stock of impudence. Molière's hero,—who, having had the ill-luck to place the heart on the wrong side (I mean the right), and being reminded of his mistake, says coolly, "*nous avons changé tout cela*"—is modesty itself compared with the brazen front of Doctor Tubb. And it tells accordingly. Patients come to him from far and near; he is the celebrated person (*l'homme marquant*) of the place. I myself have heard of him all my life as a distinguished character, although our personal acquaintance is of a comparatively recent date, and began in a manner sufficiently singular and characteristic.

On taking possession of our present abode, about four years ago, we found our garden, and all the gardens of the straggling village street in which it is situated, filled, peopled, infested by a beautiful flower, which grew in such profusion and was so difficult to keep under that (poor pretty thing!), instead of being admired and cherished and watered and supported, as it well deserves to be, and would be if it were rare, it is disregarded, affronted, maltreated, cut down, pulled up, hoed out, like a weed. I do not know the name of this elegant plant, nor have I met with any one who does; we call it the Spicer, after an old naval officer who once inhabited the white house just above, and, according to tradition, first brought the seed from foreign parts. It is a sort of large veronica, with a profusion of white gauzy flowers streaked with red, like the apple blossom. Strangers admire it prodigiously; and so do I— everywhere but in my own garden.

I never saw anything prettier than a whole bed of these spicers, which had clothed the top of a large heap of earth belonging to our little mason by the roadside. Whether the wind had carried the light seed from his garden, or it had been thrown out in the mould, none could tell; but there grew the plants as thick and close as grass in a meadow, and covered with delicate red and white blossoms like a fairy orchard. I never passed without stopping to look at them; and, however accustomed to the work of extirpation in my own territories, I was one day half-shocked to see a man, his pockets stuffed with the plants, two huge bundles under each arm, and still tugging away root and branch. "Poor pretty flower," thought I, "not even suffered to enjoy the waste by the roadside! chased from the very common of nature, where the thistle and the nettle may spread and flourish! Poor despised flower!" This devastation did not, however, as I soon found, proceed from disrespect; the spicer-gatherer being engaged in sniffing with visible satisfaction to the leaves and stalks of the plant, which (although the blossom is wholly scentless) emit when bruised a very unpleasant odour. "It has a fine venomous smell," quoth he in soliloquy, "and will certainly when stilled be good for something or other." This was my first sight of Doctor Tubb.

We have frequently met since, and are now well acquainted, although the worthy experimentalist considers me as a rival practitioner, an interloper, and hates me accordingly. He has very little cause. My quackery—for I plead guilty to a little of that aptness to offer counsel in very plain and common cases, which those who live much among poor people, and feel an unaffected interest in their health and comfort, can hardly help—my quackery, being mostly of the cautious, preventive, safe-side, common-sense order, stands no chance against the boldness and decision of his all-promising ignorance. He says, Do! I say, Do not! He deals in *stimuli*, I in sedatives; I give medicine, he gives cordial waters. Alack! alack! when could a dose of rhubarb, even although reinforced by a dole of good broth, compete with a draught of peppermint, a licensed dram? No! no! Doctor Tubb has no cause to fear my practice.

The only patient I ever won from the worthy empiric was his own wife, who had languished under his prescriptions for three mortal years, and at last stole down in the dusk of the evening to hold a private consultation with me. I was not very willing to invade the doctor's territories in my own person, and really feared to undertake a case which had proved so obstinate; I therefore offered her a ticket for the B. dispensary, an excellent charity, which has rescued many a victim from the clutches of our herbalist. But she said that her husband would never forgive such an affront to his skill, he having an especial aversion to the dispensary and its excellent medical staff, whom he was wont to call "book-doctors"; so that wise measure was perforce abandoned. My next suggestion was more to her taste; I counselled her "to throw physic to the dogs"; she did so, and by the end of the week she was another woman. I never saw such a cure. Her husband never made such a one in all the course of his practice. By the simple expedient of throwing away his decoctions, she is become as strong and hearty as I am. *N.B.*—For fear of misconstruction, it is proper to add, that I do not in the least accuse or suspect the worthy doctor of wishing to get rid of his wife —God forbid! He is a tolerable husband, as times go, and performs no murders but in the way of his profession: indeed, I think he is glad that his wife should be well again; yet he cannot quite forgive the cause of the cure, and continues boldly to assert in all companies, that it was a newly discovered fomentation of *yarbs*, applied to her by himself about a month before, which produced this surprising recovery; and I really believe that he thinks so; one secret of the implicit confidence which he inspires, is that triumphant reliance on his own infallibility with which he is possessed—

the secret perhaps of all creators of enthusiasm, from Mahomet and Cromwell to the

> "Prevailing poet, whose undoubting mind
> Believ'd the magic wonders that he sang."

As if to make some amends to this prescriber-general for the patient of whom I had deprived him, I was once induced to seek his services medically, or rather surgically, for one of my own family,—for no less a person than May, poor pretty May! One November evening, her master being on a coursing visit in Oxfordshire, and May having been left behind as too much fatigued with a recent hard day's work to stand a long, dirty journey, (note that a greyhound, besides being exceedingly susceptible of bad weather and watery ways, is a worse traveller than any other dog that breathes; a miserable little pug, or a lady's lap-dog, would, in a progress of fifty miles, tire down the slayer of hares and outrunner of race-horses),—May being, as I said, left behind slightly indisposed, the boy who has the care of her, no less a person than the runaway Henry, came suddenly into the parlour to tell me that she was dying. Now May is not only my pet but the pet of the whole house, so that the news spread universal consternation; there was a sudden rush of the female world to the stable, and a general feeling that Henry was right, when poor May was discovered stretched at full length in a stall, with no other sign of life than a tremendous and visible pulsation of the arteries about her chest—you might almost hear the poor heart beat, so violent was the action.—"Bleeding!" "She must be bled!" burst simultaneously from two of our corps; and immediately her body-servant the boy, who stood compromising his dignity by a very unmanly shower of tears, vanished, and reappeared in a few seconds, dragging Doctor Tubb by the skirts, who, as it was Saturday night, was exercising his tonsorial functions in the tap-room of the Rose, where he is accustomed to operate hebdomadally on half the beards of the parish.

The doctor made his entry apparently with considerable reluctance, enacting for the first and last time in his life the part of *Le Médecin malgré lui.* He held his razor in one hand and a shaving-brush in the other, while a barber's apron was tied round the shabby, rusty, out-at-elbow, second-hand, black coat, renewed once in three years, and the still shabbier black breeches, of which his costume usually consists. In spite of my seeming, as I really was, glad to see him, a compliment which from me had at least the charm of novelty, —in spite of a very gracious reception, I never saw the man of medicine look more completely astray. He has a pale, meagre, cadaverous face at all times, and a long lank body that seems as if he fed upon his own physic (although it is well known that gin, sheer gin, of which he is by no means sparing, is the only distilled water that finds its way down his throat):—but on this night, between fright—for Henry had taken possession of him without even explaining his errand,—and shame to be dragged into my presence whilst bearing the *insignia* of the least dignified of his professions, his very wig, the identical brown scratch which he wears by way of looking professional, actually stood on end. He was followed by a miscellaneous procession of assistants, very kind, very curious, and very troublesome, from that noisy neighbour of ours, the well-frequented Rose Inn. First marched mine host, red waistcoated and jolly as usual, bearing a huge foaming pewter pot of double X, a sovereign cure for all sublunary ills, and lighted by the limping hostler, who tried in vain to keep pace with the swift strides of his master, and held at arm's length before him a smoky horn lantern, which might well be called dark. Next tripped Miss Phœbe (this misadventure happened before the grand event of her marriage with the patten-maker) with a flaring candle in one hand and a glass of cherry-brandy, reserved by her mother for grand occasions, in the other—*autre remède!* Then followed the motley crew of the taproom, among whom figured my friend Joel, with a woman's apron tied round his neck, and his chin covered with lather, he having been the identical customer —the very shavee, whose beard happened to be under discussion when the unfortunate interruption occurred.

After the bustle and alarm had in some measure

subsided, the doctor marched up gravely to poor May, who had taken no sort of notice of the uproar.

"She must be bled!" quoth I.

"She must be fomented and physicked!" quoth the doctor; and he immediately produced from either pocket a huge bundle of dried herbs (perhaps the identical venomous-smelling spicer), which he gave to Miss Phœbe to make into a decoction *secundum artem*, and a huge horse-ball, which he proceeded to divide into boluses;—think of giving a horse-ball to my May!

"She must be bled immediately!" said I.

"She must not!" replied the doctor.

"You shall bleed her!" cried Henry.

"I won't!" rejoined the doctor. "She shall be fo——" *mented* he would have added; but her faithful attendant, thoroughly enraged, screamed out, "She sha'n't!" and a regular scolding match ensued, during which both parties entirely lost sight of the poor patient, and mine host of the Rose had very nearly succeeded in administering his specific—the double X, which would doubtless have been as fatal as any prescription of licentiate or quack. The worthy landlord had actually forced open her jaws, and was about to pour in the liquor, when I luckily interposed in time to give the ale a more natural direction down his own throat, which was almost as well accustomed to such potations as that of Boniface. He was not at all offended at my rejection of his kindness, but drank to my health and May's recovery with equal goodwill.

In the meantime the tumult was ended by my friend the cricketer, who, seeing the turn which things were taking, and quite regardless of his own plight, ran down the village to the Lea, to fetch another friend of mine, an old gamekeeper, who set us all to rights in a moment, cleared the stable of the curious impertinents, flung the horse-ball on the dunghill, and the decoction into the pond, bled poor May, and turned out the doctor; after which, it is almost needless to say that the patient recovered.

A COUNTRY BARBER

In the little primitive town of Cranley, where I spent the first few years of my life—a town, which but for the distinction of a market and a post-office, might have passed for a moderately sized village—the houses in that part of the great western road which passed through it were so tumbled about, so intermixed with garden walls, garden palings, and garden hedges, to say nothing of stables, farmyards, pigsties and barns, that it derogated nothing from the dignity of the handsome and commodious dwelling in which I had the honour to be born, that its next-door neighbour was a barber's shop, a real, genuine, old-fashioned barber's shop, consisting of a low-browed cottage, with a pole before it; a basin, as bright as Mambrino's helmet, in the window; a half-hatch always open, through which was visible a little dusty hole, where a few wigs, on battered wooden blocks, were ranged round a comfortable shaving chair; and a legend over the door, in which "William Skinner, wig-maker, hair-dresser, and barber," was set forth in yellow letters on a blue ground. I left Cranley before I was four years old; and, next to a certain huge wax-doll, called Sophy, who died the usual death of wax-dolls, by falling out of the nursery window, the most vivid and the pleasantest of my early recollections is our good neighbour Will Skinner—for by that endearing abbreviation he was called everywhere but in his own inscription. So agreeable, indeed, is the impression which he has left on my memory, that although, doubtless, the he-people find it more convenient to shave themselves, and to dispense with wigs and powder, yet I cannot help regretting, the more for his sake, the decline and extinction of a race which, besides figuring so notably in the old novels and comedies, formed so genial a link between the higher and lower orders of society; supplying to the rich the most familiar of followers and most harmless of gossips.

It certainly was not Will Skinner's beauty that caught my fancy. His person was hardly of the kind to win a lady's favour, even although that lady were only four years of age. He was an elderly man, with an infirm, feeble step, which gave him the air of being older than he was; a lank, long, stooping figure, which seemed wavering in the wind like a powder-puff; a spare, wrinkled visage, with the tremulous appearance about the mouth and cheeks which results from extreme thinness; a pale complexion; scanty white hair; and a beard considerably longer than beseemed his craft.

Neither did his apparel serve greatly to set off his lean and wrinkled person. It was usually composed, within doors, of a faded linen jacket; without, of a grey pepper-and-salt coat, repaired with black; both somewhat the worse for wear; both "a world too wide" for his shrunk sides, and both well covered with powder. Dusty as a miller was Will Skinner. Even the hat, which, by frequent reverential applications of his finger and thumb, had become moulded into a perpetual form of salutation, was almost as richly frosted as a church-warden's wig. Add to this a white apron, with a comb sticking out of the pocket; shoes clumsily patched—poor Will was his own cobbler; blue stockings, indifferently darned —he was, to boot, his own sempstress; and a ragged white cravat, marvellously badly ironed—for he was also his own washerwoman; and the picture will be complete.

Good old man! I see him in my mind's eye at this moment; lean, wrinkled, shabby, poor, slow of speech, and ungainly of aspect; yet pleasant to look at and delightful to recollect, in spite of rags, ugliness, age, and poverty. It was the contented expression of his withered countenance, the cheerful humility of his deportment, and the overflowing kindness of his temper, that rendered Will Skinner so general a favourite. There was nothing within his small power that he was not ready to undertake for anybody. At home in every house, and conversant in every business, he was the universal help of the place. Poor he was certainly, as poor as well could be, and lonely; for he had been crossed in love in his youth, and lived alone in his little tenement, with no other companions than his wig-blocks and a tame starling ("pretty company" he used to call them); but destitute as he was of worldly goods, and although people loved to talk of him with a kind of gentle pity, I have always considered him as one of the happiest persons of my acquaintance; one "who suffered all as suffering nothing"; a philosopher rather of temperament than of reason; "the only man in the parish," as mine host of the Swan used to observe, "who was foolish enough to take a drink of small-beer as thankfully as a draught of double ale."

His fortunes had, at one time, assumed a more flourishing aspect. Our little insignificant town was one of the richest livings in England, and had been held by the Bishop of ——, in conjunction with his very poor see. He resided nearly half the year at Cranley Rectory, and was the strenuous friend and patron of our friend Will. A most orthodox person at all points was the Bishop, portly, comely, and important; one who had won his way to the Bench by learning and merit, and was rather more finical about his episcopal decorations, and more jealous of his episcopal dignity, than a man early accustomed to artificial distinctions is apt to be. He omitted no opportunity of rustling and bustling in a silk apron; assumed the lawn sleeves whenever it was possible to introduce those inconvenient but pleasant appendages to the clerical costume; and was so precise in the article of perukes, as to have had one constructed in London on the exact model of the caxon worn by the then Archbishop of

Canterbury, which our orthodox divine appears to have considered as a sort of regulation wig. Now this magnificent cauliflower (for such it was) had never been frosted to his Lordship's satisfaction until it came under the hands of Will Skinner, who was immediately appointed his shaver, wig-dresser, and wig-maker in ordinary, and recommended by him to all the beards and caxons in the neighbourhood. Nor did the kindness of his right reverend patron end here. Pleased with his barber's simplicity and decency of demeanour, as well as with the zealous manner in which he led the psalmody at church, quivering forth in a high thin voice the strains of Hopkins and Sternhold, the good Bishop determined to promote him in that line; appointed him to the sextonship which happened to fall vacant; and caused him to officiate as deputy to David Hunt, the parish-clerk—a man of eighty, worn out in the service, and now bedridden with the rheumatism—with a complete understanding that he should succeed to the post as soon as David was fairly deposited in the churchyard. These were comfortable prospects. But, alas! the Bishop, a hale man of sixty, happened to die first; and his successor in the rectory, a little, thin, bald-headed person, as sharp as a needle, who shaved himself and wore no wigs, took such disgust at certain small irregularities, such as marking the evening lessons instead of the morning, forgetting to say Amen in the proper place, and other mistakes committed in his trepidation by the clerk-deputy when the new incumbent came to read in, that, instead of the translation to a higher post, which poor Will anticipated, he was within an ace of losing his sextonship, which he was only permitted to retain on condition of never raising his voice again in a stave so long as he lived; the rector, a musical amateur, having been so excruciated by Will's singing as to be fain to stop his ears. Thus ended all his hopes of church preferment.

After this disaster, the world began to go ill with him. People learnt to shave themselves, that was a great evil; they took to wearing their own hair, that was a greater; and when the French revolution and cropped heads came into fashion, and powder and hair-dressing went out, such was the defalcation of his customers, and the desolate state of his trade, that poor Will, in spite of the smallness of his wants, and the equanimity of his spirit, found himself nearly at his wits' end. In this dilemma he resolved to turn his hand to other employments; and living in the neighbourhood of a famous trout stream, and becoming possessed of a tattered copy of Izaak Walton's *Complete Angler*, he applied himself to the construction of artificial flies; in which delicate manufacture, facilitated doubtless by his dexterity in wig-weaving, he soon became deservedly eminent.

This occupation he usually followed in his territory, the churchyard, as pleasant a place to be buried in as heart could desire, occupying a gentle eminence by the side of Cranley Down, on which the cricketers of that cricketing country used to muster two elevens for practice, almost every fine evening, from Easter to Michaelmas. Thither Will, who had been a cricketer himself in his youth, and still loved the wind of a ball, used to resort on summer afternoons; perching himself on a large, square, raised monument, whose very inscription was worn away, a spreading lime-tree above his head, Izaak Walton before him, and his implements of trade at his side. I never read that delicious book without remembering how Will Skinner used to study it. Skipping the fine pastoral poetry, and still more poetical prose of the dialogues, and poring over the notes, as a housekeeper pores over the receipts in the *Cook's Oracle* or a journeyman apothecary applies himself to the London *Pharmacopeia*. Curious directions of a truth they were, and curiously followed. The very list of materials had in it something striking and outlandish; camel's hair, badger's hair, hog's wool, seal's fir, cock's hackles, a heron's neck, a starling's wing, a mallard's tail, and the crest of a peacock!

These, and a thousand such knick-knacks, a wilderness of fur and feather, were ranged beside him, with real nicety but seeming confusion; and mingled with flies, finished or in progress, and with homelier and more familiar tools, hooks, bristles, shoemaker's wax, needles, scissors, marking silk of all colours, and "barge sail for dubbing." And there he sate, now manufacturing a cannon-fly, "dubbing it with black wool, and Isabella-coloured mohair, and bright brownish bear's hair, warped on with yellow silk, shaping the wings of the feather of a woodcock's wing, and working the head of an ash-colour," and now watching Tom Taylor's unparagoned bowling, or throwing away the half-dubbed cannon-fly in admiration of Jem Willis's hits.

On this spot our intimacy commenced. A spoilt child and an only child, it was my delight to escape from nurse and nursery, and all the restraint of female management, and to follow everywhere the dear papa, my chief spoiler, who so fully returned my partiality, as to have a little pad constructed on which I used to accompany him in his excursions on horseback.

The only place at which his fondness ever allowed him to think my presence burthensome was the cricket ground, to which I used regularly to follow him in spite of all remonstrance and precaution, causing him no small perplexity, as to how to bestow me in safety during the game. Will and the monument seemed to offer exactly the desired refuge, and our good neighbour readily consented to fill the post of deputy nursery-maid for the time, assisted in his superintendence by a very beautiful and sagacious black Newfoundland dog, called Coe, who partly from a sense of duty, and partly from personal affection, used when out to take me under his particular care, and mounted guard over the monument as well as Will Skinner, who assuredly required all the aid that could be mustered to cope with my vagaries.

Poor dear old man, what a life I led him!—now playing at bo-peep on one side of the great monument, and now on the other; now crawling away amongst the green graves; now starting up between two headstones; now shouting in triumph with my small childish voice, from the low church-yard wall; now gliding round before him, and laughing up in his face as he sate. Poor dear old man! with what undeviating good-humour did he endure my naughtiness! How he would catch me away from the very shadow of danger if a ball came near! and how often did he interrupt his own labours to forward my amusement, sliding from his perch to gather lime branches to stick in Coe's collar, or to collect daisies, buttercups, or ragged-robins to make what I used to call daisy-beds for my doll.

Perhaps there might be a little self-defence in this last-mentioned kindness; the picking to pieces of flowers and making of daisy-beds being, as Will well knew, the most efficacious means of hindering me from picking to pieces his oak-flies or May-flies; or, which was still worse, of con-structing others after my own fashion out of his materials; which, with a spirit of imitation as innocently mischievous as a monkey, I used to purloin for the purpose the moment his back was turned, mixing martin's fur and otter's fur, and dipping my little fingers amongst brown and red hackles, with an audacity that would have tried the patience of Job. How Will's held out

I cannot imagine! but he never got further than a very earnest supplication that I would give over helping him, a deprecation of my assistance, a " Pray don't, dear Miss !" that on remembering the provocation seems to me a forbearance surpassing that of Grisildis. What is the desertion of a good-for-nothing husband, and even the cooking his second wedding dinner (so I believe the story runs), compared to seeing an elf of four years old mixing and oversetting the thousand and one materials of fly-making! Old Chaucer hath made the most of it, but in point of patience Grisildis was nothing to Will Skinner.

And yet, to do myself justice, my intentions towards my friend the fly-maker were perfectly friendly. Mischievous as I undoubtedly was, I did not intend to do mischief. If I filched *from* him, I filched *for* him; courted the cook for pheasant and partridge feathers; begged the old jays and black-birds which were hung up *in terrorem* in the cherry-trees from the gardener; dragged a great bit of Turkey carpet to the church-yard because I had heard him say that it made good dubbing; got into a *démêlé* with a peacock in the neighbourhood from seizing a piece of his tail to form the bodies of Will's dragon-flies; and had an affair with a pig, in an attempt to procure that staple commodity, hog's down. *N.B.*—The hog had the better of that battle; and but for the intervention of my friend Coe, who, seeing the animal in chase of me, ran to the rescue, and pulled him back by the tail, I might have rued my attack upon those pig's ears (for behind them grows the commodity in question) to this very hour.

Besides the torment that I unconsciously gave him, poor Will had not always reason to congratulate himself on the acquaintance of my faithful follower, Coe. He was, as I have said, a dog of great accomplishment and sagacity, and possessed in perfection all the tricks which boys and servants love so well to teach to this docile and noble race. Now it so happened that our barber, in the general defalcation of wig-wearers at Cranley, retained one constant customer, a wealthy grocer, who had been churchwarden ever since the Bishop's time, and still emulated that regretted prelate in the magnificence of his peruke; wearing a caxon such as I have seldom seen on any head, except that of Mr. Fawcett on the stage, and of Dr. Parr off.

Mr. Samuel Saunders, such was the name of our churchwarden, having had the calamity to lose a wife whom he had wedded some forty years before, was, as the talk went, paying his addresses to pretty Jenny Wren, the barmaid at the Swan. Samuel was a thick, short, burly person, with a red nose, a red waistcoat, and a cinnamon-coloured coat, altogether a very proper wearer of the buzz wig. If all the men in Cranley could have been ranged in a row, the wig would have been assigned to him, in right of look and demeanour, just as the hats in

one corner of Hogarth's print, " The Election Ball," can be put each on the proper head without difficulty. The man and the wig matched each other. Now Jenny Wren was no match for either. She was a pretty, airy, jaunty girl, with a merry hazel eye, a ready smile, and a nimble tongue, the arrantest flirt in Cranley, talking to every beau in the parish, but listening only to tall Thomas, our handsome groom.

An ill match for Samuel Saunders at sixty, or for Samuel Saunders's wig, was the pretty coquette Jenny Wren at eighteen! The disparity was painful to think of. But it was the old story. Samuel was wealthy and Jenny poor; and uncles, aunts, friends and cousins coaxed and remonstrated ; and poor Jenny pouted and cried, and vowed fifty times a day that she would not marry him if he were fifty times as rich ; till, at length, worn out by importunity, exhausted by the violence of her own opposition, offended by the supineness of her favourite lover, and perhaps a little moved by the splendour of the churchwarden's presents, she began to relent, and finally consented to the union.

The match was now talked of as certain by all the gossips in Cranley,—some had even gone so far as to fix the wedding-day; when one evening our handsome groom, tall Thomas, poor Jenny's favourite beau, passing by Will Skinner's shop, followed by Coe, saw a new wig of Samuel Saunders's pattern, doubtless the identical wedding wig, reposing in full friz on one of the battered wooden blocks. "High, Coe!" said Thomas making a sign with his hand; and in an instant Coe had sprung over the half-hatch into the vacant shop, had seized the well-powdered periwig, and in another instant returned with it into the street, and followed Thomas, wig in mouth, into the little bar at the Swan, where sate Mr. Samuel Saunders, making love to Jenny Wren.

The sudden apparition of his wig, borne in so unexpected a manner, wholly discomfited the unlucky suitor and even dumbfounded his fair mistress. "High, Coe! high!" repeated Thomas, and, at the word, Coe, letting drop the first caxon, sprang upon that living block, Samuel Saunders's noddle, snatched off the other wig, and deposited both his trophies at Jenny's feet!—a catastrophe, which was followed in less than a month by the marriage of the handsome groom and the pretty barmaid; for the churchwarden, who had withstood all other rebuffs, was driven for ever from the field by the peals of laughter which, after the first surprise was over, burst irrepressibly from both the lovers. In less than a month they were married; and Will Skinner and Coe, who had hitherto avoided each other by mutual consent, met as guests at the wedding-dinner; and through the good offices of the bridegroom, were completely and permanently reconciled; Coe's consciousness being far more difficult to conquer than the short-lived anger of the most placable of barbers.

OUR MAYING

As party produces party, and festival brings forth festival in higher life, so one scene of rural festivity is pretty sure to be followed by another. The boys' cricket-match at Whitsuntide, which was won most triumphantly by our parish, and luckily passed off without giving cause for a coroner's inquest, or indeed without injury of any sort except the demolition of Amos Stone's new straw-hat, the crown of which (Amos's head being fortunately at a distance) was fairly struck out by the cricket-ball; this match produced one between our eleven and the players of the neighbouring hamlet of Whitley; and being patronised by the young lord of the manor and several of the gentry round, and followed by jumping in sacks, riding donkey-races, grinning through horse-collars, and other diversions more renowned for their antiquity than their elegance, gave such general satisfaction that it was resolved to hold a Maying in full form in Whitley Wood.

Now this wood of ours happens to be a common of twenty acres, with three trees on it, and the Maying was fixed to be held between hay-time and harvest; but "what's in a name?" Whitley

Wood is a beautiful piece of greensward, surrounded on three sides by fields, and farmhouses, and cottages, and woody uplands, and on the other by a fine park; and the May-house was erected, and the May-games held in the beginning of July; the very season of leaves and roses, when the days are at the longest, and the weather at the finest, and the whole world is longing to get out of doors. Moreover, the whole festival was aided, not impeded, by the gentlemen amateurs, headed by that very genial person, our young lord of the manor; whilst the business part of the affair was confided to the well-known diligence, zeal, activity, and intelligence of that most popular of village landlords, mine host of the Rose. How could a Maying fail under such auspices? Everybody expected more sunshine and more fun, more flowers and more laughing, than ever was known at a rustic merry-making—and really, considering the manner in which expectation had been raised, the quantity of disappointment has been astonishingly small.

Landlord Sims, the master of the revels, and our very good neighbour, is a portly, bustling man, of five-and-forty, or thereabout, with a hale, jovial visage, a merry eye, a pleasant smile, and a general air of good-fellowship. This last qualification, whilst it serves greatly to recommend his ale, is apt to mislead superficial observers, who generally account him a sort of slenderer Boniface, and imagine that, like that renowed hero of the spigot, Master Sims, eats, drinks, and sleeps on his own anno domini.

They were never more mistaken in their lives; no soberer man than Master Sims within twenty miles! Except for the good of the house, he no more thinks of drinking beer than a grocer of eating figs. To be sure when the jug lags he will take a hearty pull, just by way of example, and to set the good ale a-going. But, in general, he trusts to subtler and more delicate modes of quickening its circulation. A good song, a good story, a merry jest, a hearty laugh, and a most winning habit of assentation; these are his implements. There is not a better companion or a more judicious listener in the county. His pliability is astonishing. He shall say yes to twenty different opinions on the same subject, within the hour; and so honest and cordial does his agreements seem, that no one of his customers, whether drunk or sober, ever dreams of doubting his sincerity. The hottest conflict of politics never puzzles him: Whig or Tory, he is both, or either—" the happy Mercutio, that curses both houses." Add to this gift of conformity, a cheerful, easy temper, an alacrity of attention, a zealous desire to please, which gives to his duties, as a landlord, all the grace of hospitality, and a perpetual civility and kindness, even when he has nothing to gain by them; and no one can wonder at Master Sims's popularity.

After his good wife's death, this popularity began to extend itself in a remarkable manner amongst the females of the neighbourhood; smitten with his portly person, his smooth, oily manner, and a certain soft, earnest, whispering voice, which he generally assumes when addressing one of the fairer sex, and which seems to make his very "how d'ye do" confidential and complimentary. Moreover, it was thought that the good landlord was well to do in the world, and though Betsy and Letty were good little girls, quick, civil, and active, yet, poor things, what could such young girls know of a house like the Rose? All would go to rack and ruin without the eye of a mistress! Master Sims must look out for a wife. So thought the whole female world, and, apparently, Master Sims began to think so himself.

The first fair one to whom his attention was directed was a rosy, pretty widow, a pastry-cook of the next town, who arrived in our village on a visit to her cousin, the baker, for the purpose of giving confectionery lessons to his wife. Nothing was ever so hot as that courtship. During the week that the lady of pie-crust stayed, her lover almost lived in the oven. One would have thought that he was learning to make the cream-tarts without pepper, by which Bedreddin Hassan regained his state and his princess. It would be a most suitable match, as all the parish agreed; the widow, for as pretty as she was (and one sha'n't often see a pleasanter, open countenance, or a sweeter smile), being within ten years as old as her suitor, and having had two husbands already. A most proper and suitable match, said everybody ; and when our landlord carried her back to B. in his new-painted green cart, all the village agreed that they were gone to be married, and the ringers were just setting up a peal, when Master Sims returned alone, single, crestfallen, dejected; the bells stopped of themselves, and we heard no more of the pretty pastrycook. For three months after that rebuff, mine host, albeit not addicted to aversions, testified an equal dislike to women and tartlets, widows and plum-cake. Even poor Alice Taylor, whose travelling basket of lollypops and gingerbread he had whilom patronised, was forbidden the house; and not a bun or a biscuit could be had at the Rose for love or money.

The fit, however, wore off in time; and he began again to follow the advice of his neighbours, and to look out for a wife, up street and down; whilst at each extremity a fair object presented herself, from neither of whom had he the slightest reason to dread a repetition of the repulse which he had experienced from the blooming widow. The downstreet lady was a widow also, the portly, comely relict of our drunken village blacksmith, who, in spite of her joy at her first husband's death, and an old spite at mine host of the Rose, to whose good ale and good company she was wont to ascribe most of the aberrations of the deceased, began to find her shop, her journeymen, and her eight children (six unruly, obstreperous pickles of boys, and two tomboys of girls), rather more than a lone woman could manage, and to sigh for a helpmate to ease her of her cares, collect the boys at night, see the girls to school of a morning, break the larger imps of running away to revels and fairs, and the smaller fry of birds'-nesting and orchard-robbing, and bear a part in the lectures and chastisements which she deemed necessary to preserve the young rebels from the bad end which she predicted to them twenty times a day. Master Sims was the coadjutor on whom she had inwardly pitched; and, accordingly, she threw out broad hints to that effect every time she encountered him, which, in the course of her search for boys and girls, who were sure to be missing at school-time and bed-time, happened pretty often; and Mr. Sims was far too gallant and too much in the habit of assenting to listen uumoved; for really the widow was a fine, tall, comely woman; and the whispers, and smiles, and hand-pressings, when they happened to meet, were becoming very tender; and his admonitions and head-shakings, addressed to the young crew (who, nevertheless, all liked him) quite fatherly. This was his down-street flame.

The rival lady was Miss Lydia Day, the carpenter's sister; a slim, upright maiden, not remarkable for beauty, and not quite so young as she had been, who, on inheriting a small annuity from the mistress with whom she had spent the best of her days, retired to her native village to live on her means. A genteel, demure, quiet personage, was Miss Lydia Day; much addicted to snuff and green tea, and not averse from a little gentle scandal—for the rest, a good sort of woman, and *un très-bon parti* for Master Sims, who seemed to consider it a profitable speculation, and made love to her whenever she happened to come into his head, which, it must be confessed, was hardly so often as her merits and her annuity deserved. Remiss as he was, he had no lack of encouragement to complain of—for she "to hear would seriously incline," and put on her best silk, and her best simper, and lighted up her faded complexion into something approaching to a blush, whenever he came to visit her. And this was Master Sims's up-street love.

So stood affairs at the Rose when the day of the Maying arrived; and the double flirtation, which, however dexterously managed, must have been, sometimes, one would think, rather inconvenient to the inamorato, proved on this occasion extremely useful. Each of the fair ladies contributed her aid to the festival; Miss Lydia by tying up sentimental garlands for the May-house, and scolding the carpenters into diligence in the erection of the booths; the widow by giving her whole bevy of boys and girls a holiday, and turning them loose on the neighbourhood to collect flowers as they could. Very useful auxiliaries were these light foragers; they scoured the country far and near—irresistible mendicants! pardonable thieves! coming to no harm, poor children, except that little George got a black eye in tumbling from the top of an acacia-tree at the Park, and that Sam (he's a sad pickle is Sam!) narrowly escaped a horse-whipping from the head gardener at the Hall, who detected a bunch of his new rhododendron, the only plant in the county, forming the very crown and centre of the May-pole,

Little harm did they do, poor children, with all their pilfery; and when they returned, covered with their flowery loads, like the May-day figure called "Jack of the Green," they worked at the garlands and the May-houses, as none but children ever do work, putting all their young life and their untiring spirit of noise and motion into their pleasant labour. Oh, the din of that building! Talk of the Tower of Babel! that was a quiet piece of masonry compared to the May-house of Whitley Wood, with its walls of leaves and flowers—and its canvas booths at either end for refreshments and musicians. Never was known more joyous note of preparation.

The morning rose more quietly—I had almost said more dully—and promised ill for the *fête*. The sky was gloomy, the wind cold, and the green filled as slowly as a balloon seems to do when one is watching it. The entertainments of the day were to begin with a cricket-match (two elevens to be chosen on the ground), and the wickets pitched at twelve o'clock precisely. Twelve o'clock came—but no cricketers—except, indeed, some two or three punctual and impatient gentlemen; one o'clock came, and brought no other reinforcement than two or three more of our young Etonians and Wykhamites—less punctual than their precursors, but not a whit less impatient. Very provoking, certainly—but not very uncommon. Your country cricketer, the peasant, the mere rustic, does love, on these occasions, to keep his betters waiting, if only to display his power; and when we consider that it is the one

solitary opportunity in which importance can be felt
and vanity gratified, we must acknowledge it to be
perfectly in human nature that a few airs should
be shewn. Accordingly, our best players held aloof.
Tom Coper would not come to the ground; Joel
Brent came, indeed, but would not play; Samuel
Long coquetted—he would and he would not.
Very provoking, certainly! Then two young
farmers, a tall brother and a short, Hampshire men,
cricketers born, whose good-humour and love of the
game rendered them sure cards, had been compelled
to go on business—the one, ten miles south—the
other, fifteen north—that very morning. No playing without the Goddards! No sign of either of
them on the B—— road or the F——. Most in-
tolerably provoking, beyond a doubt! Master Sims
tried his best coaxing and his best double X on the
recusant players; but all in vain. In short, there
was great danger of the match going off altogether;
when, about two o'clock, Amos Stone, who was
there with the crown of his straw hat sewed in
wrong side outward—new thatched, as it were—and
who had been set to watch the B—— highway, gave
notice that something was coming as tall as the
May-pole—which something turning out to be the
long Goddard, and his brother approaching at the
same moment in the opposite direction, hope, gaiety,
and good-humour revived again; and two elevens,
including Amos and another urchin of his calibre,
were formed on the spot.

I never saw a prettier match. The gentlemen,

the Goddards, and the boys being equally divided, the strength and luck of the parties were so well balanced, that it produced quite a neck-and-neck race, won only by two notches. Amos was completely the hero of the day, standing out half of his side, and getting five notches at one hit. His side lost—but so many of his opponents gave him their ribbons (have not I said that Master Sims bestowed a set of ribbons?) that the straw hat was quite covered with purple trophies; and Amos, stalking about the ground, with a shy and awkward vanity, looked with his decorations like the sole conqueror —the Alexander or Napoleon of the day. The boy did not speak a word; but every now and then he displayed a set of huge white teeth in a grin of inexpressible delight. By far the happiest and proudest personage of that Maying was Amos Stone.

By the time the cricket-match was over, the world began to be gay at Whitley Wood. Carts and gigs, and horses and carriages, and people of all sorts, arrived from all quarters; and, lastly, "the blessed sun himself" made his appearance, adding a triple lustre to the scene. Fiddlers, ballad-singers, cake-baskets—Punch—Master Frost, crying cherries—a Frenchman with dancing dogs—a Bavarian woman selling brooms—half a dozen stalls with fruit and frippery—and twenty noisy games of quoits, and bowls, and ninepins—boys throwing at boxes—girls playing at ball—gave to the assemblage the bustle, clatter, and gaiety of a Dutch fair, as one sees it in Teniers' pictures. Plenty of drinking and smoking on the green—plenty of eating in the booths: the gentlemen cricketers, at one end, dining off a round of beef, which made the table totter—the players, at the other, supping off a gammon of bacon—Amos Stone crammed at both—and Landlord Sims bustling everywhere with an activity that seemed to confer upon him the gift of ubiquity, assisted by the little light-footed maidens, his daughters, all smiles and curtsies, and by a pretty black-eyed young woman—name unknown—with whom, even in the midst of his hurry, he found time, as it seemed to me, for a little philandering. What would the widow and Miss Lydia have said? But they remained in happy ignorance—the one drinking tea in most decorous primness in a distant marquée, disliking to mingle with so mixed an assembly,—the other in full chase after the most unlucky of all her urchins, the boy called Sam, who had gotten into a *démêlé* with a showman, in consequence of mimicking the wooden gentleman Punch, and his wife Judy—thus, as the showman observed, bringing his exhibition into disrepute.

Meanwhile, the band struck up in the May-house, and the dance, after a little demur, was fairly set afloat—an honest English country dance—(there had been some danger of waltzing and quadrilling) —with ladies and gentlemen at the top, and country lads and lasses at the bottom; a happy mixture of cordial kindness on the one hand, and pleased respect on the other. It was droll, though, to see the beplumed and beflowered French hats, the silks and the furbelows sailing and rustling amidst the straw bonnets and cotton gowns of the humbler dancers; and not less so to catch a glimpse of the little lame clerk, shabbier than ever, peeping through the canvas opening of the booth, with a grin of ineffable delight, over the shoulder of our vicar's pretty wife. Really, considering that Mabel Green and Jem Tanner were standing together at that moment at the top of the set, so deeply engaged in making love that they forgot when they ought to begin, and that the little clerk must have seen them, I cannot help taking his grin for a favourable omen to those faithful lovers.

Well, the dance finished, the sun went down, and we departed. The Maying is over, the booths carried away, and the May-house demolished. Everything has fallen into its old position, except the love-affairs of Landlord Sims. The pretty lass with the black eyes, who first made her appearance at Whitley Wood, is actually staying at the Rose Inn, on a visit to his daughters; and the village talk goes that she is to be the mistress of that thriving hostelry, and the wife of its master; and both her rivals are jealous, after their several fashions—the widow in the tantrums, the maiden in the dumps. Nobody knows exactly who the black-eyed damsel may be,—but she's young, and pretty, and civil, and modest; and, without intending to depreciate the merits of either of her competitors, I cannot help thinking that our good neighbour has shewn his taste.

THE HARD SUMMER

AUGUST 15th—Cold, cloudy, windy, wet. Here we are, in the midst of the dog-days, clustering merrily round the warm hearth, like so many crickets, instead of chirruping in the green fields like that other merry insect the grasshopper; shivering under the influence of the *Jupiter Pluvius* of England, the watery St. Swithin; peering at that scarce personage the sun, when he happens to make his appearance, as intently as astronomers look after a comet, or the common people stare at a balloon; exclaiming against the cold weather, just as we used to exclaim against the warm. "What a change from last year!" is the first sentence you hear, go where you may. Everybody remarks it, and everybody complains of it; and yet in my mind it has its advantages, or at least its compensations, as everything in nature has, if we would only take the trouble to seek for them.

Last year, in spite of the love which we are now pleased to profess towards that ardent luminary, not one of the sun's numerous admirers had courage to look him in the face: there was no bearing the world till he had said "Good-night" to it. Then we might stir; then we began to wake and to live. All day long we languished under his influence in a strange dreaminess, too hot to work, too hot to read, too hot to write, too hot even to talk; sitting hour after hour in a green arbour, embowered in leafiness, letting thought and fancy float as they would. Those day-dreams were pretty things in their way; there is no denying that. But then, if one half of the world were to dream through a whole summer, like the Sleeping Beauty in the Wood, what would become of the other?

The only office requiring the slightest exertion, which I performed in that warm weather, was watering my flowers. Common sympathy called for that labour. The poor things withered, and faded, and pined away; they almost, so to say, panted for drought. Moreover, if I had not watered them myself, I suspect that no one else would; for water last year was nearly as precious hereabout as wine. Our land-springs were dried up; our wells were exhausted; our deep ponds were dwindling into mud; and geese, and ducks, and pigs, and laundresses used to look with a jealous and suspicious eye on the few and scanty half-buckets of that impure element, which my trusty lackey was fain to filch for my poor geraniums and campanulas and tube-roses. We were forced to smuggle them in through my faithful adherent's territories, the stable, to avoid lectures within doors; and at last even that resource failed; my garden, my blooming garden, the joy of my eyes, was forced to go waterless like its neigh-

bours, and became shrivelled, scorched, and sunburnt, like them. It really went to my heart to look at it.

On the other side of the house matters were still worse. What a dusty world it was when about sunset we became cool enough to creep into it! Flowers in the court looking fit for a *hortus siccus*; mummies of plants, dried as in an oven; hollyhocks, once pink, turned into Quakers; cloves smelling of dust. Oh, dusty world! May herself looked of that complexion; so did Lizzy; so did all the houses, windows, chickens, children, trees, and pigs in the village; so, above all, did the shoes. No foot could make three plunges into that abyss of pulverised gravel, which had the impudence to call itself a hard road, without being clothed with a coat a quarter of an inch thick. Woe to white gowns! woe to black! Drab was your only wear.

Then, when we were out of the street, what a toil it was to mount the hill, climbing with weary steps and slow upon the brown turf by the wayside, slippery, hot, and hard as a rock! And then if we happened to meet a carriage coming along the middle of the road,—the bottomless middle,—what a sandy whirlwind it was! What choking, what suffocation! No state could be more pitiable, except indeed that of the travellers who carried this misery about with them. I shall never forget the plight in which we met the coach one evening in last August, full an hour after its time, steeds and driver, carriage and passengers, all one dust.

The outsides and the horses and the coachman seemed reduced to a torpid quietness, the resignation of despair. They had left off trying to better their condition, and taken refuge in a wise and patient hopelessness, bent to endure in silence the extremity of ill. The six insides, on the contrary, were still fighting against their fate, vainly struggling to ameliorate their hapless destiny. They were visibly grumbling at the weather, scolding the dust, and heating themselves like a furnace by striving against the heat. How well I remember the fat gentleman without his coat, who was wiping his forehead, heaving up his wig, and certainly uttering that English ejaculation, which, to our national reproach, is the phrase of our language best known on the Continent. And that poor boy, red-hot, all in a flame, whose mamma, having divested her own person of all superfluous apparel, was trying to relieve his sufferings by the removal of his neckkerchief—an operation which he resisted with all his might. How perfectly I remember him, as well as the pale girl who sate opposite, fanning herself with her bonnet into an absolute fever! They vanished after a while in their own dust; but I have them all before my eyes at this moment, a companion-picture to Hogarth's "Afternoon," a standing lesson to the grumblers at cold summers.

For my part, I really like this wet season. It keeps us within, to be sure, rather more than is quite agreeable; but then we are at least awake and alive there, and the world out of doors is so much the pleasanter when we can get abroad. Everything does well, except those fastidious bipeds, men and women; corn ripens, grass grows, fruit is plentiful; there is no lack of birds to eat it, and there has not been such a wasp-season these dozen years. My garden wants no watering, and is more beautiful than ever, beating my old rival in that primitive art, the pretty wife of the little mason, out and out. Measured with mine, her flowers are nought. Look at those hollyhocks, like pyramids of roses; those garlands of the convolvulus major of all colours, hanging around that tall pole, like the wreathy hop-bine; those magnificent dusky cloves, breathing of the Spice Islands; those flaunting double dahlias; those splendid scarlet geraniums, and those fierce and warlike flowers the tiger-lilies. Oh, how beautiful they are! Besides, the weather clears sometimes — it has cleared this evening; and here are we, after a merry walk up the hill, almost as quick as in the winter, bounding lightly along the bright green turf of the pleasant common, enticed by the gay shouts of a dozen clear young voices, to linger awhile, and see the boys play at cricket.

I plead guilty to a strong partiality towards that unpopular class of beings, country-boys: I have a large acquaintance amongst them, and I can almost say, that I know good of many and harm of none. In general they are an open, spirited, good-humoured race, with a proneness to embrace the pleasures and eschew the evils of their condition, a capacity for happiness, quite unmatched in man, or woman, or girl. They are patient, too, and bear their fate as scapegoats (for all sins whatsoever are laid as matters of course to their door, whether at home or abroad) with amazing resignation; and, considering the many lies of which they are the objects, they tell wonderfully few in return. The worst that can be said of them is, that they seldom, when grown to man's estate, keep the promise of their boyhood; but that is a fault to come—a fault that may not come, and ought not to be anticipated. It is astonishing how sensible they are to notice from their betters, or those whom they think such. I do not speak of money, or gifts, or praise, or the more coarse and common briberies—they are more delicate courtiers; a word, a nod, a smile, or the mere calling of them by their names, is enough to ensure their hearts and their services. Half a dozen of them, poor urchins, have run away now to bring us chairs from their several homes. "Thank you, Joe Kirby!—you are always first—yes, that is just the place.—I shall see everything there. Have you been in yet, Joe?"—"No, ma'am! I go in next." —"Ah, I am glad of that—and now's the time Really that was a pretty ball of Jem Eusden's!— I was sure it would go to the wicket. Run, Joe! They are waiting for you." There was small need to bid Joe Kirby make haste; I think he is, next to a race-horse, or a greyhound, or a deer, the fastest creature that runs—the most completely alert and active. Joe is mine especial friend, and leader of the "tender juveniles," as Joel Brent is of the adults. In both instances this post of honour was gained by merit, even more remarkably so in Joe's case than in Joel's; for Joe is a less boy than many of his companions (some of whom are fifteeners and sixteeners, quite as tall and nearly as old as Tom Coper), and a poorer than all, as may be conjectured from the lamentable state of that patched round-frock, and the ragged condition of those unpatched shoes, which would encumber, if any thing could, the light feet that wear them. But why should I lament the poverty that never troubles him? Joe is the merriest and happiest creature that ever lived twelve years in this wicked world. Care cannot come near him. He hath a perpetual smile on his round ruddy face, and a laugh in his hazel-eye that drives the witch away. He works at yonder farm on the top of the hill, where he is in such repute for intelligence and good-humour, that he has the honour of performing all the errands of the house, of helping the maid, and the mistress, and the master, in addition to his own stated office of carter's boy. There he works hard from five till seven, and then he comes here to work still harder under the name of play—batting, bowling, and fielding, as if for life, filling the place of four boys; being, at a pinch, a whole eleven. The late Mr. Knyvett, the king's organist, who used in his own person to sing twenty parts at once of the Hallelujah Chorus, so that you would have thought he had a nest of nightingales in his throat, was but a type of Joe Kirby. There is a sort of ubiquity about him; he thinks nothing of being in two places at once, and for pitching a ball William Grey himself is nothing to him. It goes straight to the mark like a bullet. He is king of the cricketers from eight to sixteen, both inclusive, and an excellent ruler he makes. Nevertheless, in the best-ordered States there will be grumblers, and we have an opposition here in the shape of Jem Eusden.

Jem Eusden is a stunted lad of thirteen, or thereabout, lean, small, and short, yet strong and active. His face is of an extraordinary ugliness, colourless, withered, haggard, with a look of extreme age, much increased by hair so light that it might rather pass for white than flaxen. He is constantly arrayed in the blue cap and old-fashioned coat, the costume of an endowed school to which he belongs; where he sits still all day, and rushes into the field at night, fresh, untired, and ripe for action, to scold, and brawl, and storm, and bluster. He hates Joe Kirby, whose immovable good-humour, broad smiles, and knowing nods, must certainly be very provoking to so fierce and turbulent a spirit; and he has himself (being, except by rare accident, no great player) the preposterous ambition of wishing to be manager of the sports. In short, he is a demagogue in embryo, with every quality necessary to a splendid success in that vocation,—a strong voice, a fluent utterance, an incessant iteration, and a frontless impudence. He is a great "scholar," too, to use the country phrase; his "piece," as our village schoolmaster terms a fine sheet of flourishing writing, something between a valentine and a sampler, enclosed within a border of little coloured prints—his last, I remember, was encircled by an engraved history of Moses, beginning at the finding in the bulrushes, with Pharaoh's daughter, dressed in a rose-coloured gown and blue feathers —his piece is not only the admiration of the school but of the parish, and is sent triumphantly around from house to house at Christmas, to extort halfpence and sixpences from all encouragers of learning—*Montem* in miniature. The Mosaic history was so successful, that the produce enabled Jem to purchase a bat and ball, which, besides adding to his natural arrogance (for the little pedant actually began to mutter against being eclipsed by a dunce, and went so far as to challenge Joe Kirby to a trial in Practice, or the Rule of Three), gave him, when compared with the general poverty, a most unnatural preponderance in the cricket state. He had the ways and means in his hands—(for, alas! the hard winter had made sad havoc among the bats, and the best ball was a bad one)—he had the ways and means, could withhold the supplies, and his party was beginning to wax strong, when Joe received a present of two bats and a ball for the youngsters in general, and himself in particular— and Jem's adherents left him on the spot—they ratted, to a man, that very evening. Notwithstanding this desertion, their forsaken leader has in nothing relaxed from his pretensions, or his ill-humour. He still quarrels and brawls as if he had a faction to back him, and thinks nothing of contending with both sides, the ins and the outs, secure of out-talking the whole field. He has been squabbling these ten minutes, and is just marching off now with his own bat (he has never deigned to use one of Joe's) in his hand. What an ill-conditioned hobgoblin it is! And yet there is something bold and sturdy about him too. I should miss Jem Eusden.

Ah, there is another deserter from the party! my friend the little hussar—I do not know his name, and call him after his cap and jacket. He is a very remarkable person, about the age of eight years, the youngest piece of gravity and dignity I ever encountered; short, and square, and upright, and slow, with a fine bronzed flat visage, resembling those convertible signs the Broad-Face and the Saracen's Head, which, happening to be next-door neighbours in the town of B., I never know apart, resembling, indeed, any face that is open-eyed and immovable—the very sign of a boy! He stalks about with his hands in his breeches pocket, like a piece of machinery; sits leisurely down when he ought to field, and never gets farther in batting than to stop the ball. His is the only voice never heard in the *mêlée*; I doubt, indeed, if he have one, which may be partly the reason of a circumstance that I record to his honour, his fidelity to Jem

Eusden, to whom he has adhered through every change of fortune with a tenacity proceeding perhaps from an instinctive consciousness that that loquacious leader talks enough for two. He is the only thing resembling a follower that our demagogue possesses, and is cherished by him accordingly. Jem quarrels for him, scolds for him, pushes for him; and but for Joe Kirby's invincible good-humour, and a just discrimination of the innocent from the guilty, the activity of Jem's friendship would get the poor hussar ten drubbings a day.

But it is growing late. The sun has set a long time. Only see what a gorgeous colouring has spread itself over those parting masses of clouds in the west,—what a train of rosy light! We shall have a fine sunshiny day to-morrow,—a blessing not to be undervalued, in spite of my late vituperation of heat. Shall we go home now? And shall we take the longest but prettiest road, that by the green lanes? This way, to the left, round the corner of the common, past Mrs. Welles's cottage, and our path lies straight before us. How snug and comfortable that cottage looks! Its little yard all alive with the cow, and the mare, and the colt almost as large as the mare, and the young foal, and the great yard-dog, all so fat! Fenced in with hay-rick, and wheat-rick, and bean-stack, and backed by the long garden, the spacious drying-ground, the fine orchard, and that large field quartered into four different crops. How comfortable this cottage looks, and how well the owners earn their comforts! They are the most prosperous pair in the parish—she a laundress with twenty times more work than she can do, unrivalled in flounces and shirt-frills, and such delicacies of the craft; he, partly a farmer, partly a farmer's man, tilling his own ground, and then tilling other people's;—affording a proof, even in this declining age, when the circumstances of so many worthy members of the community seem to have "an alacrity in sinking," that it is possible to amend them by sheer industry. He, who was born in the workhouse, and bred up as a parish boy, has now, by mere manual labour, risen to the rank of a land-owner, pays rates and taxes, grumbles at the times, and is called Master Welles,—the title next to Mister—that by which Shakspeare was called:—what would man have more? His wife, besides being the best laundress in the county, is a comely woman still. There she stands at the spring, dipping up water for to-morrow,—the clear, deep, silent spring, which sleeps so peacefully under its high flowery bank, red with the tall spiral stalks of the foxglove and their rich pendent bells, blue with the beautiful forget-me-not, that gem-like blossom, which looks like a living jewel of turquoise and topaz. It is almost too late to see its beauty; and here is the pleasant shady lane, where the high elms will shut out the little twilight that remains. Ah, but we shall have the fairies' lamps to guide us, the stars of the earth, the glowworms! Here they are, three almost together. Do you not see them? One seems tremulous vibrating, as if on the extremity of a leaf of grass; the others are deeper in the hedge, in some green cell on which their light falls with an emerald lustre. I hope my friends the cricketers will not come this way home. I would not have the pretty creatures removed for more than I care to say, and in this matter I would hardly trust Joe Kirby—boys so love to stick them in their hats. But this lane is quite deserted. It is only a road from field to field. No one comes here at this hour. They are quite safe; and I shall walk here to-morrow and visit them again. And now, good-night! beautiful insects, lamps of the fairies, good-night!

THE MOLE-CATCHER

THERE are no more delightful or unfailing associations than those afforded by the various operations of the husbandman, and the changes on the fair face of nature. We all know that busy troops of reapers come with the yellow corn; whilst the yellow leaf brings a no less busy train of ploughmen and seedsmen preparing the ground for fresh harvests; that woodbines and wild-roses, flaunting in the blossomy hedgerows, give token of the gay bands of haymakers which enliven the meadows; and that the primroses, which begin to unfold their pale stars by the side of the green lanes, bear marks of the slow and weary female processions, the gangs of tired yet talkative bean-setters, who defile twice a day through the intricate mazes of our cross-country roads. These are general associations, as well known and as universally recognised as the union of mince-pies and Christmas. I have one, more private and peculiar, one, perhaps, the more strongly impressed on my mind, because the impression may be almost confined to myself. The full flush of violets which, about the middle of March, seldom fails to perfume the whole earth, always brings to my recollection one solitary and silent coadjutor of the husbandman's labours, as unlike a violet as possible—Isaac Bint, the mole-catcher.

I used to meet him every spring, when we lived at our old house, whose park-like paddock, with its finely clumped oaks and elms, and its richly timbered hedgerows, edging into wild, rude, and solemn fir-plantations, dark, and rough, and hoary, formed for so many years my constant and favourite walk. Here, especially under the great horse-chestnut, and where the bank rose high and naked above the lane, crowned only with a tuft of golden broom; here the sweetest and prettiest of wild-flowers, whose very name hath a charm, grew like a carpet under one's feet, enamelling the young green grass with their white and purple blossoms, and loading the air with their delicious fragrance; here I used to come almost every morning, during the violet-tide; and here almost every morning I was sure to meet Isaac Bint.

I think that he fixed himself the more firmly in my memory by his singular discrepancy with the beauty and cheerfulness of the scenery and the season. Isaac is a tall, lean, gloomy personage, with whom the clock of life seems to stand still. He has looked sixty-five for these last twenty years, although his dark hair and beard, and firm manly stride, almost contradict the evidence of his sunken cheeks and deeply lined forehead. The stride is awful: he hath the stalk of a ghost. His whole air and demeanour savour of one that comes from underground. His appearance is "of the earth, earthy." His clothes, hands, and face are of the colour of the mould in which he delves. The little round traps which hang behind him over one shoulder, as well as the strings of dead moles which embellish the other, are encrusted with dirt like a tombstone; and the staff which he plunges into the little hillocks, by which he traces the course of his small quarry, returns a hollow sound, as if tapping on the lid of a coffin. Images of the churchyard come, one does not know how, with his presence. Indeed he does officiate as assistant to the sexton in his capacity of grave-digger, chosen, as it should seem, from a natural fitness; a fine sense of congruity in good Joseph Reed, the functionary in question, who felt, without knowing why, that, of all men in the parish, Isaac Bint was best fitted to that solemn office.

His remarkable gift of silence adds much to the impression produced by his remarkable figure. I don't think that I ever heard him speak three words in my life. An approach of that bony hand to that earthy leather cap was the greatest effort of courtesy that my daily salutations could extort from him. For this silence, Isaac has reasons good. He hath a reputation to support. His words are too precious to be wasted. Our mole-catcher, ragged as he looks, is the wise man of the village, the oracle of the village inn, foresees the weather, charms away agues, tells fortunes by the stars, and writes notes upon the almanack—turning and twisting about the predictions after a fashion so ingenious, that it's a moot point which is oftenest wrong—Isaac Bint, or Francis Moore. In one eminent instance, our friend was, however, eminently right. He had the good luck to prophesy, before sundry witnesses—some of them sober—in the tap-room of the Bell—he then sitting, pipe in mouth, on the settle at the right-hand side of the fire, whilst Jacob Frost occupied the left;—he had the good fortune to foretell, on New Year's Day 1812, the downfall of Napoleon Bonaparte—a piece of soothsayership which has established his reputation, and dumbfounded all doubters and cavillers ever since; but which would certainly have been more striking if he had not annually uttered the same prediction, from the same place, from the time that the aforesaid Napoleon became First Consul. But this small circumstance is entirely overlooked by Isaac and his admirers, and they believe in him, and he believes in the stars, more firmly than ever.

Our mole-catcher is, as might be conjectured, an old bachelor. Your married man hath more of this world about him—is less, so to say, planet-struck. A thorough old bachelor is Isaac, a contemner and maligner of the sex, a complete and decided woman-hater. Female fraility is the only subject on which he hath ever been known to dilate; he will not even charm away their agues, or tell their fortunes, and, indeed, holds them to be unworthy the notice of the stars.

No woman contaminates his household. He lives on the edge of a pretty bit of woodland scenery, called the Penge, in a snug cottage of two rooms, of his own building, surrounded by a garden cribbed from the waste, well fenced with quickset, and well stocked with fruit-trees, herbs, and flowers. One large apple-tree extends over the roof—a pretty bit of colour when in blossom, contrasted with the thatch of the little dwelling, and relieved by the dark wood behind. Although the owner be solitary, his demesne is sufficiently populous. A long row of bee-hives extends along the warmest side of the garden—for Isaac's honey is celebrated far and near; a pig occupies a commodious sty at one corner; and large flocks of ducks and geese (for which the Penge, whose glades are intersected by water, is famous) are generally waiting round a back gate leading to a spacious shed, far larger than Isaac's own cottage, which serves for their feeding and roosting-place. The great tameness of all these creatures—for the ducks and geese flutter round him the moment he approaches, and the very pig follows him like a dog—gives no equivocal testimony of the kindness of our mole-catcher's nature. A circumstance of recent occurrence puts his humanity beyond doubt.

Amongst the probable causes of Isaac's dislike to women, may be reckoned the fact of his living in a female neighbourhood (for the Penge is almost peopled with duck-rearers and goose-crammers of the duck and goose gender), and being himself

unpopular amongst the fair poultry-of that watery vicinity. He beat them at their own weapons; produced at Mid-summer geese for Michaelmas; and raised ducks so precocious, the gardeners complained of them as forerun-their vegetable accompaniment; and "panting *peas* toiled after them in vain." In short, the Naïads of the Penge had the mortification to find themselves driven out of B—— market by an interloper, and that interloper a man, who had no manner of right to possess any skill in an accomplishment so exclusively feminine as duck-rearing; and being no ways inferior in another female accomplishment, called scolding, to their sister-nymphs of Billingsgate, they set up a clamour and a cackle which might rival the din of their own gooseries at feeding-time, and would inevitably have frightened from the field any competitor less impenetrable than our hero. But Isaac is not a man to shrink from so small an evil as female objurgation. He stalked through it all in mute disdain—looking now at his mole-traps, and now at the stars—pretending not to hear, and very probably not hearing. At first this scorn, more provoking than any retort, only excited his enemies to fresh attacks; but one cannot be always answering another person's silence. The flame which had blazed so fiercely, at last burnt itself out, and peace reigned once more in the green alleys of Penge Wood.

One, however, of his adversaries—his nearest neighbour—still remained unsilenced.

Margery Grover was a very old and poor woman, whom age and disease had bent almost to the earth; shaken by palsy, pinched by penury, and soured by misfortune—a moving bundle of misery and rags. Two centuries ago she would have been burnt for a witch; now she starved and grumbled on the parish allowance; trying to eke out a scanty subsistence by the dubious profits gained from the produce of two geese and a lame gander, once the unmolested tenants of a greenish pool, situate right between her dwelling and Isaac's, but whose watery dominion had been invaded by his flourishing colony.

This was the cause of feud; and although Isaac would willingly, from a mingled sense of justice and of pity, have yielded the point to the poor old creature, especially as ponds are there almost as plentiful as blackberries, yet it was not so easy to control the habits and inclinations of their feathered subjects, who all perversely fancied that particular pool; and various accidents and skirmishes occurred, in which the ill-fed and weak birds of Margery had generally the worst of the fray. One of her early goslings was drowned—an accident which may happen even to water-fowl; and her lame gander, a sort of pet with the poor old woman, injured in his well leg; and Margery vented curses as bitter as those of Sycorax; and Isaac, certainly the most superstitious personage in the parish— the most thorough believer in his own gifts and predictions—was fain to nail a horseshoe on his door for the defence of his property, and to wear one of his own ague charms about his neck for his personal protection.

Poor old Margery! A hard winter came; and the feeble, tottering creature shook in the frosty air like an aspen-leaf; and the hovel in which she dwelt—for nothing could prevail on her to try the shelter of the workhouse—shook like herself at every blast. She was not quite alone either in the world or in her poor hut: husband, children, and grandchildren had passed away; but one young and innocent being, a great grandson, the last of her descendants, remained, a helpless dependent on one almost as helpless as himself.

Little Harry Grover was a shrunken, stunted boy, of five years old; tattered and squalid, like his grandame, and, at first sight, presented almost as miserable a specimen of childhood as Margery herself did of age. There was even a likeness between them; although the fierce blue eye of Margery had, in the boy, a mild appealing look, which entirely changed the whole expression of the countenance. A gentle and a peaceful boy was Harry, and, above all, a useful. It was wonderful how many ears of corn in the autumn, and sticks in the winter, his little hands could pick up! how well he could make a fire, and boil the kettle, and sweep the hearth, and cram the goslings! Never was a handier boy or a trustier; and when the united effects of cold, and age, and rheumatism confined poor Margery to her poor bed, the child continued to perform his accustomed offices; fetching the money from the vestry, buying the loaf at the baker's, keeping house, and nursing the sick woman, with a kindness and thoughtfulness which none but those who know the careful ways to which necessity trains cottage children would deem credible; and Margery, a woman of strong passions, strong prejudices, and strong affections, who had lived in and for the desolate boy, felt the approach of death embittered by the certainty that the workhouse, always the scene of her dread and loathing, would be the only refuge for the poor orphan.

Death, however, came on visibly and rapidly; and she sent for the overseer to beseech him to put Harry to board in some decent cottage; she could not die in peace until he had promised; the fear of the innocent child's being contaminated by wicked boys and godless women preyed upon her soul; she implored, she conjured. The overseer, a kind but timid man, hesitated, and was beginning a puzzled speech about the bench and the vestry, when another voice was heard from the door of the cottage.

"Margery," said our friend Isaac, "will you trust Harry to me? I am a poor man, to be sure; but, between earning and saving, there'll be enough for me and little Harry. 'Tis as good a boy as ever lived, and I'll try to keep him so. Trust him to me, and I'll be a father to him. I can't say more."

"God bless thee, Isaac Bint! God bless thee!" was all poor Margery could reply.

They were the last words she ever spoke. And little Harry is living with our good mole-catcher, and is growing plump and rosy; and Margery's other pet, the lame gander, lives and thrives with them too.

MATTHEW SHORE

NEXT in beauty to the view over the Loddon at Aberleigh, is that from Lanton Bridge up and down the clear and winding Kennet, and this present season (the latter end of April) is perhaps the time of year which displays to the greatest advantage that fine piece of pastoral scenery. And yet it is a species of beauty difficult to convey to the reader. There is little to describe but much to feel; the sweet and genial repose of the landscape harmonises so completely with the noontide sunshine and the soft, balmy air. The river, bright and glassy, glides in beautiful curves through a rich valley of meadow-land, the view on one side of the bridge terminating at the distance of a couple of miles by the picturesque town of B. with its old towers and spires, whilst on the other the stream seems gradually to lose itself amongst the richly wooded and finely undulating grounds of Lanton Park.

But it is in the meadows themselves that the real charm is to be found: the fresh sprouting grass, bordered with hedgerows just putting on their tenderest green, dotted with wild patches of willow trees, and clumps of noble elms, gay with the

golden marsh marigold and the elegant fritillary;
alive with bees and butterflies, and the shining tribe
of water insects; and musical with the notes of a
countless variety of birds, who cease singing or
whom we cease to listen to (it comes exactly to the
same thing) the moment the nightingale begins her
matchless song. Here and there, too, farmhouses
and cottages, half hidden by cherry orchards just
in their fullest bloom, come cranking into the
meadows; and farther in the distance chimney-tops
with curling wreaths of blue smoke, or groups of
poplar, never seen but near dwellings, give a fresh
interest to the picture by the unequivocal signs of
human habitation and human sympathy.

In one of the nearest of these poplar clumps—
not above half a mile off, if it were possible for any
creature except a bird to pass the wide deep ditches
which intersect these water meadows, but which,
by thridding the narrow and intricate lanes that
form the only practicable route, we contrive to make
nearly six times as long; in that island of spiral
poplars and gigantic fruit-trees, with one corner of
the roof just peeping amongst the blossomy cherry
boughs, stands the comfortable abode of my good
friend Matthew Shore, to whose ample farm a large
portion of these rich meadows forms an appendage
of no trifling value.

Matthew is of an old yeomanry family, who have
a pedigree of their own, and are as proud of having
been for many generations the hereditary tenants
of the owners of Lanton Park, as they themselves

may be of having been for more centuries than I choose to mention the honoured possessors of that fair estate. Excellent landlords, and excellent tenants, both parties are, I believe, equally pleased with the connection, and would no more think of dissolving the union, which time and mutual service have cemented so closely, than of breaking through the ties of near relationship; although my friend Matthew, having no taste for agricultural pursuits, his genius for the cultivation of land having broken out in a different line, has devolved on his younger brother Andrew the entire management and superintendence of the farm.

Matthew and Andrew Shore are as unlike as two brothers well can be in all but their strong manly affection for each other, and go on together all the better for their dissimilarity of taste and character. Andrew is a bluff, frank, merry Benedict, blest in a comely, bustling wife, and five rosy children; somewhat too loud and boisterous in his welcomings, which come upon one like a storm, but delightful in his old-fashioned hospitality and his hearty good-humour; for the rest, a good master, a steady friend, a jovial neighbour, and the best farmer and most sagacious dealer to be found in the country-side. He must be a knowing hand who takes in Andrew Shore. He is a bold rider too, when the fox-hounds happen to come irresistibly near; and is famous for his breed of cocking spaniels, and for constantly winning the yeomanry cup at the B. coursing meeting. Such is our good neighbour Farmer Shore.

His wife is not a little like her husband; a laughing, bustling, good-humoured woman, famous for the rearing of turkeys and fattening of calves, ruling the servants and children within doors with as absolute a discretion as that with which he sways the out-door sceptre, and complaining occasionally of the power she likes so well, and which, with an ingratitude not uncommon in such cases, she is pleased to call trouble. In spite of these complaints, however, she is one of the happiest women in the parish, being amongst the very few who are neither troubled by poverty nor finery—the twin pests of the age and country. Her expenses are those of her grandmother's days; she has fourteen-shilling hyson, and double refined sugar for any friend who may drop in to tea, and a handsome silk gown to wear to church on Sundays. An annual jaunt to Ascot is all her dissipation, and a taxed cart her sole equipage. Well may Mrs. Shore be a happy woman.

The only spot about the place sacred from her authority, is that which I am come to visit,—the garden; my friend Matthew's territory, in which he spends all his days, and half his nights, and which, in spite of his strong fraternal affection, he certainly loves better than brother or sister, nephew or niece, friend or comrade; better, in short, than he loves anything else under the sun.

Matthew is an old bachelor of fifty-five, or thereaway, with a quick eye, a ruddy cheek, a delightful benevolence of countenance, a soft voice and a gentle manner. He is just what he seems, the kindest, the most generous, and the best-natured creature under the sun, the universal friend and refuge of servants, children, paupers, and delinquents of all descriptions, who fly to him for assistance and protection in every emergency, and would certainly stun him with their clamorous importunity, if he were not already as deaf as a post.

Matthew is one of the few very deaf people worth talking to. He is what is becoming scarcer every day, a florist of the first order, and of the old school, —not exactly of Mr. Evelyn's time, for in the gardening of that period, although greens were, flowers were not,—but of thirty or forty years back, the reign of pinks, tulips, auriculas, and ranunculuses, when the time and skill of the gardener were devoted to produce, in the highest imaginable perfection, a variety of two or three favoured tribes. The whole of this large garden, for the potatoes and the cabbages have been forced to retreat to a nook in the orchard, dug up in their behoof;—the whole ample garden is laid out in long beds, like those in a nursery ground, filled with these precious flowers, of the rarest sorts and in the highest culture; and as I have arrived in the midst of the hyacinth, auricula, and anemone season, with the tulips just opening, I may consider myself in great luck to see what is called in gardening language, " so grand a show." It is worth something, too, to see Matthew's delight, half compounded of vanity and kindness, as he shews them, mixed with courteous offers of seedlings and offsets, and biographical notices of the more curious flowers: " How the stock of this plant came from that noted florist Tom Bonham, the B. tailor, commonly called Tippling Tom, who once refused fifty guineas for three auriculas! and how this tulip was filched (Matthew tells this in a particularly low and confidential tone)" from a worthy merchant of Rotterdam, by an honest skipper of his acquaintance, who abstracted the root, but left five pounds in the place of it, and afterwards made over the bargain for a couple of pounds more, just to pay him for the grievous bodily fear which he had undergone between the time of this adventure, for there was no telling how the Burgomaster might relish the bargain, and his embarkation in the good schooner the *Racehorse* of Liverpool."

Perhaps the tulips, especially this pet root, are on the whole Matthew's favourites; but he is a great man at pink shows and melon feasts, and his carnations, particularly those of a sort called " the Mount Etna," which seldom comes to good in other hands, as regularly win the plate as Andrew's greyhounds. It is quite edifying to hear him run over the bead-roll of pink names, from Cleopatra to the Glory of New York. The last mentioned flowers are precisely my object to-day; for I am come to beg some of his old plants, to the great endangerment of my character as a woman of taste, I having, sooth to say, no judgment in pinks, except preferring those which are full of bloom, in which quality these old roots, which he was about to fling away, and which he is giving me with a civil reluctance to put anything so worthless into my garden, greatly excel the young plants of which he is so proud.

Notwithstanding his love for his own names, some of which are fantastical enough, Matthew wages fierce war against the cramp appellations, whether of geraniums or of other plants, introduced latterly, and indeed against all new flowers of every sort whatsoever, comprehending them all under the general denomination of trash. He contrives to get the best and the rarest, notwithstanding, and to make them blow better than anybody, and I would lay a wager——Ay, I am right! the rogue! the rogue! What is that in the window but the cactus speciosissimus, most splendid of flowers, with its large ruby cup and its ivory tassels? It is not in bloom yet, but it is showing strong and coming fast. And is not that fellow the scarlet potentilla? And that the last fuschia? And is there such a plant in the county as that newest of all the new camellia? Ah, the rogue! the rogue! He to abuse my geraniums, and call me new-fangled, with four plants in his windows that might challenge the horticultural! And when I laugh at him about it, he'll pretend not to hear, and follow the example of that other great deaf artist

"Who shifted his trumpet and only took snuff."

Ah, the rogue! the rogue! To think that fickleness should be so engrafted in man's nature, that even

Matthew Shore is not able to resist the contagion, but must fall a flirting with cactuses and camellias—let the pinks and tulips look to it! The rogue! the rogue!

If the fickleness of man were my first thought, the desire to see the camellia nearer was the second; and Mrs. Shore appearing in the porch with her clean white apron and her pleasant smile, I followed her through a large, lightsome, bricked apartment, the common room of the family, where the ample hearth, the great chairs in the chimney corner, defended from draughts by green stuff curtains, the massive oak tables, the tall japanned clock, and the huge dresser laden with pewter dishes as bright as silver, gave token of rustic comfort and opulence. Ornaments were not wanting. The dresser was also adorned with the remains of a long preserved set of tea-china, of a light rambling pattern, consisting of five cups and seven saucers, a tea-pot, neatly mended, a pitcher-like cream jug, cracked down the middle, and a sugar basin, wanting a handle; with sundry odd plates, delf, blue, and white, brown-edged and green-edged, scalloped and plain; and last, and choicest, with a grand collection of mugs—always the favourite object of housewifely vanity in every rank of rural life, from Mrs. Shore of Lanton Farm, down to her maid Debby. This collection was of a particularly ambitious nature. It filled a row and a half of the long dresser, graduated according to size, like books in a library, the gallons ranking as folios, the half pints ranging as duodecimos.

Their number made me involuntarily repeat to myself two lines from Anstey's inimitable "Pleader's Guide," meant to ridicule the fictions of the law, but here turned into a literal truth.

> "First count's for that with divers jugs,
> To wit, twelve pots, twelve cups, twelve mugs,"

but these jugs were evidently not meant to be profaned by the "certain vulgar drink called toddy," or any other drink. Half a dozen plain white ones, rather out of condition, which stood on a side-table, were clearly the drudges, the working mugs of the family. The ornamental species, the drone mugs, hung on nails by their handles, and were of every variety of shape, colour, and pattern. Some of the larger ones were adorned with portraits in medallion—Mr. Wilberforce, Lord Nelson, the Duke of Wellington, and Charles Fox. Some were gay with flowers not very like nature. Some had landscapes in red, and one a group of figures in yellow. Others again, and these were chiefly the blues, had patterns of all sorts of intricacy and involution without any visible meaning. Some had borders of many colours; and some, which looked too genteel for their company, had white cameos relieved on a brown ground. Those drinking vessels were full of the elegance and grace of the antique. I stood admiring them when Mrs. Shore called me into the parlour, where the plant I wished to see was placed. The parlour—Oh, how incomparably inferior to the kitchen!—was a little, low, square, dark box, into which we were shut by a door, painted black, dimly lighted by a casement window, quite filled by the superb camellia, and rendered even more gloomy by a dark paper of reds and greens, with an orange border. A piece of furniture called a beaufette, open and displaying a collection of glass-ware, almost equal to the pewter for age and brightness, to the mugs for variety, and to the china for joinery, a shining round mahogany table, and six hair-bottomed chairs, really seemed to crowd the little apartment; but it was impossible to look at anything except the splendid plant, with its dark shining leaves, and the pure, yet majestic, blossoms reposing on the deep verdure, as a pearly coronet on the glossy locks of some young beauty. Ah! no wonder that the pinks are a little out of favour, or that Matthew stands smiling there in utter oblivion of striped tulip or streaked carnation! such a plant as this would be an excuse for forgetting the whole vegetable creation, and my good friend Matthew (who always contrives to hear the civil things one says of his flowers, however low one may speak, and who is perfectly satisfied by my admiration on the present occasion) has just made me almost as happy as himself, by promising to rear me one of the same sort, after a method of his own discovering, which he assures me brings them to perfection twice as fast as the dwadling modes of the new school. Nothing like an old gardener after all! above all if he be as kind, as enthusiastic, and as clever as my friend Matthew Shore.

OLD MASTER GREEN

A PARTICULAR sort of mould, which in this county is scarcely to be found except in the tract of land called Chittling Moor, being wanted to form a compost for that very dear part of my small possessions, my beautiful geraniums, we determined to accompany, or rather to follow, in our pretty pony phaeton, the less aristocratic *cortège*, consisting of two boys with wheel-barrows, and old Master Green with a donkey-cart, who had been dispatched to collect it some two hours before.

The day was one of the latest in August, and the weather splendidly beautiful, clear, bright, breezy, sunny. It would have been called too warm by one half of the world, and by the other too cold, which I take to be as near an approach to perfection as our climate, or any climate, can well compass. We had been sitting in our large parlour-like greenhouse; a superb fuschia, bending with the weight of its own blossoms, reaching almost to the top of the house, on one side of the door, and a splendid campanula, with five distinct stems, covered with large yet delicate lilac bells,

on the other; the rich balmy scent of the campanula blending with the exquisite odours of tuberoses, jessamine, mignonette, full blown myrtles, and the honey-sweet clematis, and looking out on gay beds of the latest flowers, China asters, dahlias, hydrangeas blue and pink, phlox white and purple, the scarlet lobelia, and the scarlet geranium. In short, all within my little garden was autumn, beautiful autumn.

On the other side of our cottage the season seemed to have changed. The China roses and honeysuckles, with which it is nearly covered, were in the profuse bloom of early June, and the old monthly rose by the doorway (the sweetest of roses!), together with a cluster of sweet-peas that grew among its branches, were literally smelling of summer. The quantity of rain that had fallen had preserved the trees in their most vivid freshness, and the herbage by the roadside and the shorter turf on the common had all the tender verdure of spring.

As we advanced, however, through the narrow lanes, autumn and harvest reasserted their rights. Every here and there, at the corners where branches jutted out, and in the straits where the hedges closed in together, loose straws of oats and barley, torn from their different waggons, hung dangling from the boughs, mixed with straggling locks of hay, the relics of the after-crop. We ourselves were fain to drive into a ditch, to take shelter from a dingy possession of bean-carriers. My com-

panion, provoked at the ditchy indignity, which his
horse relished no better than himself, asserted that
the beans could not be fit to carry; but, to judge from
the rattling and crackling which the huge black
sheaves made in their transit, especially when the
loaded wain was jerked a little on one side, to
avoid entirely driving over our light and graceful
open carriage, which it overtopped, and threatened
to crush, as the giant in the fairy tale threatens
Tom Thumb—to judge by that noisy indication
of ripeness, ripe they were. The hedgerows, too,
gave abundant proofs in their own vegetation of
the advancing season. The fragrant hazel-nuts
were hardening in their shells, and tempting the
schoolboy's hand by their swelling clusters; the
dewberries were colouring; the yellow St. John's
wort, and the tall, mealy-leaved mullein, had
succeeded the blushing bells of the foxglove,
which, despoiled of its crimson beauty, now
brandished its long spikes of seed-vessels upon
the bank, above which the mountain-ash waved its
scarlet berries in all the glory of autumn; whilst,
as we emerged from the close, narrow lanes into
the open tract of Hartley Common, patches of
purple heath just bursting into flower, and the
gorse and broom pushing forth fresh blossom
under the influence of the late rainy weather,
waved over the light harebell, the fragrant thyme,
and the springing fungi of the season. In short,
the whole of our Berkshire world, as well as that
very dear and very tiny bit of it called my garden,

spoke of autumn, beautiful autumn, the best if not the only time for a visit to the Chittling Moor. These moors were pretty much what the word commonly indicates, a long level tract of somewhat swampy pasture-land, extending along the margin of the Kennet, which, in other parts so beautiful, rolled heavily and lazily through its abundant, but somewhat coarse, herbage; a dreary and desolate place when compared with the general scenery of our richly wooded and thickly peopled country, and one where the eye, wandering over the dull expanse, unbroken by hill, or hedge, or timber tree, conveyed, as is often the case in flat, barren, and desolate scenes, an idea of space more than commensurate with the actual extent.

The divisions of this large piece of ground are formed of wide ditches, which at once serve to drain and to irrigate these marshy moors, so frequently overflowed by the river in spring and winter, and sometimes even in summer; it being no unusual catastrophe for the coarse and heavy crops to be carried away by a sudden flood, disappointing the hopes of the farmer, and baffling the efforts of the haymaker. A weary thing was a wet summer in the Chittling Moor, with the hayfield one day a swamp and the next a lake; and the hay, or rather the poor drowned grass, that should have been hay, choking the ditches, or sailing down the stream! The best that could befall it was to be carried off in waggons in its grassy shape, and made comfortably and snugly on dry ground, in some upland meadow; but people cannot always find room for the outer integuments of three hundred acres of grass-land, and, besides that difficulty, the intersecting ditches, with their clattering, hollow-sounding wooden bridges, presented no ordinary peril to the heavy wains, so that the landlord was fain to put up with little rent, and the farmer with small profit—too happy if the subsequent grazing paid the charge or the loss of the prolonged and often fruitless hay-harvest.

A dreary scene was the Chittling Moor; a few old willow pollards, the most melancholy of trees, formed the sole break to its dull uniformity, and one small dwelling, whose curling smoke rose in the distance above a clustering orchard, was the only sign of human habitation. This small cottage had been built chiefly to suit the circumstances of the moor, which rendered a public-house necessary during the long hay-making; and it was kept by a widow, who contrived to make the profits of that watery but drouthy season pay for the want of custom during the rest of the year. Not that the Widow Knight was absolutely without customers at any period; the excellence and celebrity of her home-brewed having ensured to her a certain number of customers, who, especially on Sundays, used to walk down to the Chittling Gate (so was her domicile entitled) to partake of the luxuries of a pipe and a pot of ale, scream to the deaf widow, gossip with her comely daughter, or flirt with her pretty grandchild (for the whole establishment was female), as their several ages or dispositions might prompt.

Of this number none was more constant than our present attendant, old Master Green, and it is by no means certain whether his familiarity with the banks and pollards which afforded the true geranium mould may not have been acquired by his hebdomadal visits to the Widow Knight's snug and solitary ale-house.

Old George Green was indeed a veteran of the tap-room, one to whom strong beer had been for nearly seventy years the best friend and the worst enemy, making him happy and keeping him poor. He called himself eighty-five; and I presume, from the report of other people, as well as his own (for when approaching that age, vanity generally takes the turn of making itself older), that he might really be past fourscore. A wonderful man he was of his years, both in appearance and constitution. Hard work had counteracted the ill effects of hard drinking, as an equal quantity of labour, under the form of hard riding, sometimes used to do by a jovial, fox-hunting squire of former times, and had kept him light, vigorous, and active, as little bent or stiffened by age as the two boys who were delving out the earth under his direction. The only visible mark which age had set upon him—mark, did I say? a brand, a fire-brand—was in his nose, which was of the true Bardolphian size and colour, and a certain roll of the eye, which might perhaps, under any circumstances, have belonged to the man and his humour, but which much resembled that of a toper, when half-tipsy, and fancying himself particularly wise.

The very Nestor of village topers was Master Green, hearty, good-humoured, merry, and jolly, very civil, and a little sly. He was quite patriarchal in the number of his descendants, having had the Mahommedan allowance of four wives, although, after the Christian fashion, successively, and more children and grandchildren than he could conveniently count. Indeed, his computation varied a little, according as he happened to be drunk or sober; for he was proud of his long train of descendants, just as his betters may be proud of a long line of ancestry; and, being no disciple of the Malthusian doctrine, thought he "had done the state" (that is, the parish) "some service," in rearing up a goodly tribe of sons and daughters, many of them in their turns grandfathers and grandmothers, and most of whom had conducted themselves passably in the world, as times go—thanks probably to a circumstance which he sometimes lamented, their being, men and women, but puny tipplers compared with their jolly progenitor. Even his favourite grandson and namesake, only son and heir of the most prosperous of his innumerable family, Master Green, the thriving carpenter of East Hartley, who, like a dutiful lad, came every Sunday afternoon to the Chittling Gate to meet his grandfather, abandoning for that purpose the cricket-ground at Hartley, where he, a singularly fine young man, had long been accounted the best player—even this favourite grandson was, he declared, little better than a milk-sop, a swallower of tea and soda-water. " I verily believe," said Master Green, "that a pot of double X would upset him!"

A friend and a promoter of matrimony in all its shapes, especially in the guise of a love-match, was our worthy great-grandfather, whether in his own person or in the person of his descendants. Four wives had he had of happy memory, and he spoke of them all with mingled affection and philosophy, as good sort of women in the main, though the first was somewhat of a slut, the second ugly, the third silly, and the last a scold, which, as he observed, " might be one reason that he missed her so much, poor woman! the house seemed so quiet an *unked*"; —whereupon he sighed, and then, with a roll of his eye and a knowing twist of his Bardolphian nose, began to talk of the necessity of his looking out for a fifth helpmate.

By this the operation of collecting the geranium mould was in full activity; and the conversation of the old man and the two lively boys, to which we were authorised listeners, and in which my companion soon became an interlocutor, gave us to understand that they were in possession of some further information respecting Master Green's matrimonial intentions.

" We all know why he goes to the Chittling Gate every Sunday," said Ben, an arch, saucy lad of whom we have before heard in this volume.

"Any child may know that," responded Master Green, trying to look demure and innocent, like a young lady when rallied on her admirers; "any child can tell that. The Widow Knight brews the best ale in the parish."

"Ay, but that's not the only reason," said John, a modest youth of sixteen; "is it, Ben?"

"It's reason enough," rejoined Master Green.

"But not *the* reason," retorted Ben.

"What! the widow herself?" quoth my companion.

"Lord, no, sir," interrupted Ben.

"'Twould be a very suitable match, and a snug resting-place, only I'm afraid he would drink up all the ale in the cellar," pursued the interrogator.

"Lord, no, sir!" again exclaimed Ben. "Master Green thinks the widow too old."

"Too old! Why she's a score of years younger than himself, but I suppose he prefers the daughter?"

"No, no, sir," rejoined Ben; "she's too old, too. The granddaughter, the granddaughter! That's the match for Master Green."

"What! the young pretty girl, Susan Parker, a girl of eighteen, marry a man of eighty! nonsense, Ben."

"They've been asked in church, sir," said John quietly; "I heard it myself."

"Asked in church! But I thought the young carpenter was after Susan? Asked in church! Master Green, are you rivalling your own grandson?"

"His father the sick carpenter would not hear of that match," cried Ben, "because Susan had no money."

"And what does he say to this match, Ben?"

"Sir, he says that he likes it worse than t'other, but that he can't help this; that his father is an old fool, and must answer for his own folly."

"Well, but Susan! she never can be such a goose. It must be a mistake. Have you really been asked in church, Master Green? Have the banns actually been published?"

"Twice, sir, in full form," answered the old man gravely. "I wonder your honour did not hear them."

"And is the match really to take place?"

"Next Monday, your honour, God willing."

"Pshaw! nonsense! the thing's impossible! you are all joking."

"Time will prove, sir," rejoined Master Green, still more gravely; and, the geranium mould being now fairly collected, we parted.

And on the next Monday the marriage did take place, sure enough, though not exactly in the way anticipated, George Green the younger proving to be the bridegroom, to the surprise of bridemaid, parson, and clerk: whilst the rich carpenter, unable to resist the double pleadings of his father and his son, and somewhat pleased to be spared the scandal of so youthful a step-mother, forgave the trick and the stolen match; and old George Green, in the fulness of his delight, got tipsier than ever, in honour of his success, and toasted the Widow Knight so often and so heartily in her own home-brewed, that it's odds but he becomes the landlord of that snug ale-house, the Chittling Gate, after all.

PATTY'S NEW HAT

WANDERING about the meadows one morning last May, absorbed in the pastoral beauty of the season and the scenery, I was overtaken by a heavy shower just as I passed old Mrs. Matthews's great farmhouse, and forced to run for shelter to her hospitable porch. A pleasant shelter in good truth I found there. The green pastures dotted with fine old trees stretching all around; the clear brook winding about them turning and returning on its course, as if loath to depart; the rude cart-track leading through the ford; the neater pathway with its foot-bridge; the village spire rising amongst a cluster of cottages, all but the roofs and chimneys concealed by a grove of oaks; the woody background, and the blue hills in the distance, all so flowery and bowery in the pleasant month of May; the nightingales singing; the bells ringing; and the porch itself, around which a honeysuckle in full bloom was wreathing its sweet flowers, giving out such an odour in the rain, as in dry weather nothing but the twilight will bring forth — an atmosphere of fragrance. The whole porch was alive and musical with bees, who, happy rogues, instead of being routed by the wet, only folded their wings the closer, and dived the deeper into the honey-tubes, enjoying, as it seemed, so good an excuse for creeping still farther within their flowery lodgment. It is hard to say which enjoyed the sweet breath of the shower and the honeysuckle most, the bees or I; but the rain began to drive so fast, that at the end of five minutes I was not sorry to be discovered by a little girl belonging to the family; and, first, ushered into the spacious kitchen, with its heavy oak table, its curtained chimney corner, its bacon rack loaded with enormous flitches, and its ample dresser, glittering with crockery ware; and, finally, conducted by Mrs. Matthews herself into her own comfortable parlour, and snugly settled there with herself and her eldest granddaughter, a woman grown; whilst the younger sister, a smiling, light-footed lass of eleven or thereabouts, tripped off to find a boy to convey a message to my family, requesting them to send for me, the rain being now too decided to admit of any prospect of my walking home.

The sort of bustle which my reception had caused having subsided, I found great amusement in watching my hospitable hostess, and listening to a dialogue, if so it may be called, between her pretty granddaughter and herself, which at once let me into a little love secret, and gave me an opportunity of observing one of whose occasional oddities I had all my life heard a great deal.

Mrs. Matthews was one of the most remarkable

persons in these parts; a capital farmer, a most intelligent parish officer, and in her domestic government not a little resembling one of the finest sketches which Mr. Crabbe's graphical pen ever produced.

> "Next died the widow Goe, an active dame
> Famed ten miles round and worthy all her fame;
> She lost her husband when their loves were young,
> But kept her farm, her credit, and her tongue:
> Full thirty years she ruled with matchless skill,
> With guiding judgment and resistless will;
> Advice she scorned, rebellions she suppressed,
> And sons and servants bowed at her behest.
> No parish business in the place could stir
> Without direction or assent from her;
> In turn she took each office as it fell,
> Knew all their duties and discharged them well.
> She matched both sons and daughters to her mind,
> And lent them eyes, for love she heard was blind."
>
> *Parish Register.*

Great power of body and mind was visible in her robust person and massive countenance; and there was both humour and intelligence in her acute smile, and in the keen grey eye that glanced from under her spectacles. All that she said bore the stamp of sense; but at this time she was in no talking mood, and on my begging that I might cause no interruption, resumed her seat and her labours in silent composure. She sat at a little table mending a fustian jacket belonging to one of her sons—a sort of masculine job which suited her much better than a more delicate piece of sempstressship would probably have done; indeed the tailor's needle, which she brandished with great skill, the whitey-brown thread tied round her neck, and the huge, dull-looking *shears* (one can't make up one's mind to call such a machine scissors), which, in company with an enormous pincushion, dangled from her apron-string, figuring as the pendant to a most formidable bunch of keys, formed altogether such a working apparatus as shall hardly be matched in these days of polished cutlery and cobwebby cotton-thread.

On the other side of the little table sat her pretty granddaughter Patty, a black-eyed young woman, with a bright complexion, a neat trim figure, and a general air of gentility considerably above her station. She was trimming a very smart straw hat with pink ribbons; trimming and untrimming, for the bows were tied and untied, taken off and put on, and taken off again, with a look of impatience and discontent, not common to a damsel of seventeen when contemplating a new piece of finery. The poor little lass was evidently out of sorts. She sighed, and quirked, and fidgeted, and seemed ready to cry; whilst her grandmother just glanced at her from under her spectacles, pursed up her mouth, and contrived with some difficulty not to laugh. At last Patty spoke.

"Now, grandmother, you will let me go to Chapel Row revel this afternoon, won't you?"

"Humph!" said Mrs. Matthews.

"It hardly rains at all, grandmother!"

"Humph!" again said Mrs. Matthews, opening the prodigious scissors with which she was amputating, so to say, a button, and directing the rounded end significantly to my wet shawl, whilst the sharp point was reverted towards the dripping honeysuckle. " Humph!"

"There's no dirt to signify!"

Another "Humph!" and another point to the draggled tail of my white gown.

"At all events, it's going to clear."

Two "Humphs!" and two points, one to the clouds, and one to the barometer.

"It's only seven miles," said Patty; "and if the horses are wanted, I can walk."

"Humph!" quoth Mrs. Matthews.

"My aunt Ellis will be there, and my cousin Mary."

"Humph!" again said Mrs. Matthews.

"And if a person is coming here on business, what can I be wanted for when you are at home, grandmother?"

"Humph!" once again was the answer.

"What business can any one have with me?"

Another "Humph!"

"My cousin Mary will be so disappointed!"

".Humph!"

"And I half promised my cousin William—poor William!"

"Humph!" again.

"Poor William! Oh, grandmother, do let me go! And I've got my new hat and all—just such a hat as William likes! Poor William! You will let me go, grandmother?"

And receiving no answer but a very unequivocal "Humph!" poor Patty threw down her straw hat, fetched a deep sigh, and sate in a most disconsolate attitude, snipping her pink ribbon to pieces; Mrs. Matthews went on manfully with her "stitchery"; and for ten minutes there was a dead pause. It was at length broken by my little friend and introducer, Susan, who was standing at the window, and exclaimed—"Who is this riding up the meadow all through the rain? Look!—see!—I do think—no, it can't be—yes, it is—it is certainly my cousin William Ellis! Look, grandmother!"

"Humph!" said Mrs. Matthews.

"What can cousin William be coming for?" continued Susan.

"Humph!" quoth Mrs. Matthews.

"Oh, I know!—I know!" screamed Susan, clapping her hands and jumping for joy as she saw the changed expression of Patty's countenance,—the beaming delight succeeded by a pretty, downcast shamefacedness, as she turned away from her grandmother's arch smile and archer nod. "I know!—I know!" shouted Susan.

"Humph!" said Mrs. Matthews.

"For shame, Susan! Pray don't, grandmother!" said Patty imploringly.

"For shame! Why, I did not say he was coming to court Patty! Did I, grandmother?" returned Susan.

"And I take this good lady to witness," replied Mrs. Matthews, as Patty, gathering up her hat and her scraps of ribbon, prepared to make her escape—"I take you all to witness that I have said nothing of any sort. Get along with you, Patty!" added she, "you have spoiled your pink trimming; but I think you are likely to want white ribbons next, and, if you put me in mind, I'll buy them for you!" And, smiling in spite of herself, the happy girl ran out of the room.

NUTTING

SEPTEMBER 26th.—One of those delicious autumnal days, when the air, the sky, and the earth seem lulled into an universal calm, softer and milder even than May. We sallied forth for a walk, in a mood congenial to the weather and the season, avoiding, by mutual consent, the bright and sunny common, and the gay high road, and stealing through shady, unfrequented lanes, where we were not likely to meet any one,—not even the pretty family procession which in other years we used to contemplate with so much interest—the father, mother, and children, returning from the wheat-field, the little ones laden with bristling close-tied bunches of wheat-ears, their own gleanings, or a bottle and a basket which had contained their frugal dinner, whilst the mother would carry her babe, hushing and lulling it, and the father and an elder child trudged after with the cradle, all seeming weary, and all happy. We shall not see such a procession as this to-day; for the harvest is nearly over, the fields are deserted, the silence may almost be felt. Except the wintry notes of the redbreast, nature herself is mute. But how beautiful, how gentle, how harmonious, how rich! The rain has preserved to the herbage all the freshness and verdure of spring, and the world of leaves has lost nothing of its midsummer brightness, and the harebell is on the banks and the woodbine in the hedges, and the low furze, which the lambs cropped in the spring, has burst again into its golden blossoms.

All is beautiful that the eye can see; perhaps the more beautiful for being shut in with a forest-like closeness. We have no prospect in this labyrinth of lanes, cross-roads, mere cart-ways, leading to the innumerable little farms into which this part of the parish is divided. Uphill or down, these quiet woody lanes scarcely give us a peep at the world, except when, leaning over a gate, we look into one of the small enclosures, hemmed in with hedgerows, so closely set with growing timber, that the meadowy opening looks almost like a glade in a wood, or when some cottage, planted at a corner of one of the little greens formed by the meeting of these cross-ways, almost startles us by the unexpected sight of the dwellings of men in such a solitude. But that we have more of hill and dale, and that our cross-roads are excellent in their kind, this side of our parish would resemble the description given of La Vendée, in Madame Larochejacquelin's most interesting book.[1] I am

[1] An almost equally interesting account of that very peculiar and interesting scenery, may be found in *The Maid of La Vendée*, an English novel, remarkable for its simplicity and truth of painting,

sure if wood can entitle a country to be called Le Bocage, none can have a better right to the name. Even this pretty, snug farmhouse on the hillside, with its front covered with the rich vine, which goes wreathing up to the very top of the clustered chimney, and its sloping orchard full of fruit—even this pretty, quiet nest can hardly peep out of its leaves. Ah! they are gathering in the orchard-harvest. Look at that young rogue in the old mossy apple-tree—that great tree, bending with the weight of its golden-rennets—see how he pelts his little sister beneath with apples as red and as round as her own cheeks, while she, with her outstretched frock, is trying to catch them, and laughing and offering to pelt again as often as one bobs against her; and look at that still younger imp, who, as grave as a judge, is creeping on hands and knees under the tree, picking up the apples as they fall so deedily,[1] and depositing them so honestly in the great basket on the grass, already fixed so firmly and opened so widely, and filled almost to overflowing by the brown rough fruitage of the golden rennet's next neighbour the russeting; and

---

written by Mrs. Le Noir, the daughter of Christopher Smart, and inheritrix of much of his talent. Her works deserve to be better known.

[1] "Deedily,"—I am not quite sure that this word is good English; but it is genuine Hampshire, and is used by the most correct of female writers, Miss Austen. It means (and it is no small merit that it has no exact synonym) anything done with a profound and plodding attention, an action which engrosses all the powers of mind and body.

see that smallest urchin of all, seated apart in infantine state on the turfy bank, with that toothsome piece of deformity a crumpling in each hand, now biting from one sweet, hard, juicy morsel, and now from another.—Is not that a pretty English picture? And then, farther up the orchard, that bold hardy lad, the eldest-born, who has scaled (Heaven knows how!) the tall, straight upper branch of that great pear-tree, and is sitting there as securely and as fearlessly, in as much real safety and apparent danger, as a sailor on the top-mast. Now he shakes the tree with a mighty swing that brings down a pelting shower of stony bergamots, which the father gathers rapidly up, whilst the mother can hardly assist for her motherly fear,—a fear which only spurs the spirited boy to bolder ventures. Is not that a pretty picture? And they are such a handsome family, too, the Brookers. I do not know that there is any gipsy blood, but there is the true gipsy complexion, richly brown, with cheeks and lips so deeply red, black hair curling close to their heads in short crisp rings, white shining teeth—and such eyes!—That sort of beauty entirely eclipses your mere roses and lilies. Even Lizzy, the prettiest of fair children, would look poor and watery by the side of Willy Brooker, the sober little personage who is picking up the apples with his small chubby hands, and filling the basket so orderly, next to his father the most useful man in the field. "Willy!" He hears without seeing; for we are quite hidden by the high bank, and a spreading hawthorn-bush that overtops it, though between the lower branches and the grass we have found a convenient peephole. "Willy!" The voice sounds to him like some fairy dream, and the black eyes are raised from the ground with sudden wonder, the long silky eyelashes thrown back till they rest on the delicate brow, and a deeper blush is burning in those dark cheeks, and a smile is dimpling about those scarlet lips. But the voice is silent now, and the little quiet boy, after a moment's pause, is gone coolly to work again. He is indeed a most lovely child. I think some day or other he must marry Lizzy; I shall propose the match to their respective mammas. At present the parties are rather too young for a wedding—the intended bridegroom being, as I should judge, six, or thereabout, and the fair bride barely five,—but at least we might have a betrothment after the royal fashion,—there could be no harm in that. Miss Lizzy, I have no doubt, would be as demure and coquettish as if ten winters more had gone over her head, and poor Willy would open his innocent black eyes, and wonder what was going forward. They would be the very Oberon and Titania of the village, the fairy king and queen.

Ah! here is the hedge along which the periwinkle wreathes and twines so profusely, with its ever-green leaves shining like the myrtle, and its starry blue flowers. It is seldom found wild in this part of England; but, when we do meet with it, it is so abundant and so welcome,—the very robin-redbreast of flowers, a winter friend. Unless in those unfrequent frosts which destroy all vegetation, it blossoms from September to June, surviving the last lingering crane's-bill, forerunning the earliest primrose, hardier even than the mountain daisy,—peeping out from beneath the snow, looking at itself in the ice, smiling through the tempests of life, and yet welcoming and enjoying the sunbeams. Oh, to be like that flower!

The little spring that has been bubbling under the hedge all along the hillside begins, now that we have mounted the eminence and are imperceptibly descending, to deviate into a capricious variety of clear, deep pools and channels, so narrow and so choked with weeds that a child might overstep them. The hedge has also changed its character. It is no longer the close, compact, vegetable wall of hawthorn, and maple, and briar roses, intertwined with bramble and woodbine, and crowned with large elms or thickly set saplings. No! the pretty meadow which rises high above us, backed and almost surrounded by a tall coppice, needs no defence on our side but its own steep bank, garnished with tufts of broom, with pollard oaks wreathed with ivy, and here and there with long patches of hazel overhanging the water. "Ah, there are still nuts on that bough!" and in an instant my dear companion, active and eager and delighted as a boy, has hooked down with his walking-stick one of the lissome hazel stalks, and cleared it of its tawny clusters, and in another moment he has mounted the bank, and is in the midst of the nuttery, now transferring the spoil from the lower branches into that vast variety of pockets which gentlemen carry about them, now bending the tall tops into the lane, holding them down by main force, so that I might reach them and enjoy the pleasure of collecting some of the plunder myself. A very great pleasure he knew it would be. I doffed my shawl, tucked up my flounces, turned my straw bonnet into a basket, and began gathering and scrambling—for, manage it how you may, nutting is scrambling work,—those boughs, however tightly you may grasp them by the young fragrant twigs and the bright green leaves, will recoil and burst away; but there is a pleasure even in that; so on we go, scrambling and gathering with all our might and all our glee. Oh, what an enjoyment! All my life long I have had a passion for that sort of seeking which implies finding (the secret, I believe, of the love of field-sports, which is in man's mind a natural impulse), —therefore I love violeting,—therefore, when we had a fine garden I used to love to gather strawberries, and cut asparagus, and, above all, to collect the filberts from the shrubberies: but this hedgerow nutting beats that sport all to nothing. That was a make-believe thing compared with this; there was no surprise, no suspense, no unexpectedness—it was as inferior to this wild nutting as the turning out of a bag-fox is to unearthing the fellow in the eyes of a staunch fox-hunter.

Oh, what an enjoyment this nut-gathering is! They are in such abundance, that it seems as if there were not a boy in the parish, nor a young man, nor a young woman,—for a basket of nuts is the universal tribute of country gallantry; our pretty damsel Harriet has had at least half a dozen this season; but no one has found out these. And they are so full too, we lose half of them from over-ripeness; they drop from the socket at the slightest motion. If we lose, there is one who finds. May is as fond of nuts as a squirrel, and cracks the shell and extracts the kernel with equal dexterity. Her white glossy head is upturned now to watch them as they fall. See how her neck is thrown back like that of a swan, and how beautifully her folded ears quiver with expectation, and how her quick eye follows the rustling noise, and her light feet dance and pat the ground, and leap up with eagerness, seeming almost sustained in the air, just as I have seen her when Brush is beating a hedgerow, and she knows from his questing that there is a hare afoot. See, she has caught that nut just before it touched the water; but the water would have been no defence,—she fishes them from the bottom, she delves after them amongst the matted grass— even my bonnet—how beggingly she looks at that! "Oh, what a pleasure nutting is!—Is it not, May? But the pockets are almost full, and so is the basket-bonnet, and that bright watch the sun says it is late;—and after all it is wrong to rob the poor boys—'pleasant but wrong'—is it not, May?"—May shakes her graceful head denyingly, as if she understood the question.—" And we must go home now—must we not? But we will come nutting again some time or other—shall we not, my May?"

A NEW MARRIED COUPLE

THERE is no pleasanter country sound than that of a peal of village bells, as they come vibrating through the air, giving token of marriage and merriment; nor ever was that pleasant sound more welcome than on this still, foggy, gloomy November morning, when all nature stood as if at pause; the large drops hanging on the thatch without falling; the sere leaves dangling on the trees; the birds mute and motionless on the boughs; turkeys, children, geese and pigs unnaturally silent; the whole world quiet and melancholy as some of the enchanted places in the Arabian tales. That merry peal seemed at once to break the spell, and to awaken sound, and life, and motion. It had a peculiar welcome too, as stirring up one of the most active passions in woman or in man, and rousing the rational part of creation from the torpor induced by the season and the weather at the thrilling touch of curiosity. Never was a completer puzzle. Nobody in our village had heard that a wedding was expected; no unaccustomed conveyance, from a coach to a wheel-barrow, had been observed passing up the vicarage lane; no banns had been published in church—no marriage of gentility, that is to say, of license, talked of, or thought of; none of our village beaux had been seen, as village beaux are apt to be on such occasions, smirking and fidgety; none of our village belles ashamed and shy. It was the prettiest puzzle that had occurred since Grace Neville's time; and, regardless of the weather, half the gossips of the street— in other words, half the inhabitants — gathered together in knots and clusters, to discuss flirtations and calculate possibilities.

Still the bells rang merrily on, and still the pleasant game of guessing continued until the appearance of a well-known, but most unsuspected equipage, descending the hill from the church, and shewing dimly through the fog the most unequivocal signs of bridal finery, supplied exactly the solution which all riddles ought to have, adding a grand climax of amazement to the previous suspense—the new married couple being precisely the two most unlikely persons to commit matrimony in the whole neighbourhood; the only two whose names had never come in question during the discussion, both bride and bridegroom having been long considered the most confirmed and resolute old maid and old bachelor to be found in the country-side.

Master Jacob Frost is an itinerant chapman, somewhere on the wrong side of sixty, who traverses the counties of Hants, Berks, and Oxon, with a noisy lumbering cart full of panniers, containing the heterogeneous commodities of fruit and fish, driving during the summer a regular and profitable barter between the coast on one side of us and the cherry country on the other. We who live about midway between these two extreme points of his peregrination, have the benefit of both kinds of merchandise going and coming; and there is not a man, woman, or child in the parish who does not know Master Frost's heavy cart and old grey mare half a mile off, as well as the stentorian cry of "Cherries, crabs, and salmon," sometimes pickled, and sometimes fresh, with which he makes the common and village re-echo; for, with an indefatigable perseverance, he cries his goods along the whole line of road, picking up customers where a man of less experience would despair, and so used to utter those sounds while marching beside his rumbling equipage, that it would not be at all surprising if he were to cry "Cherries — salmon! salmon — cherries!" in his sleep. As to fatigue, that is entirely out of the question. Jacob is a man of iron; a tall, lean, gaunt figure, all bone and sinew, constantly clad in a tight brown jacket with breeches to match, long leather gaiters, and a leather cap; his face and hair tanned by constant exposure to the weather into a tint so nearly resembling his vestments that he looks all of a colour, like the statue ghost in *Don Giovanni*, although the hue be different from that renowned spectre—Jacob being a brown man. Perhaps Master Peter in *Don Quixote*, him of the ape and the chamois doublet, were the apter comparison; or, with all reverence be it spoken, the ape himself. His visage is spare, and lean, and saturnine, enlivened by a slight cast in the dexter eye, and diversified by a partial loss of his teeth, all those on the left hand having been knocked out by a cricket ball, which, aided by the before-mentioned obliquity of vision, gives a peculiar one-sided expression to his physiognomy.

His tongue is well hung and oily, as suits his vocation. No better man at a bargain than Master Frost: he would persuade you that brill was turbot, and that black cherries were Maydukes; and yet, to be an itinerant vendor of fish the rogue hath a conscience. Try to beat him down, and he cheats you without scruple or mercy; but put him on his honour, and he shall deal as fairly with you as the honestest man in Billingsgate. Neither doth he ever impose on children, with whom, in the matter of shrimps, periwinkles, nuts, apples, and such boyish ware, he hath frequent traffic. He is liberal to the urchins; and I have sometimes been amused to see the Wat Tyler and Robin Hood kind of spirit with which he will fling to some wistful, pennyless brat the identical handful of cherries which, at the risk of his character and his customer, he hath cribbed from the scales when weighing out a long-contested bargain with some clamorous housewife.

Also he is an approved judge and devoted lover of country sports; attends all pony races, donkey races, wrestling and cricket matches, an amateur and arbiter of the very first water. At every revel or Maying within six miles of his beat, may Master Frost be seen, pretending to the world, and doubtless to his own conscience (for of all lies those that one tells to that stern monitor are the most frequent), that he is only there in the way of business; whilst in reality the cart and the old white mare, who perfectly understands the affair, may generally be found in happy quietude under some shady hedge; whilst a black sheep-dog, his constant and trusty follower, keeps guard over the panniers, Master Frost himself being seated in full state amidst the thickest of the throng, gravest of umpires, most impartial and learned of referees, utterly oblivious of cart and horse, panniers and sheep-dog. The veriest old woman that ever stood before a stall, or carried a fruit-basket, would beat our shrewd merchant out of the field on such a day as that; he hath not even time to bestow a dole on his usual pensioners the children. Unprofitable days to him, of a surety, so far as blameless pleasure can be called unprofitable; but it is worth something to a spectator to behold him in his glory, to see the earnest gravity, the solemn importance with which he will ponder the rival claims of two runners tied in sacks, or two grinners through a horse-collar.

Such were the habits, the business, and the amusements of our old acquaintance Master Frost. Home he had none, nor family, save the old sheep-dog, and the old grey horse, who lived, like himself, on the road; for it was his frequent boast that he never entered a house, but ate, drank, and slept in the cart, his only dwelling-place. Who would ever have dreamt of Jacob's marrying! And yet he it is that has just driven down the vicarage lane, seated in, not walking beside, that rumbling conveyance, the mare and the sheep-dog decked in white satin favours, already somewhat soiled, and wondering at their own finery; himself adorned in a new suit of brown exactly of the old cut, adding by a smirk and a wink to the usual knowingness of his squinting visage. There he goes, a happy bridegroom, perceiving and enjoying the wonder that he has caused, and chuckling over it in low whispers to his fair bride, whose marriage seems to the puzzled villagers more astonishing still.

In one corner of an irregular and solitary green, communicating by intricate and seldom-trodden lanes with a long chain of commons, stands a thatched and white-washed cottage, whose little dove-cot windows, high chimneys, and honey-suckled porch, stand out picturesquely from a richly wooded background; whilst a magnificent yew-tree, and a clear bright pond on one side of the house, and a clump of horse-chestnuts overhanging some low, weather-stained outbuildings on the other, form altogether an assemblage of objects that would tempt the pencil of a landscape-painter, if ever painter could penetrate to a nook so utterly obscure. There is no road across the green, but a well trodden footpath leads to the door of the dwelling, which the sign of a bell suspended from the yew-tree, and a board over the door announcing "Hester Hewit's home-brewed Beer," denote to be a small public-house.

Everybody is surprised to see even the humblest village hostel in such a situation; but the Bell is in reality a house of great resort, not only on account of Hester's home-brewed, which is said to be the best ale in the county, but because, in point of fact, that apparently lonely and trackless common is the very high road of the drovers who come from different points of the west to the great mart, London. Seldom would that green be found without a flock of Welch sheep, footsore and weary, and yet tempted into grazing by the short fine grass dispersed over its surface, or a drove of gaunt Irish pigs sleeping in a corner, or a score of Devonshire cows straggling in all directions, picking the long grass from the surrounding ditches; whilst dog and man, shepherd and drover, might be seen basking in the sun before the porch, or stretched on the settles by the fire, according to the weather and the season.

The damsel who, assisted by an old Chelsea pensioner minus a leg, and followed by a little, stunted, red-haired, parish girl and a huge tabby cat, presided over this flourishing hostelry, was a spinster of some fifty years standing, with a reputation as upright as her person; a woman of slow speech and civil demeanour, neat, prim, precise and orderly, stiff-starched and strait-laced as any maiden gentlewoman within a hundred miles. In her youth she must have been handsome; even now, abstract the exceeding primness, the pursed-up mouth, and the bolt-upright carriage,

is far from uncomely, for her complexion and her features are regular. And besides her comeliness and her good ale, to do in the world, has money in the stocks, seventy pounds, a fortune in furniture, mattresses, tables, presses and chairs shining walnut-tree, to say nothing of a store of ome-spun linen and the united wardrobes of three aiden aunts. A wealthy damsel was Hester, and er suitors must probably have exceeded in number nd boldness those of any lady in the land. Welch drovers, Scotch pedlars, shepherds from Salisbury Plain, and pig-drivers from Ireland—all these had she resisted for five-and-thirty years, determined to live and die " in single blessedness," and " leave the world no copy."

And she it is whom Jacob has won, from Scotchman and Irishman, pig-dealer and shepherd, she who now sits at his side in sober finery, a demure and blushing bride! Who would ever have thought of Hester's marrying! And when can the wooing have been? And how will they go on together? Will Master Frost still travel the country, or will he sink quietly into the landlord of the Bell? And was the match for love or for money? And what will become of the lame ostler? And how will Jacob's sheep-dog agree with Hester's cat? These, and a thousand such, are the questions of the village, whilst the bells ring merrily, and the new married couple wend peaceably home.

A CHRISTMAS PARTY

THE wedding of Jacob Frost and Hester Hewit took place on a Monday morning; and, on the next day (Tuesday), as I was walking along the common—blown along would be the properer phrase, for it was a wind that impelled one onward like a steam engine—what should I see but the well-known fish-cart sailing in the teeth of that raging gale, and Jacob and his old companions, the grey mare and the black sheep-dog, breasting, as well as they might, the fury of the tempest. As we neared, I caught occasional sounds of " Herrings—oysters!—oysters—herrings!" although the words, being as it were blown away, came scatteringly and feebly on the ear; and when we at last met, and he began in his old way to recommend, as was his wont, these oysters of a week old (note, that the rogue was journeying coastwise, outward-bound), with a profusion of praises and asseverations which he never vented on them when fresh,—and when I also perceived that Jacob had donned his old garments, and that his company had doffed their bridal favours,—it became clear that our man of oysters did not intend to retire yet awhile to the landlord-ship of the Bell; and it was soon equally certain that the fair bride, thus deserted in the very outset of the honeymoon, intended to maintain a full and undisputed dominion over her own territories—she herself, and her whole establishment—the lame ostler, who still called her Mistress Hester—the red-haired charity girl, and the tabby cat, still remaining in full activity; whilst the very inscription of her maiden days, "Hester Hewit's home-brewed," still continued to figure above the door of that respectable hostelry. Two days after the wedding, that happy event seemed to be most comfortably forgotten by all the parties concerned—the only persons who took any note of the affair being precisely those who had nothing to do with the matter; that is to say, all the gossips of the neighbourhood, male and female—who did, it must be confessed, lift up their hands, and shake their heads, and bless themselves, and wonder what this world would come to.

On the succeeding Saturday, however, his regular day, Jacob reappeared on the road, and, after a pretty long traffic in the village, took his way to the Bell; and, the next morning, the whole *cortège*, bride and bridegroom, lame ostler, red-haired lass, grey mare, and black sheep-dog, adorned exactly as on the preceding Monday, made their appearance at church; Jacob looking, as aforetime, very knowing—Hester, as usual, very demure. After the service there was a grand assemblage of Master Frost's acquaintances; for, between his customers and his playmates, Jacob was on intimate terms with half the parish—and many jokes were prepared on his smuggled marriage and subsequent desertion;—but he of the brown jerkin evaded them all, by handing his fair lady into the cart, lifting the poor parish girl beside her, and even lending a friendly hoist to the lame ostler; after which he drove off, with a knowing nod, in total silence; being thereunto prompted partly by his wife's entreaties, partly by a sound more powerful over his associations—an impatient neigh from the old grey mare, who, never having attended church before, had begun to weary of the length of the service, and to wonder on what new course of duty she and her master were entering.

By this dispatch, our new married-couple certainly contrived to evade the main broadside of jokes prepared for their reception; but a few random jests, flung after them at a venture, hit notwithstanding; and one amongst them, containing an insinuation that Jacob had stolen a match to avoid keeping the wedding, touched our bridegroom, a man of mettle in his way, on the very point of honour—the more especially as it proceeded from a bluff old bachelor of his own standing—honest George Bridgwater, of the Lea—at whose hospitable gate he had discussed many a jug of ale and knoll of bacon, whilst hearing and telling the news of the country-side. George Bridgwater to suspect him of stinginess!—the thought was insupportable. Before he reached the Bell he had formed, and communicated to Hester, the spirited resolution of giving a splendid party in the Christmas week—a sort of wedding-feast or house-warming; consisting of smoking and cards for the old, dancing and singing for the young, and eating and drinking for all ages; and, in spite of Hester's decided disapprobation, invitations were given and preparations entered on forthwith.

Sooth to say, such are the sad contradictions of poor human nature, that Mrs. Frost's displeasure, albeit a bride in the honeymoon, not only entirely failed in persuading Master Frost to change his plan, but even seemed to render him more confirmed and resolute in his purpose. Hester was a thrifty housewife; and although Jacob was apparently, after his fashion, a very gallant and affectionate husband, and although her interest had now become his—and of his own interest none had ever suspected him to be careless—yet he did certainly take a certain sly pleasure in making an attack at once on her hoards and her habits, and forcing her into a gaiety and an outlay which made the poor bride start back aghast.

The full extent of Hester's misfortune in this ball did not, however, come upon her at once. She had been accustomed to the speculating hospitality of the Christmas parties at the Rose, whose host was wont at tide times to give a supper to his customers, that is to say, to furnish the eatables thereof—the leg of mutton and turnips, the fat goose and apple-sauce, and the huge plum-puddings—of which light viands that meal usually consisted, on an understanding that the aforesaid customers were to pay for the drinkables therewith consumed; and, from the length of the sittings, as well as the reports current on such occasions, Hester was pretty well assured that the expenditure had been most judicious, and that the leg of mutton and trimmings had been paid for over and over. She herself being, as she expressed it, "a lone woman, and apt to be put upon," had never gone further in these matters than a cup of hyson and muffins, and a glass of hot elder-wine, to some of her cronies in the neighbourhood; but, having considerable confidence both in the extent of Jacob's connections and their tippling propensities, as well as in that faculty of getting tipsy and making tipsy in Jacob himself, which she regarded "with one auspicious and one dropping eye," as good and bad for her trade, she had at first no very great objection to try for once the experiment of a Christmas party; nor was she so much startled at the idea of a dance —dancing, as she observed, being a mighty provoker of thirst; neither did she very greatly object to her husband's engaging old Timothy, the fiddler, to officiate for the evening, on condition of giving him as much ale as he chose to drink, although she perfectly well knew what that promise implied; Timothy's example being valuable on such an occasion. But when the dreadful truth stared her in the face, that this entertainment was to be a *bonâ fide* treat—that not only the leg of mutton, the fat goose, and the plum puddings, but the ale, wine, spirits and tobacco were to come out of her coffers, then party, dancing, and fiddler became nuisances past endurance, the latter above all.

Old Timothy was a person of some note in our parish, known to every man, woman, and child in the place, of which, indeed, he was a native. He had been a soldier in his youth, and having had the good luck to receive a sabre wound on his skull, had been discharged from the service as infirm of mind, and passed to his parish accordingly; where he led a wandering, pleasant sort of life, sometimes in one public-house, sometimes in another—tolerated, as Hester said, for his bad example, until he had run up a score that became intolerable, at which times he was turned out, with the workhouse to go to, for a *pis aller*, and a comfortable prospect that his good-humour, his good-fellowship, and his fiddle, would in process of time be missed and wanted, and that he might return to his old haunts and run up a fresh score. When half tipsy, which happened nearly every day in the week, and at all hours, he would ramble up and down the village, playing snatches of tunes at every corner, and collecting about him a never-failing audience of eight and ten-year-old urchins of either sex, amongst which small mob old Timothy, with his jokes, his songs, and his antics, was incredibly popular. Against Justice and Constable, treadmill and stocks, the sabre-cut was a protection, although, I must candidly confess, that I do not think the crack in the crown ever made itself visible in his demeanour until a sufficient quantity of ale had gone down his throat, to account for any aberration of conduct, supposing the broadsword in question never to have approached his skull. That weapon served, however, as a most useful shield to our modern Timotheus, who, when detected in any outrageous fit of drunkenness, would immediately summon sufficient recollection to sigh and look pitiful, and put his poor, shaking, withered hand to the seam which the wound had left, with an air of appeal, which even I, with all my scepticism, felt to be irresistible.

In short, old Timothy was a privileged person; and terrible sot though he were, he almost deserved to be so, for his good-humour, his contentedness, his constant festivity of temper, and his goodwill towards every living thing—a goodwill which met with its usual reward in being heartily and universally returned. Everybody liked old Timothy, with the solitary exception of the hostess of the Bell, who, having once had him as an inmate during three weeks, had been so scandalised by his disorderly habits, that, after having with some difficulty turned him out of her house, she had never admitted him into it again, having actually resorted to the expedient of buying off her intended customer, even when he presented himself pence in hand, by the gift of a pint of home-brewed at the door, rather than suffer him to effect a lodgment in her taproom—a mode of dismissal so much to Timothy's taste, that his incursions had become more and more frequent, insomuch that "to get rid of the fiddler and other scapegraces, who were apt to put upon a lone woman," formed a main article in the catalogue of reasons assigned by Hester to herself and the world for her marriage with Jacob Frost. Accordingly, the moment she heard that Timothy's irregularities and ill example were likely to prove altogether unprofitable, she revived her old objection to the poor fiddler's morals, rescinded her consent to his admission, and insisted so vehemently on his being unordered, that her astonished husband, fairly out-talked and out-scolded, was fain to purchase a quiet evening by a promise of obedience. Having carried this point, she forthwith, according to the example of all prudent wives, began an attack on another, and, having compassed the unordering of Timothy, began to bargain for uninviting her next neighbour, the Widow Glen.

Mrs. Martha Glen kept a baker's and chandler's shop in a wide lane, known by the name of the Broadway, and adorned with a noble avenue of oaks, terminating in the green whereon stood the Bell, a lane which, by dint of two or three cottages peeping out from amongst the trees, and two or three farmhouses, the smoke from whose chimneys sailed curlingly amongst them, might, in comparison with that lonely nook, pass for inhabited. Martha was a buxom widow, of about the same standing with Mistress Frost. She had had her share of this world's changes, being the happy relict of three several spouses; and was now a comely, rosy dame, with a laughing eye and a merry tongue. Why Hester should hate Martha Glen was one of the puzzles of the parish. Hate her she did, with that venomous and deadly hatred that never comes to words; and Martha repaid the obligation in kind, as much as a naturally genial and relenting temper would allow, although certainly the balance of aversion was much in favour of Mrs. Frost. An exceedingly smooth, genteel, and civil hatred it was on both sides; such an one as would have done honour to a more polished society. They dealt with each other, curtsied to each other, sate in the same pew at church, and employed the same charwoman —which last accordance, by the way, may partly account for the long duration of discord between the parties. Betty Clarke, the help in question, being a sharp, shrewish, vixenish woman, with a positive taste for quarrels, who regularly reported every cool innuendo uttered by the slow and soft-spoken Mrs. Frost, and every hot retort elicited from the rash and hasty Martha, and contrived to infuse her own spirit into each. With such an auxiliary on either side, there could be no great wonder at the continuance of this animosity; how it began was still undecided. There were, indeed, rumours of an early rivalry between the fair dames for the heart of a certain gay shepherd, the first husband of Martha; other reports assigned as a reason the unlucky tricks of Tom Higgs, the only son of Mrs. Glen by her penultimate spouse, and the greatest pickle within twenty miles; a third party had, since the marriage, discovered the jealousy of Jacob to be the proximate cause, Martha Glen having been long his constant customer, dealing with him in all sorts of fishery and fruitery for herself and her shop, from red-herrings to golden pippins; whilst a fourth party, still more scandalous, placed the jealousy, to which they also attributed the aversion, to the score of a young and strapping Scotch pedlar, Sandy Frazer by name, who travelled the country with muslins and cottons, and for whom certain malicious gossips asserted both ladies to entertain a lurking *penchant*, and whose insensibility towards the maiden was said to have been the real origin of her match with Jacob Frost, whose proffer she had accepted out of spite. For my own part, I disbelieve all and each of these stories, and hold it very hard that an innocent woman cannot entertain a little harmless aversion towards her next neighbour without being called to account for so natural a feeling. It seems that Jacob thought so too—for on Hester's conditioning that Mrs. Glen should be excluded from the party, he just gave himself a wink and a nod, twisted his mouth a little more on one side than usual, and assented without a word; and with the same facility did he relinquish the bough of misletoe, which he had purposed to suspend from the bacon-rack—the ancient mistletoe bough, on passing under which our village lads are apt to snatch a kiss from the village maidens: a ceremony which offended Hester's nicety, and which Jacob promised to abrogate; and, pacified by these concessions, the bride promised to make due preparation for the ball, whilst the bridegroom departed on his usual expedition to the coast.

Of the unrest of that week of bustling preparation, words can give but a faint image. Oh, the scourings, the cleanings, the sandings, the dustings, the scoldings of that disastrous week! The lame ostler and the red-haired parish girl were worked off their feet —" even Sunday shone no Sabbath day to them "— for then did the lame ostler trudge eight miles to the church of a neighbouring parish, to procure the attendance of a celebrated bassoon player to officiate in lieu of Timothy; whilst the poor little maid was sent nearly as far to the next town, in quest of an itinerant show-woman, of whom report had spoken at the Bell, to beat the tambourine. The showwoman proved undiscoverable; but the bassoon player having promised to come, and to bring with him a clarionet, Mrs. Frost was at ease as to her music; and having provided more victuals than the whole village could have discussed at a sitting, and having, moreover, adorned her house with berried holly, china roses, and chrysanthemums after the most tasteful manner, began to enter into the spirit of the thing, and to wish for the return of her husband, to admire and to praise.

Late on the great day Jacob arrived, his cart laden with marine stores for his share of the festival. Never had our goodly village witnessed such a display of oysters, muscles, periwinkles and cockles, to say nothing of apples and nuts, and two little kegs, snugly covered up, which looked exceedingly as if they had cheated the revenue, a packet of green tea, which had something of the same air, and a new silk gown, of a flaming salmon colour, straight from Paris, which he insisted on Hester's retiring to assume, whilst he remained to arrange the table and receive the company, who, it being now about four o'clock p.m.—our good rustics can never have enough of a good thing—were beginning to assemble for the ball.

The afternoon was fair and cold, and dry and frosty, and Matthews's, Bridgwaters, Whites, and Jones's, in short the whole farmerage and shop-keepery of the place, with a goodly proportion of wives and daughters, came pouring in apace. Jacob received them with much gallantry, uncloaking and unbonnetting the ladies, assisted by his two staring and awkward auxiliaries, welcoming their husbands and fathers, and apologising, as best he might, for the absence of his helpmate; who, "perplexed in the extreme" by her new finery, which, happening to button down the back, she was fain to put on hind side before, did not make her appearance till the greater part of the company had arrived, and the music had struck up a country dance. An evil moment, alas! did poor Hester choose for her entry! for the first sound that met her ear was Timothy's fiddle, forming a strange trio with the bassoon and the clarionet: and the first persons whom she saw were Tom Higgs cracking walnuts at the chimney-side, and Sandy Frazer saluting the Widow Glen under the mistletoe. How she survived such sights and sounds does appear wonderful—but survive them she did—for at three o'clock a.m., when our reporter left the party, she was engaged in a sociable game at cards, which, by the description, seems to have been long whist, with the identical Widow Glen, Sandy Frazer, and William Ford, and had actually won fivepence-halfpenny of Martha's money; the young folks were still dancing gaily, to the sound of Timothy's fiddle, which fiddle had the good quality of going on almost as well drunk as sober, and it was now playing solo, the clarionet being *hors-de-combat* and the bassoon under the table. Tom Higgs, after shewing off more tricks than a monkey, amongst the rest sewing the whole card-party together by the skirts, to the probable damage of Mrs. Frost's gay gown, had returned to his old post by the fire, and his old amusement of cracking walnuts, with the shells of which he was pelting the little parish girl, who sate fast asleep on the other side; and Jacob Frost in all his glory, sate in a cloud of tobacco smoke, roaring out catches with his old friend George Bridgwater, and half a dozen other "drowthy cronies," whilst "ay the ale was growing better," and the Christmas party went merrily on.

TOM HOPKINS

THEY who knew the little town of Cranley some thirty years ago, must needs remember Tom Hopkins, the loudest, if not the greatest man in the place, and one of the most celebrated sportsmen in that sporting neighbourhood, which he had honoured with his residence for a longer time than he—still in the prime of life, and as tenacious of his pretensions to youth as a fading beauty—cared to hear tell of. Tom, whose family was none of the most illustrious, his ancestors having been from time immemorial grocers in the town, had had the good luck, before he was out of petticoats, to take the fancy of a rich relation, a grand-aunt, who, captivated as grand-aunts are wont to be, by a happy union of prettiness and mischief, rosy cheeks and naughty tricks, the usual merits of a spoilt child, installed the chubby-faced Pickle into the post of present pet and future heir,—sent him to school at her own expense, and declared her intention to make a gentleman of him in proper time,—a prospect which, as her hopeful grand-nephew happily conceived the immunities and privileges of gentility to consist of. idleness and field-sports, proved sufficiently delightful to reconcile him to the previous formality of learning "small Latin and less Greek," and bore him safely through the forms, with no worse reputation than that of being the greatest dunce that ever quitted the school. When that happy time arrived, however, there was some difference of opinion as to his destination, Tom having set his heart on one mode of killing, whilst his grand-aunt had decided on another. " I will be a soldier," cried Tom, already enamoured of the art of gunnery. "You shall be an apothecary," replied Aunt Deborah, equally devoted to the draught and the pill. Physic and arms fought a pitched battle, and long and obstinate was the contest; there was even some danger that the dispute might have ended in disinheritance, to the probable benefit of the county hospital, when a discreet friend prudently suggested the possibility of uniting the two modes of putting people out of the world, and Tom consented to don the apron and sleeves and become *un garçon apothicaire*, under promise of flourishing at some future period as an army surgeon—a promise which, though not kept to the letter, was at least so far realised as to make him a surgeon of militia, and obtain for him the enviable privilege of wearing a red coat, and meddling with fire-arms. These delights, however ecstatic, soon lost their gloss and their novelty; Tom speedily discovered that hunting and shooting were his real vocation; and Aunt Deborah happening to die and to leave him a comfortable independence, he retired from

spent in country quarters, returned to his native town, built himself a   set up an establishment, consisting of a couple of hunters, a brace of pointers, a servant   and an old woman, and began to make war on the hares, foxes, pheasants, partridges, and other *feræ naturæ*, under the character of a sportsman, which he filled with eminent ability and success, being universally reckoned one of the boldest riders and best shots in the county.

At the time of which I speak he was of an age somewhat equivocal; public fame called him forty, whilst he himself stuck obstinately at thirty-two; of a stout active figure, rather manly than gentlemanly, and a bold jovial visage, in excellent keeping with his person, distinguished by round, bright, stupid black eyes, an aquiline nose, a knowing smile, and a general comely vulgarity of aspect. His voice was hoarse and deep, his manner bluff and blunt, and his conversation loud and boisterous. With all these natural impediments to good company, the lowness of his origin recent in their memories, and the flagrant fact of his residence in a country town, staring them in the face, Mr. Tom Hopkins made his way into almost every family of consideration in the neighbourhood. Sportsmanship, sheer sportsmanship, the qualification that, more than any other, commands the respect of your great English landholder, surmounted every obstacle. There was not a man in the * * shire hunt who fenced so well, or went so fast over a country; and every table in the county was open to so eminent a personage.

With the ladies, he made his way by different qualities; in the first place he was a character, an oddity, and the audacity of his vulgarity was tolerated where a man only half as boisterous would have been scouted; then he was gallant in his way, affected, perhaps felt, a great devotion to the sex, and they were half amused, half pleased, with the rough flattery which seemed, and probably was, so sincere. Then they liked, as all women like, his sturdiness of character, his boldness, his staunchness, and his zeal. He won Lady Frances's heart by canvassing for her husband in a contested election, during which he performed more riding, drinking, and roaring, told more lies and made more noise than any ten of the fee'd agents; he achieved the Countess's good graces by restoring her fat, asthmatic lap-dog to health, appetite, and activity;— *N.B.*—As Mr. Thomas Hopkins took Chloe home to Cranley to be nursed, it is likely that the Abernethy system may fairly claim the merit of that cure;— and he even made a favourable impression on a young Marchioness, by riding to London, above seventy miles, in order to match a shade of netting silk, thereby winning a considerable wager against time of the Marquis. In short, Tom Hopkins was so general a favourite with the female world that, but for three or four flat refusals, consequent on as many very presumptuous offers, he would certainly have fallen into the mistake of thinking he might marry whom he would. As it was, he kept his own counsel, only betraying his soreness by a transient avoidance of ladies' company, and a proneness to descant at the Hunt dinners on the comforts of a single state, and the manifold evils of matrimony.

His house was an ugly brick dwelling of his own erection, situate in the principal street of Cranley, and adorned with a green door and a brass knocker, giving entrance into a stone passage, which, there being no other way to the stable, served both for himself, and that very dear part of himself, his horses, whose dwelling was certainly far more commodious than their master's. His accommodations were simple enough. The dining-parlour, which might pass for his only sitting-room,—for the little dark den which he called his drawing-room was not entered three times a year,—the dining-parlour was a small square room, coloured pea-green with a gold moulding, adorned with a series of four prints on shooting, and four on hunting, together with two or three portraits of eminent racers, riders, hunters, and grooms. Guns and fishing-rods were suspended over the mantelpiece; powder-horns, shot-belts, and game-bags scattered about; a choice collection of flies for angling lay in one corner, whips and bridles in another, and a pile of books and papers, —*Colonel Thornton's Tour*, Daniel's *Rural Sports*, and a heap of *Racing Calendars*, occupied a third; Ponto and Carlo lay basking on the hearth-rug, and a famous little cocking spaniel, Flora by name, a conscious favourite, was generally stretched in state on an arm-chair.

Here, except when the owner was absent on a sporting expedition, which, between fishing, shooting, hunting, and racing, did, it must be confessed, happen pretty often; here his friends were sure to find a hearty welcome, a good beefsteak (his old housekeeper was famous for cookery !), and as much excellent port and super-excellent Madeira (Tom, like most of his school, eschewed claret and other thin potations) as their host could prevail on them to swallow. Many a good fellow hath "heard the chimes at midnight" in this little room. Here Tom sate in his glory, telling interminable stories of his own exploits, and those of his dogs and horses; stories in every sense of the word, but yet as innocent as falsehoods well can be—in the first place, because they were always lies of vanity, not lies of malice, and could do harm to no creature upon earth; in the second, because the orator, being somewhat lengthy and prosy, his hearers were apt to be troubled with "the disease of not listening, the malady of not marking," and seldom knew what he was talking about. Moreover, having told fibs of this sort all his life, I don't think he could help it; I don't even believe that he knew when he did it, or that he could, to save his life, have separated the true from the false, in any one of his legends. He was incurable. It did not even hurt his conscience to be found out.

Such was Tom Hopkins; and such, allowing for

the difference of thirty years, Tom Hopkins is still. Some changes are however observable in that gallant sportsman, such changes as thirty years are wont to bring. He sits somewhat heavier in the saddle, and mounts somewhat seldomer,—has well-nigh given up fishing and shooting,—has exchanged fox-hunting for coursing,—sold his hunters and purchased a staid roadster,—keeps a brace of greyhounds of whose pedigree he vaunts much,—belongs to two coursing meetings, and swears every year that his dog was cheated out of the cup.

This is his winter amusement. In the summer he diverts himself like other idle gentlemen; cons over the *Sporting Magazine*, and the newspaper of the day; lounges to the inn to see the coaches change horses, and observes to a second whether the Regulator or the Defiance keeps time best; or stands sentinel in the garden, firing, from time to time, to keep the sparrows from the cherry trees. On wet days he is often seized with a fancy for mending and altering, and walks about the house, with a hammer sticking out of his pocket, doing no good, or a carpenter at his heels doing harm; sometimes dozes in his easy-chair, and sometimes complains of a twinge of the gout. He has nearly given up country visiting, but is a great man at the Cranley Club, where he tells longer stories than ever of the chases, the hounds, and the hunters of his youth; of the great contested election; of matchless belles, now, alas! no more, and lords who have not left their fellow; rails at the degeneracy of the times, the decline of beauty, the increase of dandyism, the adulteration of port wine, and the decrease of good-fellowship; gets half tipsy, and finally staggers home, escorted by his maid Dorothy, a rosy-cheeked damsel, of whose handiness and skill in cookery (his old house-keeper having long been dead), he boasts almost as much as of the breed of his greyhounds, and whom the President of the Cranley Club has betted with his Vice, "that old Tom Hopkins" (so he irreverently calls him), "with all his talk of Duchesses and Countesses, will marry before the year is out"; and truly I think so too.

A WIDOW GENTLEWOMAN

I HAVE never had much acquaintance with a country-town life, an ignorance which I regret exceedingly, not merely because such a life comprises so much of the intelligence, cultivation, and moral excellence of that most intelligent, cultivated, and excellent body of persons, the middle classes, as they are called, of England; but because, so far as authorship is concerned, it is decidedly the sphere which presents most novelty, and would be most valuable as affording a series of unhackneyed studies to an observer and delineator of common nature. To the novelist, indeed, an English provincial town offers ground almost untrodden; and the bold man who shall first adventure from the tempting regions of high life, or low life, or Irish life, or life abroad, or life in the olden times, into that sphere where he has hitherto found so many readers and so few subjects, will, if he write with truth and vividness, find his reward in the strong and clinging interest which we never fail to feel when everyday objects are presented to us under a new and striking form—the deep and genuine gratification excited by an union of the original and the familiar. But when will such an adventurer arise? Who shall dare to delineate the humours of an apothecary? or the parties of his wife? or the loves of his daughter? Who will have courage to make a hero of an attorney? or to throw the halo of imagination around the head of a country brewer? Alas! alas! until a grand literary reform shall take place, boroughs and county towns must be content to remain in obscurity, represented in the house indeed, but absolute nullities in the library.

My acquaintance with the subject, slight as I have acknowledged it to be, has the further disadvantage of being almost wholly recollective, referring to persons who have long passed away, and to a state of things which I suspect has no present existence —for in country towns, as in other places, society has been progressing (if I may borrow that expressive Americanism) at a very rapid rate, for the last twenty years; and when I go into the goodly streets of B. (where I still possess some few younger friends) I cannot help looking around me, and wondering whether the very race of my old acquaintance be not extinct with the individuals, or whether there be still a class of respectable, elderly gentlewomen, who, with no apparent object or interest in life, do yet contrive to live, and to live happily, by the help of a little innocent gossiping, and a great deal of visiting and cards.

One of the most notable specimens of this class that I recollect—and I remember her as long as I can remember anything—was my mother's old friend, Mrs. Nicholson. She was the childless widow of a former vicar of St. John's parish in B., and her husband's successor residing on another living, and the curate, a single man, preferring to board with a friend in the town, she still retained possession of the vicarage-house, in which she had presided for so many years, and which a limited but sufficient income enabled her to keep up on a small but comfortable scale. The house, indeed, was not of a sort to make any serious demands on her purse. It was a low, dark, dingy dwelling, situate in an angle between St. John's Church and the lofty town-hall, the windows of which overtopped the very chimneys; enclosed within high walls, and looking out into a triangular court, where a few dusty poplars and yellow, frost-bitten laurels combined to exclude the daylight from the little low rooms, whose small heavy sashes, of a glass older and thicker than common, afforded another protection against the beams of the blessed sun. The parlour in which she usually sat had also a triangular appearance, resulting from the chimney being placed in one corner—the little chimney faced with tiny Dutch tiles divided by a small low brass fender from a narrow hearthrug of Mrs. Nicholson's own work, the lion rampant in the middle of which was particularly like a sandy cat, and fronted by a very dark, very bright, very old-fashioned mahogany table, hardly large enough to hold the frame on which she performed her worsted embroidery. The opposite corner displayed a beaufet, adorned with ornamental glass and china in various states of preservation; one side boasted an old settee, and another an indescribable piece of furniture called a commode, consisting of three drawers of dark mahogany, perched upon long legs, and surmounted by four shelves enclosed within glass doors, and containing a miscellaneous collection of odds and ends, one half-shelf being filled with books, Fordyce's *Sermons*, Young's *Night Thoughts*, Mrs. Glass's *Cookery*, and other works placed there for show and use, and the rest filled with a stuffed parrot, a shell-work grotto, some specimens of spars and ores, particularly dusty, and a curious collection of filigree.

The usual inhabitants of this apartment were Mrs. Nicholson, a huge, overgrown dame, dressed in a style which twenty years ago had been twenty years out of fashion, with powdered hair and fly-caps and lappets, and a black lace tippet, looking exactly like a head-dress cut out of an old pocket-book, all bustle and speechifying, and fidget and fuss; and a very sedate, demure, pale, sallow little woman (everything in the house was on a small scale except its mistress), whom Mrs. Nicholson called Madge, but whose real name was Miss Day, and who filled an equivocal post in the household, half handmaiden and half companion—or rather who performed the duties of both offices—dressing her lady, waiting upon her, combing her dog, and making up caps, lappets, and tippets, in the former capacity; and writing her notes, reading her to sleep, sitting with her, and listening to her (for with reply, or anything that implied talking, Miss Day had little to do), in the latter.

There they dwelt, Miss Nicholson and Miss Day, with the dog Viper, an astonishingly ugly terrier, most unnaturally fat, a little footboy in clerical livery, and an ancient maid-of-all-work—there they lived, patterns of decorum (even the boy Tom, and Viper the terrier, were most staid and orderly specimens of their usually obstreperous class);—there they lived, with a regularity so punctual, that they might have set the church clock, had that important functionary been out of order, and the sun unwilling to present himself. At half-past seven they rose, at eight they breakfasted, at three they dined, at six they drank tea, at half-past six they sat down to cards, at half-past nine the pool (for quadrille was the game) finished as by instinct, and at ten precisely they went to bed. As the watchman called half-past ten they lay down, and before he cried eleven the whole household, from Mrs. Nicholson to Viper, might be fairly presumed to be at rest.

Sunday made little variation in this routine, except the episode of going to church, the change in the dinner-hour from three to half-past one, and the substitution of Miss Day's reading the late doctor's manuscript sermons during the time which, on the other six days, was devoted to quadrille. The stock of sermons was not very large; and three hours' reading, weekly, soon got through them; but Mrs. Nicholson, to whom Miss Day once humbly and submissively suggested Blair, would by no manner of means consent to a change: and the good lady was right; she had been used to go to sleep to these sermons in the time of her late husband, of happy memory, and knew their quality. Blair might have kept her awake.

For the rest, Mrs. Nicholson was a good woman and a kind, fond of Viper, civil to her acquaintance, and tolerably considerate towards Miss Day; who, for as little as she looked like the heroine of a novel, had that prime requisite of one, which consists in being in love; though whether that phrase may be applied to a twenty years' attachment, for such was the date of Miss Day's engagement to Mr. Thomas Cooke, writing-master in B., and parish-clerk of St. John's, may be doubtful. If fortune frowned, Mrs. Nicholson did not. She asked him how he did every Sunday, invited him to take a glass of wine every Christmas Day, and presented him with a kettle-holder of her own best worsted work, as a token of favour and remembrance.

In the duties of acquaintanceship Mrs. Nicholson was pre-eminent. Never was woman so regular in paying and returning visits, whether morning or evening—in sending to inquire after the sick, to condole on deaths, and congratulate on marriages. At the very moment prescribed by etiquette (the etiquette of a country town many years ago), the rat-tat-tat of the little footboy was heard at the door, and the pit-a-pat of the clogs, or the heavy clamp of the sedan-chair—a much more dignified conveyance for a dowager of weight in the world than any of the race of flies, whether horse-fly or man-fly—resounded in the passage. She was the very pattern of all acquaintances.

But visiting, although it was much to her, was not quite all; she had something more of the salt of life to season her summer and winter worsted-work, in the shape of two sentiments, both excellent as preservatives from *ennui*—a close and ancient friendship, and a gentle, harmless, innocent, gentlewomanly, Mrs. Grundy sort of hatred. Nobody that had the honour of belonging to Mrs. Nicholson's society, but must have heard of Mrs. Quelch, her aversion, and Lady Daly, her friend. Mrs. Quelch was not, as in the course of things it seemed right that she should have been, her next neighbour; on the contrary, she lived fifty miles off, so completely out of the way, that it really seemed surprising how Mrs. Nicholson could manage to pick up, as pick up she did, so many stories about her; of the number of new bonnets she bought in the year, and the number of servants she turned away—how she was cross to the governess, and spoiled the children—and how, above all, she prevented the doctor (for Mrs. Quelch was the wife of the then vicar of St. John's, and in some circumstance arising from that juxtaposition had arisen Mrs. Nicholson's enmity) from increasing Thomas Cooke's salary, and giving a new gown to the sexton. Well! hatred and malice are, commonly speaking, very bad things, and far be it from me to enter into a general vindication of them. But in this particular instance I cannot help having a leaning towards the "simple sin"; for it was certainly a great comfort and amusement to Mrs. Nicholson, and could do Mrs. Quelch no harm, that lady being, as I have good cause to believe, happily ignorant that such a sentiment was entertained towards her by the ex-vicaress of St. John's, and for the most part, I fear, entirely oblivious of the very existence of the personage in question. Why might not Mrs. Nicholson hate Mrs. Quelch? especially as her expression of the feeling, and sometimes its affected suppression, were by far the most amusing parts of her conversation.

Her friendship for Lady Daly, although more amiable in itself, was, as far as her acquaintance were concerned, a much greater evil. Lady Daly's name, and Lady Daly's news, and Lady Daly's letters, were bores of the first magnitude. There was no escaping them either. It was impossible. As soon as you entered, she began with the name, and then she told you the news, and then (incredible barbarity!) after having told you every syllable of the contents, she inflicted on you the epistles in full—such epistles too! Lady Daly seems to have been that astounding person—a sensible woman, a good sort of sensible woman! and her letters were those tremendous compositions called sensible letters, well-written letters, excellent letters! words of praise which, being translated, are commonly found to signify the most elaborate specimens of dulness that are to be met with out of print. Her ladyship's epistles might pass for lessons on the art of amplification. It was wonderful how little meaning she could contrive to spread over four pages. They wanted even the seasoning of malice. Doubtless Mrs. Nicholson's answers were more amusing—she had Mrs. Quelch to hate. I know no harm of Lady Daly, poor woman, but I never saw one of her neat-looking packets, franked by her son Sir John (the son's M.P.-ship had probably tended to make his mamma epistolary), emerge from her correspondent's huge pocket without wishing them both in the Red Sea.

In other respects Mrs. Nicholson's conversation was pretty much like that of other elderly gentlewomen. She talked of her good husband, the doctor, and showed his portrait in a bracelet—a faded miniature in full canonicals—displaying at the same time a chalk drawing of herself as a shepherdess, which had been taken at the same period by an artist of similar talent. She praised the weather of her youth, and abused that of the present time, as everybody begins to do who has turned the point of forty; she was afraid of the opposition, and attached to the ministry; did not like the taxes, but hated the French; disliked new fashions; deprecated late hours; always petted Viper, and sometimes snubbed Miss Day.

MY GODFATHER

IT is now nearly twenty years ago, that I, a young girl just freed from the trammels of schooldom, went into a remote and distant county, on a visit to my godfather, to make acquaintance with a large colony of my relations, and behold new scenes and new faces; a pleasure, certainly; but a formidable and awful pleasure, to a shy and home-loving girl. Nothing could have reconciled me to the prospect of encountering so many strange cousins, for they were all strangers, but my strong desire to see my dear and venerable god-papa, for whom, although we had never met since the christening, I entertained the most lively affection,—an affection nourished on his part by kindnesses of every sort, from the huge wax-doll, and the letter in print-hand, proper to the damsel of six years old, down to the pretty verses and elegant necklace, his birthday greeting to the young lady of sixteen. He was no stranger, that dear god-papa! I was quite sure I should know him at first sight, quite sure that I should love him better than ever; both which predictions were verified to the letter. It would have been strange indeed if they had not.

Mr. Evelyn, for so I shall call him, was a gentleman of an ancient family and considerable fortune, residing in a small town in the north of England; where he had occupied for the last fifty years the best house, and the highest station, the object of universal respect and affection from high and low. He was that beautiful thing, a healthy and happy old man. Shakspeare, the master painter, has partly described him for me, in the words of old Adam,—

> "Therefore my age is as a lusty winter
> Frosty but kindly."

Never was wintry day, with the sun smiling upon the icicles, so bright or so keen. At eighty-four, he had an unbent, vigorous person, a fresh colour, long, curling, milk-white hair, and regular features, lighted up by eyes as brilliant and as piercing as those of a hawk; his foot was as light, his voice as clear, and his speech as joyous as at twenty. He had a life of mind, an alertness of spirit, a brilliant and unfading hilarity, which were to him like the quick blood of youth. Time had been rather his friend than his foe; had stolen nothing as far as I could discover; and had given such a licence to his jokes and his humour, that he was when I knew him as privileged a person as a court-jester in days of yore. Perhaps he was always so; for, independently of fortune and station, high animal spirits, invincible good-humour, and a certain bustling officiousness, are pretty sure to make their way in the world, especially when they seek only for petty distinctions. He was always the first personage of his small circle; president of half the clubs in the neighbourhood; steward to the races; chairman of the bench; father of the corporation; and would undoubtedly have been member for the town, if that ancient borough had not had the ill luck to be disfranchised in some stormy period of our national history.

But that was no great loss to my dear godfather. Even the bench and the vestry, although he presided at them with sufficient reputation, were too grave matters to suit his taste. He would have made a bad police magistrate; his sympathies ran directly the contrary way. Accordingly he used to be accused of certain merciful abuses of his office of justice of the peace; such as winking at vagrants and vagabonds, encouraging the Merry Andrew, and the droll fellow Punch, and feeing the constable, *not* to take up a certain drunken fiddler, who had haunted the town, man and boy, these forty years.

Races and balls were more his element. There he would walk about with his hands behind him, and a pleasant word for every one; his keen eye sparkling with gaiety, and his chuckling laugh heard above all, the unwearied patron and promoter of festivity in all its branches; rather than the dance should languish, he would stand up himself. This indulgence to the young, or rather this sympathy with enjoyment wherever he found it, was not confined to the rich; he liked a fair or a revel quite as well as an assembly, perhaps better, because the merriment there was noisier, heartier, more completely free from restraint. How he would chuck the rosy country lasses under the chin, and question them about their sweethearts! And how the little coquettes would smile, and blush, and curtsy, and cry "fie" and enjoy it! That was certainly an octogenarian privilege and one worth a score or two of years, in his estimation.

But these diversions, thoroughly as he entered into their spirit, were by no means necessary to his individual amusement. His cheerfulness needed no external stimuli. The day was too short—life itself, although so prolonged, was too brief for his busy idleness. He had nothing to do, followed no calling, belonged to no profession, had no estate to improve, no children to establish, and yet from morning to night he was employed about some vagary or other, with as much ardour as if the fate of the nation depended on his speed. Fishing and fiddling, shooting and coursing, turning and varnishing, making bird-cages and picture-frames, and cabbage-nets, and flies for angling, constructing charades, and tagging verses, were only a few of his occupations. Then he dallied with science, and flirted with art; was in a small way a connoisseur, had a tolerable collection of prints, and a very bad one of paintings, and was, moreover, a sort of virtuoso. I had not been two days in the house before my good godfather introduced me to his museum, a long room or rather gallery, where, as he boasted, and I well believe, neither mop, nor broom, nor housemaid had ever entered.

This museum was certainly the dirtiest den into which I ever set foot; dark, to a pitch, which took away for awhile all power of distinguishing objects, and so dusty as to annihilate colour, and confuse form. I have a slight notion that this indistinctness was, in the present instance, rather favourable than otherwise to the collection, which I cannot help suspecting was a thought less valuable than its owner opined. It consisted, I believe (for one cannot be very sure), of sundry birds in glass-cases exceedingly ragged and dingy; of sundry stuffed beasts among which the moth had made great havoc; of sundry reptiles, and other curiosities, preserved, pickled—(what is the proper word?)—in glass bottles; of a great heap of ores, and shells, and spars, covered with cobwebs; of some copper coins, all rust; of half a mummy; and a bit of cloth made of asbestos. The only time I ever got into a scrape with my good-humoured host was on the score of this last-mentioned treasure. Being assured by him that it was the veritable, undoubted asbestos, which not only resists the action of fire, but is actually cleansed by that element, I proposed, seeing how very much it needed purification, that it should undergo a fiery ablution forthwith; but that ordeal was rejected as too dangerous; and I myself certainly considered for five minutes as dangerous too—something of an incendiary, a female Guy Vaux—I was lucky enough to do away the impression by admiring, very honestly, some newly caught butterflies,—pretty insects, and not yet spoiled,—which occupied one side of a long table. They were backed, to my great consternation, by a row of skulls, which, Mr. Evelyn having lately met with Dr. Gall's book, and being much smitten with Cranio—I beg its new name's pardon—Phrenology —had purchased at five shillings a head, of the sexton, and now descanted on in a vein as unlike Hamlet's as possible.

The museum was hung round with festoons of bird's-eggs, strung necklace-fashion, as boys are wont to thread them, being the part of its contents which, next perhaps to his new playthings the skulls, its owner valued most. Indeed they had an additional charm in his eyes, by being mostly the trophies of his own exploits from childhood downwards. Bird-nesting, always his favourite sport, had been, since he had dabbled in natural history, invested with the dignity of a pursuit. He loved it as well as any child in the parish; had as keen an eye to his game, and as much intrepidity in its acquisition; climbed trees, delved into hedgerows, and no more minded a rent garment, or a tumble into a ditch than an urchin of eight years old. The butterflies too, were, for the most part, of his own catching. I have myself seen a chase after a moth, that might serve as a companion to that grand Peter-Pindaric, "Sir Joseph Banks and the Emperor of Morocco," but my godfather had the better of the sport, he knocked down *his* insect.

To return to our museum. The last article that I remember, was a prodigious bundle of autographs, particularly unselect; where Thomas Smith, date unknown, figured by the side of Oliver Cromwell; and John Brown, equally incognito, had the honour of being tied up with Queen Elizabeth. I would not be very certain either that there might not be an occasional forgery among the greater names; not on the part of the possessor, he would as soon have thought of forging a bank bill, but on that of the several vendors, or donors, which last class generally came, autograph in hand, to beg a favour. Never was any human being so complete a subject for imposition—so entirely devoid of guile himself, so utterly unsuspicious of its existence in others. He lived as if there were not a lie in the world;— blessed result of a frank and ardent temperament, and of a memory so happily constituted that it retained no more trace of past evil than of last year's clouds.

His living collection was quite as large, and almost as out-of-the-way, as his dead one. He was an eminent bird-fancier, and had all sorts of "smale foules" as old Chaucer calls them, in every variety of combination, and in different stages of education; for your professed bird-fancier, like your professed florist, is seldom content to let nature alone. Starlings, jays, and magpies, learning to talk; bullfinches and goldfinches learning tunes from a barrel-organ; linnets brought up under a wood-lark, unlearning their own notes and studying his; nightingales, some of the earliest known in those parts, learning to live north of Trent; all sorts of canaries, and mule birds, and nests full of young things not yet distinguishable from each other, made up the miscellaneous contents of his aviary. He had also some white mice, a tame squirrel, and a very sagacious hedge-hog; and he had had a tortoise, which by an extraordinary exertion of ingenuity he had contrived to kill,—a feat which a road waggon, going over the poor animal, would have failed to perform. This was the manner. The tortoise, as most people know, is for about six months in the year torpid, and generally retires under ground to enjoy his half year's nap: he had been missing some days, when the old gardener dug him up out of a cabbage bed, and brought him in for dead. My godfather, forgetting his protégé's habits, and just fresh from reading some book on the efficacy of the warm bath (he was a great man for specifics), soused the unlucky land-crab into hot water, and killed him outright. All that could be done to repair the mischief was tried, and he was finally replaced in his old burrow, the cabbage bed, but even burying him failed to bring him to life again. This misadventure rather damped Mr. Evelyn's zest for outlandish favourites. After all, his real and abiding pets were children—children of all ages, from six months old to twelve years. He had much of the child in his own composition; his sweet and simple nature, his restlessness and merriment, harmonised with theirs most completely. He loved a game at romps too, as well as they did, and would join in all their sports from battledore and shuttlecock, to puss in the corner. He had no child of his own—(have I not said that he was married?)—no child whom he had an absolute right to spoil; but he made all the children of the place serve his turn, and right happy were they to be spoiled by Mr. Evelyn.

They all flocked around him, guided by that remarkable instinct, by which the veriest baby can detect a person who really loves it; ran after him when he rode on horseback, thrust their little hands into his when he walked, and hung round the stone porch in which he had the habit of sitting on a summer afternoon, reading the newspaper in the sun, and chatting to the passers-by (for he knew every soul in the place gentle or simple), holding a long dialogue with one, sending a jest after another, and a kind nod to the third. Thither his clients, the children, would resort every evening, as much, I verily believe, for love of their patron as for the gingerbread, apples, and half-pence,—the tops, marbles, and balls, which used to issue from those capacious magazines, his pockets.

The house, to which this porch belonged, was well suited to the tastes and station of its owner;—stately, old-fashioned, and spacious; situate in the principal street, and commanding the market-place,—a mansion in a town. Behind was a formal garden in the Dutch style,—terraces, and beds of flowers, and tall yew hedges, and holly and box cut into various puzzling shapes, dragons, peacocks, lions, and swans. Within doors all was equally precise and out of date, being (except the museum) under the special and exclusive dominion of the lady of the house.

Mrs. Evelyn formed just the contrast with her husband which is said to tell best in matrimony. She was nearly twenty years younger in actual age, but seemed twenty years older from the mere absence of his vivacity. In all essential points they agreed perfectly; were equally charitable, generous, hospitable, and just; but of their minor differences there was no end. She was grave, and slow, and formal—upright, thin, and pale; dressed with a sort of sober splendour; wore a great quantity of old-fashioned jewellery; went airing every day; and got up, breakfasted, dined, supped, and went to bed at exactly the same minute, the whole year round,—clock work was never more regular. Then she was addicted to a fussing and fidgety neatness, such as is held proper to old maids and Dutch women, and kept the house afloat with perpetual scourings. Moreover she had a hatred of motion and idleness, and pursued as a duty some long, tiresome, useless piece of handy work. Knitting a carpet, for instance, or netting a veil, or constructing that hideous piece of female joinery, a patch-work counterpane. The room in which I slept bore notable testimony to her industry; the whole fringe of the bed and window-curtains being composed of her knotting, and the hearth-rug of her work, as well as a chair, miscalled easy, stuffed into a hardness bumping against you in every direction, and covered with huge flowers, in small tent stitch, flowers that would have done honour to the gardens of Brobdingnag. Besides this she was a genealogist, and used to bewilder herself and her hearers in a labyrinth of pedigree, which, even at this distance of time, it gives me a headache to think of; nay, she was so unmerciful as to expect that I should understand and recollect all the intricacies of my own descent, and how I came to be of kin to the innumerable cousins to whom she introduced me,— I could as soon have learnt that despair of my childhood, the multiplication table.

All this might seem to compose no very desirable companion for an idle girl of sixteen; but I had not been a week in the house before I loved her very nearly as well as my dear godfather, although in a different way. Her thorough goodness made itself felt; and she was so perfectly a gentlewoman, so constantly considerate and kind, liberal and charitable, in deed and word, that nobody could help loving Mrs. Evelyn. Besides, we had one taste in common, a fondness for her peculiar territory, the orchard, a large grassy spot covered with fine old fruit-trees, divided from the flower garden on the north by a magnificent yew hedge, bounded on one side by a filbert walk, on the other by the high, ivied stone wall of the potagerie, and sloping down on the south to a broad sparkling rivulet, which went dancing along like a thing of life (as your northern rivulet is apt to do), forming a thousand tiny bays and promontories, and letting in a prospect of matchless beauty. Fancy a winding woodland valley, a rural bridge, a village, with its Gothic church, and a steep acclivity crowned with the ruins of a venerable castle, thrown together with a felicity of form and colouring which might beseem a landscape-painter's dream, and you will have a faint idea of the view from that orchard. Under the yew hedge, on a sunny bank thickly set with roses and honeysuckles, and flowers and sweet herbs, were Mrs. Evelyn's pets, her only pets, the bees. She was so fond of them, and visited them so often, that I used to wonder that she allowed them to be taken; but her love of bees was balanced by her extraordinary predilection for honey: honey, especially when eaten in the comb, was, in her mind, a specific for all diseases, an universal panacea, the true elixir vitæ. She imputed her own good health entirely to this salutary regimen; and was sure to trace every illness she heard of to some neglect of honey-eating. That she never could prevail on her husband to taste this natural balsam (as she was wont to call it) must have been the great evil of her matrimonial life. Every morning did she predict death or disease to the sturdy recusant; and every morning was she answered by the same keen glance of the laughing hazel eye, and the same arch nod of defiance. There he sat, a living witness that man might thrive without honey. It was really too provoking.

Another point in dispute between them arose out of Mr. Evelyn's extraordinary addiction to match-making. He always insisted on calling marriage a happy ceremony, although one should think he had attended weddings enough to know that a funeral is generally lively in the comparison; and I am persuaded that dear as he held his genuine asbestos, a piece of bride-cake, drawn nine times through the ring, would for the time being have been held the greater treasure. Accordingly he was the general confidant of all courtships of gentility within ten miles, and even, with all deference be it spoken, of some wooings which had no gentility to boast; for his taste being known, and his abilities in that line duly appreciated, half the youths in the town came bowing to his honour to beg his good word. To his honour's good word and his own goodly person did John Bell, head waiter of the Greyhound, owe the felicity of calling the buxom Widow Wilson, the rich landlady of that well-accustomed inn, Mrs. Bell. To his honour's good word, and a threatened loss of custom, was Robert Heron, the smart young linen-draper, indebted for the fair hand of Margaret Car, sole heiress of Archy Car, Scotchman, and barber, between whom and old Robert Heron a Capulet and Montagu feud, originating in a quarrel about their respective countries, had subsisted for a dozen years. Nothing short of my godfather's threatening to learn to shave could have brought that Romeo and Juliet together. His honour related these exploits with great complacency, whilst his wife did not fail to remind him of the less fortunate exertions of his talent. How his influence gained poor Will the blacksmith his shrew, or Jem the gardener his daudle. But such accidents will befall the ablest diplomatists. The grand object of his schemes at present was an union between two individuals of his own household. Mrs. Evelyn's personal attendant was a stiff, perpendicular old maid, bony and meagre in her person, with red hair, and something of a vinegar aspect,—for the rest a well-intentioned woman, and a voluable servant. Mr. Evelyn had been looking out for a sweetheart for this amiable damsel (Mrs. Embleton by name) for the last ten years, and had begun to despair of success, when all at once it occurred to him to strike up a match between her and his fat coachman, Samuel—a round, jolly old bachelor, blunt and bluff, with a broad red face, a knowing grin, and a most magnificent coachmanlike wig. He began in due form by rallying Mrs. Embleton on her conquest. Mrs. Embleton minced and simpered,—no objection in that quarter! Then he consulted Mrs. Evelyn,—Mrs. Evelyn remonstrated; that however, he knew by experience, might be overcome. Then he laughed at Samuel,—Samuel whistled;—that was rather dismaying. The next day he returned to the charge—and again Samuel whistled,—worse and worse!—A third time his master attacked him, and a third time did Samuel whistle;—and anybody but my godfather would have despaired. He, however, did not. At this point stood the game, when I left the north; and the very first letter I received from Mrs. Evelyn told me that the marriage was settled, the wedding-day fixed, and the bride-cake purchased. And the next brought tidings (for I still had my doubts of Samuel) that the ceremony was actually performed, and the happy knot tied; and Mrs. Evelyn seemed pacified, and the bridegroom resigned. No withstanding my dear godfather!

MY GODFATHER'S MAN-ŒUVRING

I HAVE said that my dear godfather was a great match-maker. One of his exploits in this way, which occurred during my second visit to him and Mrs. Evelyn, I am now about to relate.

Amongst the many distant cousins to whom I was introduced in that northern region, was a young kinswoman of the name of Hervey—Lucy Hervey—an orphan heiress of considerable fortune, who lived in the same town and the same street with my godfather, under the protection of a lady who had been the governess of her childhood, and continued with her as the friend of her youth. Sooth to say, their friendship was of that tender and sentimental sort at which the world, the wicked world, is so naughty as to laugh. Miss Reid and Miss Hervey were names quite as inseparable as goose and apple-sauce, or tongue and chicken. They regularly made their appearance together, and there would have appeared I know not what of impropriety in speaking of either singly; it would have looked like a tearing asunder of the "double cherry," respecting which, in their case, even the "seeming parted" would have been held too disjunctive a phrase, so tender and inseparable was their union; although, as far as resemblance went, no simile could be more inapplicable. Never were two people more unlike in mind and person.

Lucy Hervey was a pretty little woman of six and twenty; but from a delicate figure, delicate features, and a most delicate complexion, looking much younger. Perhaps the total absence of strong expression, the mildness and simplicity of her countenance, and the artlessness and docility of her manner might conduce to the mistake. She was a sweet, gentle creature, generous and affectionate; and not wanting in sense, although her entire reliance on her friend's judgment, and constant habit of obedience to her wishes, rendered the use of it somewhat rare.

Miss Reid was a tall, awkward woman, raw-boned, lank and huge, just what one fancies a man would be in petticoats; with a face that, except the beard (certainly she had no beard), might have favoured the supposition; so brown and bony and stern and ill-favoured was her unfortunate visage. In one point, she was lucky. There was no guessing at her age, certainly not within ten years; nor within twenty. She looked old: but with that figure, those features, and that complexion, she must have looked old at eighteen. To guess her age was impossible. Her voice was deep and dictatorial; her manner rough and assuming; and her conversation unmercifully sensible and oracular—"full of wise saws and modern instances." For the rest, in spite of her inauspicious exterior she was a good sort of disagreeable woman: charitable and kind in her way; genuinely fond of Lucy Hervey, whom she petted and scolded and coaxed and managed just as a nurse manages a child; and tolerably well liked of all her acquaintance—except Mr. Evelyn, who had been at war with her for the last nine years, on the subject of his fair cousin's marriage; and had, at last, come to regard her pretty much as a prime minister may look on an opposition leader,—as a regular opponent, an obstacle to be put down, or swept away. I verily believe that he hated her as much as his kindly nature could hate anybody.

To be sure, it was no slight grievance to have so fair a subject for his matrimonial speculations, a kinswoman too, just under his very eye, and to find all his plans thwarted by that inexorable *gouvernante*—more especially as, without her aid, it was morally certain that the pretty Lucy would never have had the heart to say *no* to anybody. Ever since Miss Hervey was seventeen, my dear god-papa had been scheming for her advantage It was quite melancholy to hear him count up the husbands she might have had,—beginning with the Duke's son, her partner at her first race-ball,— and ending with the young, newly arrived physician, his last protégé: "now," he said, "she might die an old maid; he had done with her." And there did actually appear to be a cessation of all his matrimonial plans in that quarter. Miss Reid herself laid aside her mistrust of him; and a truce, if not a peace, was tacitly concluded between these sturdy antagonists. Mr. Evelyn seemed to have given up the game—a strange thing for him to do whilst he had a pawn left! But so it was. His adversary had the board all to herself; and was in as good humour as a winning player generally is. Miss Reid was never remembered so amiable. We saw them almost every day, as the fashion is amongst neighbours in small towns, and used to ride and walk together continually—although Lucy, whose health was delicate, frequently declined accompanying us on our more distant excursions.

Our usual beau, besides the dear god-papa, was a Mr. Morris, the curate of the parish—an uncouth, gawky, lengthy man, with an astounding Westmoreland dialect, and a most portentous laugh. Really his Ha! ha! was quite a shock to the nerves—a sort of oral shower-bath; so sudden and so startling was the explosion. In loudness, it resembled half a dozen ordinary laughs "rolled into one"; and as the gentleman was of a facetious disposition, and chorused his own good things, as well as those of other people, with this awful cachinnation, it was no joking matter. But he was so excellent a person, so cordial, so jovial, so simple-hearted, and so contented with a lot none of the most prosperous, that one could not help liking him, laugh and all. He was a widower, with one only son, a Cambridge scholar, of whom he was deservedly proud. Edward

Morris, besides his academical honours (I think he had been senior wrangler of his year), was a very fine young man, with an intelligent countenance, but exceedingly shy, silent and abstracted. I could not help thinking the poor youth was in love; but his father and Mr. Evelyn laid the whole blame on the mathematics. He would sit sometimes for an hour together, immersed, as they said, in his calculations, with his eyes fixed on Lucy Hervey, as if her sweet face had been the problem he was solving. But your mathematicians are privileged people; and so apparently my fair cousin thought, for she took no notice, unless by blushing a shade the deeper. It was worth while to look at Lucy Hervey, when Edward Morris was gazing on her in his absent fits; her cheeks were as red as a rose.

How these blushes came to escape the notice of Miss Reid, I cannot tell,—unless she might happen to have her own attention engrossed by Edward's father. For certain that original paid her, in his odd way, great attention; was her constant beau in our walking parties; sate by her side at dinner; and manœuvred to get her for his partner at whist. She had the benefit of his best bon-mots, and his loudest laughs; and she seemed to me not to dislike that portentous sound so much as might have been expected from a lady of her particularity. I ventured to hint my observations to Mr. Evelyn; who chuckled, laid his forefinger against his nose, rubbed his hands, and called me a simpleton.

Affairs were in this position, when one night

just at going to bed, my good godfather, with a little air of mystery (no uncommon preparation to his most trifling plans), made an appointment to walk with me before breakfast as far as a pet farm about a mile out of the town, the superintendence of which was one of his greatest amusements. Early the next morning, the housemaid, who usually attended me, made her appearance, and told me that her master was waiting for me, that I must make haste, and that he desired I would be smart, as he expected a party to breakfast at the farm. This sort of injunction is seldom thrown away on a damsel of eighteen; accordingly, I adjusted, with all dispatch, a new blue silk pelisse, and sallied forth into the corridor, which I heard him pacing as impatiently as might be. There, to my no small consternation, instead of the usual gallant compliments of the most gallant of godfathers, I was received with very disapproving glances: told that I looked like an old woman in that dowdy-coloured pelisse, and conjured to exchange it for a white gown. Half affronted, I nevertheless obeyed; doffed the pelisse, and donned the white gown, as ordered: and being greeted this time with a bright smile, and a chuck under the chin, we set out in high good-humour on our expedition.

Instead, however, of proceeding straight to the farm, Mr. Evelyn made a slight deviation from our course, turning down the market-place, and into the warehouse of a certain Mrs. Bennet, milliner and mantua-maker, a dashing, over-dressed dame, who presided over the fashions for ten miles round, and marshalled a compter full of caps and bonnets at one side of the shop, whilst her husband, an obsequious, civil, bowing tradesman, dealt out gloves and stockings at the other. A little dark parlour behind was common to both. Into this den was I ushered; and Mrs. Bennet, with many apologies, began, at a signal from my godfather, to divest me of all my superfluous blueness, silk handkerchief, sash and wrist-ribbons (for, with the constancy which is born of opposition, I had, in relinquishing my obnoxious pelisse, clung firmly to the obnoxious colour), replacing them by white satin ribbons and a beautiful white shawl; and, finally, exchanging my straw bonnet for one of white silk, with a deep lace veil—that piece of delicate finery which all women delight in. Whilst I was now admiring the richness of the genuine Brussels point, and now looking at myself in a little glass which Mrs. Bennet was holding to my face, for the better display of her millinery,—the bonnet, to do her justice, was pretty and becoming,—during this engrossing contemplation, her smooth silky husband crept behind me with the stealthy pace of a cat, and relying, as it seems, on my preoccupation, actually drew my York-tan gloves from my astonished hands, and substituted a pair of his own best white kid. This operation being completed, my god-papa, putting his forefinger to his lip in token of secrecy, hurried me, with a look of great triumph, from the shop.

He walked at a rapid pace; and, between quick motion and amazement, I was too much out of breath to utter a word, till we had passed the old Gothic castle at the end of the town, and crossed the long bridge that spans its wide and winding river. I then rained questions on my dear old friend, who chuckled and nodded, and vented two or three half laughs, but vouchsafed nothing tending to a reply. At length we came to a spot where the road turned suddenly to the left (the way to the farm), whilst right before us rose a knoll, on which stood the church, a large, heavy, massive building, almost a cathedral, finely relieved by the range of woody hills which shut in the landscape. A turning gate, with a tall straight cypress on either side, led into the churchyard; and through this gate Mr. Evelyn passed. The church door was a little ajar, and, through the crevice was seen peeping the long red nose of the old clerk, a Bardolphian personage, to whom my godfather, who loved to oblige people in their own way, sometimes did the questionable service of clearing off his score at the Greyhound; his red nose and a skirt of his shabby black coat peeped through the porch; whilst behind one of the buttresses glimmered, for an instant, the white drapery of a female figure. I did not need these indications to convince me that a wedding was the object in view; that had been certain from the first cashiering of my blue ribbons; but I was still at a loss as to the parties; and felt quite relieved by Mr. Evelyn's question, "Pray, my dear, were you ever a bridesmaid?"—since, in the extremity of my perplexity, I had had something like an apprehension that an unknown beau might appear at the call of this mighty manager, and I be destined to play the part of bride myself. Comforted to find that I was only to enact the confidante, I had now leisure to be exceedingly curious as to my prima donna. My curiosity was speedily gratified.

On entering the church we had found only a neighbouring clergyman, not Mr. Morris, at the altar; and, looking round at the opening of another door, I perceived the worthy curate in a jetty, clerical suit, bristling with newness, leading Miss Reid, be-flounced and be-scarfed and be-veiled and be-plumed, and all in a flutter of bridal finery, in great state, up the aisle. Mr. Evelyn advanced to meet them, took the lady's fair hand from Mr. Morris, and led her along with all the grace of an old courtier; I fell into the procession at the proper place; the amiable pair were duly married, and I thought my office over. I was never more mistaken in my life.

In the midst of the customary confusion of kissing and wishing joy, and writing and signing registers and certificates, which form so important and disagreeable a part of that disagreeable and important ceremony, Mr. Evelyn had vanished; and just as the bride was inquiring for him, with the intention of leaving the church, he reappeared, through the very same side-door which had admitted the first happy couple, leading Lucy Hervey, and followed by Edward Morris. The father evidently expected them; the new stepmother as evidently did not. Never did a thief, taken in the manner, seem more astonished than that sage *gouvernante*! Lucy, on her part, blushed and hung back, and looked shyer and prettier than ever; the old clerk grinned; the clergyman, who had shewn some symptoms of astonishment at the first wedding, now smiled to Mr. Evelyn, as if this accounted and made amends for it; whilst the dear god-papa himself chuckled and nodded and rubbed his hands, and chucked both bride and bridesmaid under the chin, and seemed ready to cut capers for joy. Again the book was opened at the page of destiny; again I held the milk-white glove; and after nine years of unsuccessful manœuvring, my cousin Lucy was married. It was, undoubtedly, the most triumphant event of the good old man's life; and I don't believe that either couple ever saw cause to regret the dexterity in the art of match-making which produced their double union. They have been as happy as people usually are in this workaday world, especially the young mathematician and his pretty wife; and their wedding-day is still remembered in W.; for besides his munificence to singer, ringer, sexton and clerk, Mr. Evelyn roasted two sheep on the occasion, gave away ten bride-cakes, and made the whole town tipsy.

www.ingramcontent.com/pod-product-compliance
Lightning Source LLC
Chambersburg PA
CBHW041438300426
44114CB00026B/2932